SIGNS OF REVIVAL

Revival is a part of God's plan –

Renewing – the faithful...

Reviving – the church...

Awakening – a nation...

Redeeming – the world...

God, send us a season of glorious disorder. Oh, for a sweep of the wind that will set the seas in motion, and make our ironclad brethren, now lying so quietly at anchor, to roll from stem to stern! Oh, for the fire to fall again – fire which shall affect the most solid! Oh, that such fire might first sit upon the disciples, and then fall on all around! O God, Thou art ready to work with us today even as Thou didst then. Stay not, we beseech Thee, but work at once. Break down every barrier that hinders the incoming of Thy might! Give us now both hearts of flame and tongues of fire to preach Thy reconciling word, for Jesus' sake! Amen!

C. H. Spurgeon (1834-1892)

By the same author:
  The Truth About AIDS
  AIDS and You
  HIV: It's Your Choice (booklet)
  The Genetic Revolution

Signs
of
Revival

PATRICK DIXON

KINGSWAY PUBLICATIONS
EASTBOURNE

ISBN 0 85476 539 5

Produced by Bookprint Creative Services
P.O. Box 827, BN21 3YJ, England, for
KINGSWAY PUBLICATIONS LTD
Lottbridge Drove, Eastbourne, E. Sussex BN23 6NT.
Printed in Great Britain.

Contents

Acknowledgements

This book has been a joint attempt by many to record for future generations and for now some of the remarkable things that God is doing today, in the light of all that has gone before. So much has been happening every day that memories of how this current move of God began are already fading.

A large number of people have provided personal accounts of what happened to them or to others in their churches during 1994, while many others have sent press cuttings, diary notes, or observations, or have directed me to other sources. Others have helped debate the issues and given them an historical and biblical context. I am deeply grateful to them all. I am also indebted to those who have graciously allowed extracts to be printed from published work as part of this unique collection of history in the making, and of the past. In particular I would like to thank Gerald Coates, leader of the Pioneer network of churches, for his unfailing support, encouragement and practical help in gathering material.

Thank you also to William Atkinson, Norman and Grace Barnes, Stuart Bell, Celia Bowring, Chris Cartwright, Charlie Cleverley, Steve Clifford, Colin Dye, Roger and

Margaret Ellis, Andrew Fergusson, Nicky Gumbel (for kind permission to use extracts from *HTB In Focus*), Allistair Graham, Clifford Hill, Tim Hill, Sarah Jerath, R. T. Kendall, Jeff Lucas, Peter Lynne, Sandy Millar, Derek Munday, Philippa Pearson Miles, John Noble, Roger Popplestone, David Pytches, Mick and Liz Ray, Dave Roberts, Pete Sanderson, Martin Scott, Roger Stephenson, Marjie Sutton, Phil Vogel, Adrian Warnock and Michael Williams.

I hope the reader will forgive any minor factual inaccuracies and omissions and will help me to correct them in later editions. New material is welcomed on the past and present.

I am indebted to the following for kind and generous permission to use extensive extracts or quotations from important works on revival: Estates of C. Vulliamy for extracts from *Wesley*; of Donald Gee for *Wind and Flame*; of Arthur Wallis for *In the Day of Thy Power*; and to WEC for *This Is That*. Indeed I am grateful to every source.

Thanks are due to all the team at Kingsway who have been very encouraging and have worked near miracles to get the book printed quickly. I am also very grateful to the librarians of both the Evangelical Library and Charing Cross Hospital Medical School. Finally, I would also like to thank Sheila my wife, for her help and advice in editing and checking the manuscript as well as in support and encouragement, and John, Caroline, Elizabeth and Paul, who were patient and understanding throughout.

October 1994

I

News of Laughter

On Saturday 18th June 1994 over 10,000 readers of the *Church of England Newspaper* were astounded to read of disturbing scenes of near chaos in a large Anglican church in London; of an outbreak of convulsive laughter, people falling over, weeping and uncontrollable movements. The communion service could not continue and some who heard were scandalised.

The Times carried the same extraordinary story that day to a further half a million, under the headline 'Spread of hysteria fad worries church – Toronto blessings', describing a 'religious craze' spreading from Canada. Hysteria, however, was not an adequate diagnosis of what was going on.

The church in question, Holy Trinity Brompton in London, was normally quite full, so much so that two other nearby churches had been filled by their overflowing growth. The evening services in particular were informal and often lively, but this was something quite different in scale to anything seen before.

The following morning, on Sunday 19th June 1994, over a million people in Britain were even more surprised when they read the headline in *The Sunday Telegraph*: 'Faithful fall for power of the Spirit – revival of evangelism sweeps

round world from Airport Church'. Fred Langan and Paul
Goodman reported from Toronto and London of thousands
of people from all over the world who were flooding into the
Toronto   Airport   branch   of   the   Vineyard   Christian
Fellowship.

The Sunday Telegraph described how almost every night
of the week there were 'astounding scenes of people shaking
with laughter, slipping into a trance, falling to the floor, and
crying'. While most of the crowds were from Toronto itself,
a quarter were from the United States and Europe, and many
of those were British. Another source estimated that there
were fifty from the UK every night.

> And now, there is rising speculation among charismatic
> evangelicals that what may be happening is more than a
> renewal, more even than a revival. The world, it is said, may in
> fact be on the verge of a fully-fledged awakening – something
> on the scale of the great Wesleyan movement that swept
> England during the early 19th century.

This distinction in terms between renewal, revival and
awakening is helpful, and has been adopted by Edwin Orr,
an authority on revival, and by the Oxford Association for
Research on Revival. The word 'revival' has been used over
the centuries to describe anything from a church trebling
in size in a year to the conversion of a million people
across a nation.

The journalists from *The Sunday Telegraph* reported that
the meetings started at 7.30pm but went on until the early
hours, with worship led by a small band with two guitars and
a keyboard.

> Arms are stretched out, people shout 'Amen', 'Yes, Jesus' and
> 'Hallelujah'. After the singing, Mr Arnott gets up and gives a

small talk – and then the phenomena begin. A woman in a blue sun-dress talks about her experience with cancer. She faints and falls into a trance on the floor. Then a pastor speaks. He swoons, and is caught before he hits the floor.

'I've never seen anything like this,' says Ewen Huffman, 31, a pastor from Carshalton Beeches Baptist Free Church, in Surrey. In front of him seven grown men are writhing on the floor.

'We were praying for something to happen, but we don't know why God picked our dumb little church among so many others,' says one of the pastors. 'We don't advertise, and we have people from Germany, Switzerland, England, Australia even Singapore and Hong Kong.'

The evening builds into a finale. People clear away chairs from the first few rows. Some come up to the stage where Mr Arnott touches some of them, and in a couple of minutes the floor in front of the stage is littered with bodies.

So was this just a limited phenomenon? Was this a sign of revival to come? Was it merely emotional excess and crowd manipulation? The Revd Sandy Millar, Vicar at Holy Trinity Brompton, went out to Toronto himself. Although he did not know it at the time, the whole of church life was to become dominated by these new experiences throughout the summer and on into the autumn. Once the media circus began to roll there were journalists in almost every service, and hundreds of observers, either curious, hostile, indifferent or hungry for their own personal 'times of refreshing from the presence of the Lord',[1] for personal revival.

Sandy Millar had no idea then that within twelve weeks the crowds would grow so big that regular church members would need to be issued with special tickets to allow them a chance of entering the building – and even then only if they arrived early.

His first direct experience of what was happening came as a result of a phone call on Tuesday 24th May just after 4pm. He was sitting in a meeting at the Evangelical Alliance (EA) chaired by Clive Calver, General Secretary, when he was summoned to an urgent phone call.[2] On the line was a member of his church staff who reported that the entire church team were in the office on the floor unable to get up, having been prayed for. Sandy asked her how she had managed then to get to the phone. 'I crawled!' she replied.

Some of Sandy's first thoughts were these, published in June:

> It's premature to talk of a revival, let alone of an awakening, although I obviously have my hopes. However, there are clearly lots of signs that God is at work. I would describe what is happening now as a time of refreshment for the Church. Obviously, lots of people will find what is happening – such as the laughter, which is quite new on this scale in Britain – disturbing and even shocking. We must continue to pray for understanding, and judge these events by their fruit.[3]

So let us rewind the video-tape, as it were, and take a closer look at what has mushroomed into a global phenomenon. First, I want to take us into a leader's home in Kingston, Surrey, just five hours before that telephone call to Sandy.

Earlier on the same day as Sandy's meeting at EA, Tuesday 24th May at 11.30, Eleanor Mumford had gathered a small number of friends to hear about her trip to the Vineyard church at Toronto Airport. Eleanor is part of the leadership team of the Putney Vineyard Church in South London. John Mumford, her husband, has responsibility for the oversight of all the Vineyard churches in Britain.

Some of those Eleanor had invited were leaders of other churches. She explained her remarkable experiences of

God's power and prayed for them to be filled with the Spirit. Everyone present was affected profoundly. At 2pm, Nicky Gumbel, Curate at Holy Trinity Brompton, rushed back from Kingston to the church office in South Kensington, rather late for the staff lunchtime meeting. It was almost over, but they asked him to pray a concluding prayer. The church newspaper records:

> The effect was instantaneous. People fell to the ground again and again. There were remarkable scenes as the Holy Spirit touched all those present in ways few had ever experienced or seen. Staff members walking past the room were also affected. Two hours later some of those present went to tell others in different offices and prayed with them where they found them. They too were powerfully affected by the Holy Spirit – many falling to the ground. Prayer was still continuing after 5pm.[4]

Sandy Millar arrived back shortly afterwards to find people somewhat in a state of shock, surprised at what had happened. The leaders then invited Eleanor Mumford to preach at Holy Trinity Brompton (HTB) that Sunday (29th May), at both morning and evening services. After each talk there was silence as she asked the Holy Spirit to come. In a few minutes laughter and other manifestations began, with people still in the church at 1.30pm after the morning service, and until 9.30pm after the evening service.

Two days later, on 31st May, Sandy Millar flew out with HTB's Pastoral Director, Jeremy Jennings, to Toronto. That night they saw remarkable scenes take place at the Airport Vineyard. Meanwhile, the following day back in London those at the staff prayer meeting continued to experience similar things. Jeremy and Sandy flew home on Friday 3rd June, and Jeremy left immediately to join a residential Alpha weekend, run by the church for new believers and enquirers.

That Sunday morning (5th June), Nicky Gumbel shared what had been happening to him, and others also described their experiences. Once again, many manifestations appeared among the congregation – so many in fact that the normal communion service could not continue.

That night the church was completely full, with around 1,200 people. As people prayed, the main church area gradually became covered with people lying on the floor, requiring hundreds of chairs to be stacked away. More than 100 people were still praying in the church at 10pm.[5] Someone remarked: 'The word "revival" is on everyone's lips.'

It would be wrong, however, to think from the press reports that the famous Holy Trinity church was the first to be affected in Britain. Traces of what became widespread were present over the previous fifteen years or more.

Rodney Howard-Browne's name has been closely associated in many people's minds with what is happening, especially when it comes to outbreaks of laughter. He is a South African evangelist in his early thirties, previously an associate pastor at Rhema Church in Johannesburg, which has 13,000 members. He became more widely known after a series of meetings in spring 1993 in Lakeland, Florida, where he was invited by an Assemblies of God pastor to speak at Carpenter's Home Church.

Every time he got up to speak, people broke out laughing. This first started in April 1989 when he was preaching in a church near Albany, New York, but only happened from time to time from 1989 to 1993. Rodney was puzzled and disturbed by the laughter at first, but gradually came to the conclusion that God was touching people as they laughed, and that he should stop fighting it, even though laughter was often intrusive in the meetings.

I have seen a video of one of the meetings he spoke at in 1993. His style is informal, conversational even, as he wanders cheerfully around the platform and among the front few rows in the large auditorium. Laughter, shaking, crying and weeping break out spontaneously, particularly among those he is interviewing, praying for or talking to – and it affects him too.

The scenes look very strange and bizarre, with people quivering, shaking, contorting, jumping and falling. It is all strikingly familiar, however, to those who have attended similar meetings in the UK in 1994. Rodney Howard-Browne is seen on the tape trying to give a talk, but breaking down with laughter and speaking a mix of English and tongues jumbled together.

So what about the Toronto connection? Marc Du Pont is one of the Vineyard Team at the Airport Vineyard in Toronto. He was interviewed recently by Dave Roberts, editor of *Alpha* magazine. He explained there were two main influences: one from Argentina and the other from the US:

John Arnott attended a conference that Argentinian pastors Ed Silvoso, Claudio Freidzon and Hector Jiminez staged for North American pastors (November 1993). These men are experiencing a move of God in Argentina. Claudio Freidzon prayed for John.

Another Vineyard pastor Randy Clark was finding 1993 a hard year. He was near to burnout and he was quite desperate for God's touch. A friend encouraged him to go to a Rodney Howard-Browne meeting. Randy was really helped after prayer at a meeting in Tulsa. John Arnott heard about Randy's experience and that of several others including a pastor called Happy Leman, via Vineyard pastors' grapevine conference.

John contacted Randy and scheduled a series of meetings beginning January 20. Randy has a godly desire to see revival released. He took a team up to Toronto and everything began to break out. We have often seen falling, shaking, deliverances and healings so the phenomenon wasn't new to us but what was new was that it was going on and on.

This was much more intense. There were far more people getting drunk in the Spirit, far more people overcome with laughter, which we haven't seen much of. That was rather new to us. The meetings aren't the most powerful things I have ever seen but the sense of the presence of God is so strong. What is so overwhelming about it is not the physical phenomena but the phenomenal hunger for the Lord expressed in worship.

I haven't fallen in the Spirit, I haven't shaken in the Spirit, I haven't laughed uncontrollably, I haven't been weeping in meetings, I haven't had anything happen to me overtly. On the other hand since mid-January, when I spent time alone with God and felt he spoke to me of his love for me, his hope for me, his friendship for me, I know that my own prayer life has been much more consistent than in the past.

John Arnott is a tremendous risk-taker. We're totally not in a seeker-sensitive mode – we're quite radical by Vineyard standards. John is very close friends with Benny Hinn which gives an indication of what his priorities are in terms of the Holy Spirit.

We try to be careful about the physical phenomena. The roots can be the Holy Spirit, the flesh or the Devil. Things are always mixed, you know. If it's not from God and it's not disturbing the meeting I'll talk to the person later. But if they are drawing attention away from the Lord, we'll just tell them to be quiet – in fact I did that twice last night.

There are times when you just have to diplomatically say, 'Not now.' We also don't want to do any deliverance during the ministry meetings in Toronto. We'll either bind the demonic spirit or take people out of the meetings.[6]

On the 20th January the Holy Spirit began to fall on members of the Airport Vineyard Church in Toronto in a new way. They began to hold services each weekday evening. By March 1994 the word was spreading across Vineyard churches throughout the world of an extraordinary outpouring of the Holy Spirit in Toronto, and by April, hundreds of church leaders began to arrive to see what was happening and experience it for themselves.

It would be tempting to do what we all tend to do, which is to 'box' the experience and label what is happening as somehow a product of this man's ministry, or of John Wimber's ministry in Vineyard, or of Benny Hinn's ministry – thought by some to have sparked things off in Argentina, or at least accelerated them.

Labelling makes us feel good; it helps us to feel in control of our world, dismissing things, people, situations and revivals even, into tidy pigeon-holes where they are safely tucked away. Unfortunately such simplistic explanations are hopelessly naïve and incorrect historically, as we will see. It would be more accurate to say that the world conditions and the state of the church in some nations have been such that the 'tinder was dry'. It just needed a spark.

Despite the undoubted impact of the ministry of one or two key people, what is happening now in Britain and other nations is almost entirely independent of personalities. This was seen quite dramatically in June 1994 when Rodney Howard-Browne visited the UK to hold a national conference and in September when John Wimber did the same.[7] Both have been seen by many as closely linked to current phenomena. Considering the huge momentum among UK churches to see the 'times of refreshing' encouraged, the conferences were marked by relatively low attendance. Whatever is going on has been transmitted by hundreds or thousands of individuals from place to place, carrying their own personal experience of the power of God.

While perhaps 1,500 British church leaders had been to Toronto from Britain by September 1994 (just some of the 35,000 visiting that church over the first nine months of the year), it is also true that what is happening has been thoroughly anglicised as it has spread around the UK.

Things were already happening in the UK on a smaller scale long before anyone had heard of a church at Toronto Airport as we will see in the next chapter. For example, falling, shaking and laughter in 1987 at the Wales Bible Week (Bryn Jones), but more immediately, in October 1993, when a number of people in Kensington Temple were affected by 'holy laughter', including one woman who was almost unable to make the bus journey home, embarrassing her friend because she looked so drunk.

In December 1993, a team from Argentina arrived in Brighton, and a church there experienced weeping, laughter and shaking. In the same month, a church in Penzance was also affected through contact with the ministry of Rodney Howard-Browne. Small numbers of people were affected by strange new manifestations in the Covenant Ministry churches overseen by Bryn Jones. In April 1984, without any related transatlantic contact, a small prayer meeting of students in Southampton, part of Tony Morton's church, started laughing and falling over. But these were all small events, limited in scope and duration, and at the time were not thought to be particularly significant.

Despite these and other minor outbreaks over previous years, it would be true to say that most of the new manifestations happening in Britain in May or June 1994 could be traced to transatlantic influence.

In April 1994 Dave Holden from New Frontiers International was visiting Terry Virgo's church in Columbia, where Rodney Howard-Browne had recently preached. He was greatly affected by what happened and returned home. On Sunday 1st May, Dave spoke at a church in Cambridge where the same things started happening. While at a related church in Brighton (Church of Christ the King), another leader spoke having just returned from Toronto. The phenomena hit the church immediately.

On the following Wednesday another New Frontiers church in Sidcup experienced laughter and falling at a church meeting attended by Dave. The following day (5th May) around fifty leaders from New Frontiers churches in South East England met at Sidcup and many were affected.

Three days later, on Sunday 8th May, Gerald Coates, leader of the Pioneer group of churches, went to speak at the Vineyard church in Putney. At the time he knew very little of what was going on in Toronto, but when he arrived he was told that Eleanor Mumford was out there. After he spoke he was surprised at what happened. All kinds of phenomena broke out. While these had been seen before in some measure in some Vineyard churches in Britain, and to a slight degree in Putney the previous week, this was with a new intensity. Gerald gradually saw a pattern in recent trips to Geneva, Dublin and Sweden over the previous five weeks. At Orebro, Sweden, many had begun laughing, 'drunk'. He had felt for some time that 'something was going to break', but had been unclear what that meant. That night similar things began to happen to a small degree in Gerald's own church, Pioneer People, and at Queen's Road Baptist in Wimbledon. Here the congregation was greatly affected by a woman weeping who described a vision in which she saw the whole church on the ground in repentance and then with their hands joined together around the church.[8] Norman Moss, the minister, told them he believed this to be of great significance. News was already beginning to spread of

events in Toronto, and the following weekend he
flew out there.

Two days after that Sunday at Queen's Road Baptist, the
Ichthus 'Building Together' conference began (10th-12th
May) for a small number of leaders linked with them in
church-planting initiatives. Ichthus is yet another growing
network of new churches, with greatest numerical strength in
South East London. Many at this conference were touched
by a fresh sense of God's power and with manifestations of
various kinds. A similar conference for New Frontiers
leaders began on the same day elsewhere and the same
things happened.

Roger Mitchell, one of the leaders of Ichthus, had seen
such things in Argentina six months before. He had flown
out in November 1993 with four others to take part in a big
conference in Buenos Aires organised by Harvest
Evangelism, with Ed Silvoso, himself Argentinian but based
in California. John Arnott was also there from the Vineyard
in Toronto.

Roger and the others were profoundly affected by what
happened. They saw a great move of God taking place in the
country with thousands turning to Christ across the nation,
people falling over, laughing, trembling and manifesting in
other ways. The country had been experiencing very rapid
church growth for a number of years. It was as if a new
power had been unleashed throughout the country. Revival
had come.

The team returned, telling others of the 'life-changing
experience' they had had. However, what happened at their
10th-12th May church-planting conference was just a taste
of what was to come later at Ichthus.

While that Ichthus conference was going on (Wednesday
11th May), a few people from Queen's Road Baptist got

together to hear someone from the Church of Christ the King talk about the new move of the Holy Spirit. Several were affected by laughter and falling down. The following Sunday (15th May), the church was asked to stand quietly in prayer. Norman Moss was still in Toronto. The person leading the meeting fell onto the floor after a few minutes, where he remained for an hour-and-a-half, while many others began to be affected in various ways.

On Tuesday 17th May, around 200 New Frontiers leaders met with Terry Virgo (back from the US) and Dave Holden for a day of prayer and fasting. Most were overcome by God's presence. That Sunday, various manifestations broke out in many more churches. In the evening, Queen's Road Baptist was suddenly hit by an outbreak of manifestations, which spread week by week until the effect on the whole church was profound. On one occasion over 200 people were on the floor, weeping, laughing or 'resting in the Spirit', some for several hours.

Many were overwhelmed by a sense of God's judgement and a concern for the lost. Others began to read their Bibles with a new hunger. Norman Moss reported that over the following weeks at least 100 lapsed Christians reaffirmed their faith at special meetings attended by up to 600 people, with a small number of conversions.

Lewin Road Baptist Church in Streatham was also quickly affected, with a new sense of the holiness of God and a deeper hunger for God and the Bible. Likewise, Herne Hill Baptist was one of the first groups of churches to experience these things, people 'falling down under the weight of the glory of God'. Rob Warner, the minister, was reported as saying in June 1994: 'I have never experienced such a profound outpouring of the Spirit, but this is not yet a revival. The signs are hopeful that what we are seeing now is not superficial or trivial, but the acid test will be whether it leads to conversions.'[9]

At the beginning of June (3rd-4th) all the churches linked to Ichthus sent leaders to a conference where again new things began to happen at the final celebration in Westminster Chapel after Sandy Millar spoke to them. From that time Ichthus church members began to be increasingly affected.

On Tuesday 7th June there was a leaders' meeting at Kensington Temple. After half an hour most present were on the floor, unable to stand, with many also filled with laughter. One woman present said she received physical healing.

On Friday 10th June, Bishop David Pytches called an urgent meeting at St Andrew's Chorleywood to explain what had happened to him and his wife over the previous few days in Toronto. Many were affected.

The same day, all the local leaders from Ichthus in London drove down to Ashburnham for their twice yearly weekend together where once again things began to happen.

On Sunday 12th June, the New Frontiers church in Sidcup was swamped by around 900 people, with the hall and side hall both completely full. 'Hundreds' were turned away that night, and so many fell on the floor that you could hardly walk among them. On the same day, seventy miles south west, Tony Morton's church in Southampton experienced a flood of new phenomena, despite lack of contact with anyone from Toronto or other places directly affected. Perhaps twenty or thirty other churches were already seeing similar things that day alone. We will never know.

Things were certainly happening in two other places that same Sunday – at Bookham Baptist Church in Surrey, and of course at Holy Trinity Brompton. On the previous Friday (10th June) the minister of Bookham Baptist was enjoying a day off, gardening. He was hit by shaking as he tried to work. It was so intense that he had to stop and sit down. At the time he did not think it was anything to do with the work of the Holy Spirit. A few days earlier he had called the church to prayer after it had been going through a particularly difficult time.

The following Sunday (12th June), at the end of the evening service, he invited people to stand and 'wait upon the Lord'. Almost at once he fell forwards off the platform, landing on the floor, conscious but unable to move. Others, meanwhile, began to weep and laugh as they prayed for each other.[10]

Meanwhile, earlier that Sunday, Nicholas Monson from *The Daily Telegraph* went to Holy Trinity Brompton's morning service. Under the headline 'Congregation rolling in the aisle', he wrote:

First there was a sing-along, next a reading from Corinthians, then up stood the vicar, the Reverend Sandy Millar. He reminded us of 'the strange things that had happened the previous Sunday' and requested witnesses to step forward to recount their experiences. A young man duly came forward and told of the ecstatic sensations he had had after Mr Millar had touched him and he had fallen to the floor the previous week. It was like being held in the arms of an adoring father, he said. 'I was overwhelmed with a sensation of love.'

'Shall we try it again?' asked Mr Millar. The man assented. Mr Millar prayed. We held our breath. Mr Millar touched the man's forehead and then bam! Right on cue, his eyelids fluttered, his knees buckled and he was lowered to the floor where he started to gibber.

Soon there were four bodies on the floor, two giggling, one gibbering and one silent. Then, curates began passing down the aisles praying and touching the congregation, which was now falling about me.

To my right a young man in shorts was in hysterics, rolling about the floor holding the hand of another who joined him in a fit of spiritual merriment. A grinning girl sat over this scene almost in a trance, with both her hands shaking out in front of her.

Alarmed, I moved away from my seat towards the back of the church but my exit was blocked by a large plump lady lying face down in the aisle, being prayed over by six people. Then the curate touched me on the back. I may have been imagining it but I felt a sensation of heat coming from the curate's hand. I started to giggle. Why? I don't know. Nerves, I think. I am not sure.[11]

On Monday 13th June, at a conference organised by Woodgates Assembly of God Church in Birmingham, Rodney Howard-Browne began teaching people about the new work of the Holy Spirit as he had been experiencing it in the US, particularly since 1993. A number from Ichthus were profoundly affected by the meetings that week, as were many others from across the country, so that a large number of other churches began to see things happen on Sunday 19th June.

On Wednesday 15th June, Bryn Jones of Covenant Ministries had gathered seventy of his leaders from across the country for one of their regular times together at Nettle Hill near Coventry. Gerald Coates had been invited to spend the day with them – something which had not happened in a long time, and a sign of the many new bridges of trust and friendship being built across the country between many national leaders throughout 1993 and 1994. Those links of fellowship greatly accelerated the spread of the new move of God across the whole country, through different denominations and groupings.

Gerald spoke in the morning, and over lunch the conversation moved to Toronto and the ministry of Rodney

Howard-Browne to whom Bryn had gone to listen in Birmingham on the first night of the conference two days before. Gerald explained his understanding of what had happened to him since speaking at Putney Vineyard five weeks previously. They asked him to talk about it to all the leaders after lunch. Many were prayed for and deeply touched in a new way that afternoon.

That evening both Gerald and Bryn went together to the Rodney Howard-Browne conference, taking the other leaders with them. Many experienced different manifestations and carried what had happened back to their churches, with a great sense of expectancy that God was about to do something very significant in the nation.

At about this time a five-line letter rolled out of the fax machine in a UK church office sent by John Arnott in Toronto, to confirm travel arrangements for one of the team. At the bottom was a one-line greeting. As soon as the leader to whom it was addressed read it he was struck with overwhelming laughter which affected his secretary too.[12]

At the Sunday meeting he showed the letter to a friend without mentioning a word about the 'faxed laughter'. Immediately his friend began to laugh. He fell over and continued to roar with laughter. The man was so utterly intoxicated that at the end of the meeting he had to be carried out by three others.

A few days later another letter arrived from a church in Scotland where such things were also being experienced. Once again both the leader and his secretary were totally overcome with mirth as he held the letter in his hand, unable to let go. He ended up on the floor.

Kensington Temple is possibly the fastest growing church in the UK, having grown from around 500 to 6,000 in fewer than fifteen years. (Incidentally, in the last century any church growing from 500 to 6,000 so quickly would have been described as experiencing revival. Sometimes we are too close to events to notice what is happening, or too grudging to admit to the 'success' that others experience.)

With a multinational congregation from across London, and a strong emphasis on charismatic gifts, Kensington Temple had been seeing people fall over in meetings for a number of years, and also, since 1991, episodes of laughter. However, 1994 saw a new wave of emotion in the church, a fresh sense of God's presence, his power, holiness and blessing – but following a visit from the US, not via Toronto.

We pick up the story in June 1994, from the church publication, *City News*.

LAUGHTER HITS MUSIC DIRECTOR

KT's director of music, Richard Lewis, confesses that after the visit of US ministers, Charles & Frances Hunter, he was somewhat disappointed that none of the holy laughter experienced by some – including our dignified senior minister – had come his way. It seemed that he just wasn't the sort to experience such spiritual phenomena.

This all changed when on the 1st June he bumped into an old friend, who shared with him the exciting acts of the Holy Spirit taking place in his church. Having heard all this Richard said: 'Well, for goodness sake pray for me so that I can enter into this blessing too.' Bob retorted, 'I'm not sure that I'm qualified, and besides, you Pentecostals experience this all the time.'

Touched by the humility of this Anglican brother Richard assured him that he was indeed qualified to pray for him. 'We Pentecostals are out for anything we can get,' added Richard. So, Bob laid hands on him and about an hour later, while praying at home, Richard collapsed in hysterical holy laughter which continued for at least 20 minutes.

That evening [June 1st] the Wednesday night prayer meeting

erupted in holy chaos with people falling under the mighty presence of God, many laughing or just totally 'out' in the Spirit. The following Sunday 11am service [June 5th] was one of those rare occasions where senior minister Colin Dye was unable to finish a sermon as this great move of the Holy Spirit manifested powerfully.

Some folk were seen doing the most extraordinary things, including one man who looked as though he was swimming, first on his back and then later in breast stroke style! The 5pm service on the weekend of March for Jesus (June 26th) was particularly powerful. After some wonderful healings, all heaven broke loose with people falling and laughing all over the church.

Holy Trinity Brompton, Queen's Road Baptist and the Putney and Twickenham Vineyards were among the first of many churches to be hit by this new wave of God's power, with Pioneer, Ichthus and New Frontiers now affected too. The common feeling is that this is a time of refreshing for the churches in preparation for the greater manifestation of God's power.

The word 'hysterical', used to describe the laughter in the extract above, is common but perhaps unhelpful since it has two very separate and distinct uses which are tending to become confused. In popular usage it means 'loud, overwhelming, over the top, side-splitting' when, say, describing laughter. However, the same word is also used by doctors to describe a particular type of mental illness which may require urgent attention from a psychiatrist!

The medical syndrome of hysteria describes a highly abnormal mental state. Confusion over terms has led unqualified observers to muddle the two uses together, and then dismiss what is happening as hysteria. I am certain that they are largely mistaken, for reasons we will see later.

Why not me?

The issue of the disappointment of people coming away from meetings 'untouched' is a very important one. Meetings like these can create great expectations and pressures, with two effects. First, some may be inclined to imitate consciously or unconsciously what is happening to others. Secondly, others may feel failures or inadequate because God seems somehow to have passed them by. Indeed, slight depression in mood is a very common feeling in those who observe the ecstasy of those around them but are left relatively unaffected. Then there are those who react strongly against the disturbances and are repelled by the thought of being drawn into what they see as emotional fanaticism.

No words can convey the impact of being in some of these meetings, standing next to someone who is swaying, shrieking, yelling out, laughing wildly, bellowing, bouncing up and down or writhing as if controlled by an unseen force, rolling on the ground or thrashing about. Such close proximity can indeed be hazardous. In extreme cases you may have to move well away or risk being accidentally hit in the face, barged into or knocked down. These can be violent phenomena.

Many leaders who months ago used to feel reasonably confident about telling the difference between the work of the Holy Spirit, human emotionalism and demonic activity, have been baffled by some of the phenomena. At first a common reaction has been that most if not all of the more extreme manifestations have been demonic in origin, but after a few weeks of observation and talking to those of their congregations who have been affected, many are becoming far less sure about such instant labelling. The reason is the fruit.

Often those manifesting in these ways have testified to an

overwhelming experience of God's love, power, holiness or authority. Many describe that the strange movements have had a particular symbolic significance in what God was saying to them. Most important of all has been that the changes in people's lives appear to be profound, positive and long lasting, and that these manifestations are often happening to mature leaders who have led churches for years. Even an Anglican bishop (David Pytches) has been heard 'roaring like a lion' loudly for a long period. It is therefore far less easy to make a blanket diagnosis.

But what about these animal noises – barking, roaring, mooing or crowing? Some remain very puzzled, others are alarmed. Many who are positive generally about what has been happening have drawn the line at these things, although in practice when manifestations break out all over a meeting it is hard to encourage one type and suppress others.

The key seems to be having adequate numbers of experienced ministry team members who can quickly come alongside someone who is manifesting, make some kind of assessment and deal with the situation with prayer and firm but gentle counsel if necessary. At the same time it is important that the meeting continues to be led, and that the ministry team is directed.

The trouble is that when the phenomena first hit a church it has happened that many of the team, including the musicians, have themselves been incapacitated – on the floor or otherwise out of action – and those responsible for leading the meeting have been drawn into praying for individuals. The result has sometimes been disorder and confusion as a bewildered congregation tries to interpret what is happening, with no lead at all from the front.

For critics of the movement, such bizarre sights as grown men crawling about the floor making loud animal noises or imitating animal movements have merely confirmed their worst fears that what might conceivably have started out long ago as a move of God, is now going rapidly off the rails, divorced from scriptural reason and mature godly common sense.

The manifestations are so striking, so visible, so overwhelming, so dominant that it is easy to forget our call to worship Jesus and to concentrate on the visible, and assume that shaking or laughter is now a sign of holiness, hysteria or demons, depending on your perspective. The reality is that in some cases it could merely be a sign of insecurity in a person – a result of emotional vulnerability or even exhibitionism. It could also be a simple result of disinhibition following intoxication. As we will see later, what is happening is certainly affecting the brain as profoundly as a big dose of alcohol – it's powerful stuff. The only way to evaluate thoroughly is through long-term follow up. Fruit.

We will return to these pressures, dilemmas and guidelines for the future later on.

On Friday 17th June 1994 the *Church of England Newspaper* ran the headline: 'Revival breaks out in London', describing bewilderment among church leaders as manifestations affected business and staff meetings, as well as church services.

From Monday 20th June Ichthus began special 'receiving meetings' every weekday evening for two weeks, and after a break of a week, again from 11th-22nd July. Hundreds of lives were touched. Throughout August the special meetings continued on Mondays and Wednesdays. From 21st to 24th June Ichthus also held a prayer and fasting conference at Sizewell Hall. Stuart Bell from New Life Christian Fellowship in Lincoln arrived on the final morning to speak.

The day before, R. T. Kendall from Westminster Chapel had been in Lincoln and had offered to pray for Stuart after describing how his own scepticism about the new 'move of God' had melted away.

Stuart had not fallen over, laughed or been in any way obviously affected at the time. However, on arrival at the Ichthus meeting:

I asked whether any of the phenomena that had been seen in other London churches had impacted Ichthus, and Roger [Forster] told me that for the past week they had had special meetings and people were being blessed and touched by the Spirit.

It is rather difficult to explain what exactly happened, but there was a sense of the spiritual climate rising in the room, and I was asked to pray specifically for two people, one of them Roger. About halfway through my prayer I was totally taken by surprise as Roger and I were knocked to the floor for about 20 minutes.

I personally felt the power and love of God like 'warm waves' over me. Most of the leaders who were present experienced various kinds of reactions to the power of the Holy Spirit. There was laughter, tears, confession of sin, humbleness, brokenness, and we had the privilege of being in what turned out to be about five hours of the very evident blessing of God upon our lives.

We then drove to Newark, where I was booked to speak to leaders of the Baptist Church. We went to the (evening) meeting where I shared in a very low-key manner, then at about 10pm the leaders asked if we would pray for them before leaving. As we prayed, again the power of God was released, and the leaders all ended up with laughter, and again we witnessed a very deep work of the Spirit in people's lives. At 11pm we struggled to the car to go home.

Since that time, almost every day things have happened at

various levels. We have witnessed shaking, tears, laughter, confession of sin, and people's testimonies are being shared that are of a deeper nature than I have personally ever witnessed. A number have spoken of sensing they were having a 'spiritual scan' as they laid on the floor, as God worked into areas that had been hidden, or hurts going back to childhood.

I wrote to Dr Kendall, believing that his prayer when he came to Lincoln released blessing into our locality. We have, since that time, prayed with leaders from across the region, and many of the churches in the area have been impacted through this new move of the Spirit.

So was Stuart affected by the prayers of R. T. Kendall, or just swept up in what had been developing in Ichthus over the previous month? That is the sort of question that is being asked over and over again across the country. The 'we had it first' syndrome in those who approve of what is happening, or 'that man's influence again' in those who disapprove.

It is possible that from time to time some leaders may have tended to play down the degree to which the current wave of the Holy Spirit has occurred through the ministry of another person affecting their church. It is important that we graciously honour each other in this move of God when God has so graciously used others to bring us this blessing, as indeed both Ichthus leadership and Stuart Bell have done.

I have encountered all these reactions over and over again in collecting material for this book. They can be linked to pride, feelings of superiority or even resentment about the huge profile being enjoyed in some places. God is sovereign. Who are we to claim his glory or deny his right to exercise power as he wills?

Yet history shows clearly that the date churches have been affected has depended largely on who visited where and when. The experience of God's power has been transmitted through lines of relationship – of friendship – rather than through extra devotion to Jesus.

It is surely very dangerous to say a church is full of holy and obedient people, just because its meetings were one of the first to be filled by laughter, shaking or other manifestations. The opposite could be true if the experiences and disinhibition were to lead to sexual excesses and heresy, as happened in the Latter Rain Movement earlier this century in America. Manifestations alone prove nothing.

However, it is also true that some churches are full of cynical, faithless people who despise all traces of Christian emotion and who have abandoned biblical truth and morality in favour of their own intellectual opinions. They are hardly likely suddenly to experience an overwhelming sense of the presence of God.

On the 26th June, *The Sunday Telegraph* reported that George Carey, Archbishop of Canterbury, had declined to visit the Toronto Vineyard church, although asked to do so by Canon Michael Green. The Archbishop was booked to visit other churches in the city as part of his busy international schedule. The paper reported:

'It would be very helpful and significant if he [Dr Carey] went along,' said Canon Michael Green, joint coordinator of Dr Carey's Operation Springboard initiative for the Decade of Evangelism. 'What's going on is perfectly legitimate and people need encouraging. Privately, Dr Carey is understood to be delighted by talk of a revival but is reluctant to give his backing to what some view as self-induced hysteria.

'The Archbishop does not want to downplay what is going on but there are many ways that God's Spirit manifests itself [*sic*],' said his spokesman. 'He has to be careful about identifying himself with one form of charismatic manifestation.'

The Archdeacon of York, the Ven George Austin, took a sharply different view:

'If you want these things to happen they will... Some think you are not a proper Christian unless you roll around the floor in laughter,' he said. Meanwhile, a Baptist minister in Matlock, Derbyshire, has published a leaflet warning against the current religious excitement. 'This phenomenon does not provide any evidence of a genuine Christian revival,' said the Reverend Alan Morrison. 'Thousands of professing Christians are being hoodwinked by a psycho-religious phenomenon that is completely unrelated to genuine Christian spirituality.

'Not only is this harmful to the emotional and spiritual health of those who fall under its compelling power, but the rampant encouragement of such experiences is bringing the gospel and church of Jesus Christ into disrepute.'

On the same day as this *Sunday Telegraph* report appeared (26th June), an Anglican vicar, adviser to Clifford Hill's team (Prophecy Word Ministries), went to see for himself what was happening at Holy Trinity Brompton.

I visited HTB for the 6.30pm service on Sunday 26 June with two colleagues from our leadership team. We went to observe, but were willing to respond in any way that the Lord wanted us to. The service itself was quite low-key, short and more formal than we had expected. The worship was not very noisy, and there was no corporate singing in tongues. Sandy Millar preached.

Before doing so he called, one by one, two women and two men to the front. They had already begun to shake and as each received ministry from members of the ministry team they fell to the ground and continued shaking, laughing, roaring or crying out in various ways for some time while Sandy continued preaching.

I was at the back of the gallery (the church was absolutely full) so could not see well, but it seemed to me that others were being similarly affected as Sandy preached.

The sermon was very much off the cuff and loosely based on Nehemiah 8:5-12. Sandy quite often referred to the people receiving ministry at the front while he spoke. The theme was the joy of knowing the reality of God's forgiveness. He spoke for about 20 minutes and then after spending a few moments reassuring everyone that anything that might happen was safely in God's hands he prayed briefly and simply that God would send the Holy Spirit among us.

Gradually more and more people began to display quite a wide variety of manifestations. From our perch in the gallery we watched with prayerful interest. After a while first one colleague and then the other, one on each side of me, began shaking and laughing. Both were lowered to their seats by members of the HTB ministry team.

I have quite often ministered to the demonised, but I had no sense whatever of anything demonic about what was happening on each side of me. Indeed, I had a strong sense that it was entirely good and healthy. I too felt the Lord's presence weighing heavily on me and fell to my knees in rather tearful adoration. My male colleague and I recovered rather sooner than the other, who for about 35-40 minutes alternately rested peacefully, or laughed loudly, stamping her feet and waving her arms.

By this time around 75-100 people out of (I would guess) 1500 present were receiving ministry. Some were laughing, others were weeping, while still others did show signs of demonic manifestations of the kind that I would associate with effective deliverance.

Afterwards, both of my colleagues spoke of a sense of great and joyful liberation, of feeling willing to do anything for the Lord. My colleague's wife, in particular, had a great sense of her sin and of the holiness of God, but had quickly been overwhelmed by the wonderful certainty of forgiveness.

I am sure that there was some mixture of influences at the meeting (when isn't there?) but that taken all in all, we had witnessed a healthy move of the Spirit of God.

I believe that it is not revival, but if properly received and channelled with a cool head for the possibilities of deception, then this move could mark the first stage of revival. In particular, I noticed that repentance did find a significant place in the preaching.[13]

Two days later (Tuesday 28th June), five miles further west, an evening meeting was held in an Anglican church in Ealing, West London, for any leaders interested to hear about what was happening. At only a few days' notice several hundred turned up, including members of my church, my wife and a number of close friends from other places.

That night I was speaking to the Movement of Christian Democracy in the House of Lords. I returned home where I waited until almost midnight for people to come back. My wife was delayed because the driver of the car was so overcome with laughter – as were all the passengers – that they had to stop to recover.

On the same evening, on the other side of the world, the evangelist Billy Graham told a conference of evangelists in Louisville, USA that he was excited about the increasing signs of what he saw as nothing less than world revival: 'This is a wonderful day to be alive ... I've never seen so many people come to salvation in such a short period of time.'

Gerald Coates, director of Pioneer, a national network of new churches, was interviewed in June 1994 regarding the new move of God. Commenting on the changes taking place for some years previously in Britain, he said:

Whoever would have thought that around 15 million people would take to the streets to pray for the world on June 25th

1994 (March for Jesus)? We should be astounded this initiative came from the UK. So there is at last something happening in the West.

It is touching the USA, Canada and now the UK. This 'new thing' is being expressed in uproarious laughter, tears, confession of sin and apparent drunkenness.

Q. What has the Holy Spirit come to do? What is the purpose of laughter and these other manifestations of the Holy Spirit? Is this another Wimber phenomenon?

A. For us in Pioneer People there are stories of personal revival. But for the church I believe it is simply 'times of refreshing from the presence of the Lord' (Acts 3:19). There are over 30 references to laughter in Scripture. God laughs. There is a 'time to laugh' (Ecc 3:4). This must be one of those times! Jesus promised laughter (Luke 6:21). Therefore we must be very careful about perspectives such as the 'Wimber phenomenon'. If you reduce what is happening to that then much of the New Testament was the 'Paul phenomenon'.

Q. Maybe this is a sovereign move of God, but it comes through people. What should our response to this be? Do we just allow it to happen or can we take hold of God's purposes?

A. It has come in answer to prayer. We have seen London's Royal Albert Hall filled with over 5,000 for prayer, and I have been privileged to be present at the National Exhibition Centre in Birmingham when around 15,000 were present to pray. Prayer has been a main feature of our own church for years. But our responses will vary. Ultimately we must humble ourselves before God, knowing that whatever He does is to equip us to fulfil the task of nourishing the church and reaching the lost.

One leader for example did not go forward on the 5th June when I gave an appeal. But she was deluged by the Spirit, fell into her chair so drunk that when she opened her mouth nothing would come out! She is not exactly known for those sorts of things. When another leader was prayed for the same night at Tooting, he was not expecting what happened. He ended up on the floor roaring with laughter. The real test will be the fruit of these manifestations in people's lives.

Q. Many people are fearful of the phenomena of the Holy Spirit. What would you say to them? Could this be seen as mass hysteria?

A. Strangely most people are not fearful. Laughter destroys fear! Most think it is lovely, like heaven. I have an increasing number of stories from people telling me how their awareness of God's presence has been remarkably increased. They want to read the Scriptures, can't stop praying – it has put a new zest into their relationships. It is happening to very sensible people and, dare I say it, to the sceptics. These are people not easily led. By the way, the dictionary explains hysteria as 'morbid excitement', but this is the last thing I have experienced as I have seen the Holy Spirit move in such diverse places as Dublin, Geneva, Orebro in Sweden, Frankfurt and now here.

Q. If nothing has happened to me have I missed out? Is there something wrong with me?

A. No! One man I know of sat in this sort of thing for a total of 12 hours and absolutely nothing happened to him. But it looks as though the work of God's Spirit was such that he is now praying for hundreds of people and is one of the main instruments at this time blessing others. He is a wise, sensible pastor.

Q. Many children are being touched by God. How should we be helping them?

A. I suggest we take time to read relevant scriptures about laughter, the coming of the Holy Spirit and other unusual things Jesus did. Our children need to know that this is not new. This has gone on in almost every revival. At two meetings children have actually asked me if they can come forward and if I would pray for them. They love it. One lad confessed in tears that he was telling his parents lies and was ashamed of it and as a result he put things right with them. Repentance is always at the core of personal and corporate revival.

Q. What should we expect to see as a result of this move of God?

A. As the leaders of Pioneer People know, I have been privileged to see this sort of thing for the last three months in different places I have visited around the world. Throughout May I often found myself in tears with some of them as I felt something was 'about to break'. I was not aware that at the end of May this would break out in a number of churches known to me personally.

It is not that we have wanted to keep this from the church but we do not want the power of auto suggestion to rule. Martin was aware that I knew something was going to break on the first Sunday of June and we shouldn't be surprised at what we saw. But I expect increased faith in Christ, a growing love for the Scriptures, care for people, courtesy in relationships, and I would be surprised if we don't find public confession of sin and a request for forgiveness, as well as an increasing heart for the lost.

I am convinced this is a visitation from God and my prayer is it will last as long as I live![14]

Terry Virgo wrote in the July issue of New Frontiers magazine how the church in Columbia, USA had also been touched since April:

Our church meetings were totally transformed and a new release of the Holy Spirit has overtaken us. I have never seen lives changed so rapidly and the atmosphere of a church altered so swiftly … The continuing impact on people's lives has been magnificent! The blessing of God seems to be very widespread.

He describes how C. J. Mahaney had arrived at the church to speak and had just started with: 'The story of Solomon is one of the most tragic in the whole Bible.' That was as far as he got. He was interrupted by an outbreak of sudden laughter from several people. Terry was embarrassed and C. J. Mahaney was uncertain what to do. The laughter continued for a while and those affected were invited to come forward. No sooner had they arrived at the front than they collapsed to the ground in more convulsive laughter. The laughter spread across the congregation and continued until almost midnight, with many people praying for each other.

Bryn Jones, leader of the Covenant Ministries network of churches in the UK, reported an outpouring of the Holy Spirit in Bradford, the Wirral, Manchester, Chester, Leicester and other places.[15] Across the country the phenomena spread rapidly. By June and July, Sunday meetings in perhaps 200 churches were already affected in England alone, with individuals touched in up to 1,000 others. Noel Stanton of the Jesus Fellowship group of churches wrote in *Jesus Lifestyle* magazine:

> It's reminiscent of the charismatic buzz of the '60s and '70s which swept around the UK. There have been many waves since, but the present wave could well be the big one. This really is God reviving His people. This is a charismatic revival movement which will spread through the nation.

The Jesus Army mission in London during July was marked by a lot of laughter among the team during the week, but at the Sunday morning meeting:

> There was a general wave of repentance, with many people weeping and crying out to God. 'People carried a new sense of tenderness to God. I became aware of many little things which had seemed right before but now I knew just weren't,' said Julie. The next meeting was full of laughter once again. Such was the Holy Spirit 'drunkenness' that passers-by came into the meeting,

looking for the bar, only to be amazed by the power of God!

'Drunken' or 'intoxicated' behaviour became a common feature of life after meetings in various churches in West London, particularly among those connected with the Vineyard, such as the Vineyard churches in Putney and in Twickenham, which were among the first to be affected in London.

Some found themselves temporarily incapacitated and unable to drive home, needing to take time to 'sober up', while others were so overcome with paroxysmal laughter that they too were unable to drive.[16] Taxis began to find extra work after services at Holy Trinity Brompton. Speech becomes slurred, movements become clumsy, and there is a great feeling of merriment and happiness, like being intoxicated with too much beer or wine.

Noel Stanton of the Jesus Army has been quick to point out that laughter 'in the Spirit' is nothing new in his own experience of British charismatic church life.

We started laughing (in the Spirit!) 25 years ago. People in our meetings have been laughing (at irregular intervals) ever since. Occasionally it has spread, and we have been engulfed in outbursts of sometimes uncontrollable laughter, with people rolling on the floor and making loud persistent belly laughs! But the laughter can also be relatively quiet. 'Falling under the power' happens even more frequently.

The New Testament describes it as 'rejoicing with unutterable and exalted joy'. The first Christians were intoxicated with power and joy. So when I see and hear people laughing with joy in the Spirit, or when some of our leaders roll about consumed by mirth, I am neither surprised nor concerned. It's almost always genuine and exalts Jesus.

Spiritual intoxication happens when believers are first

baptised with the Holy Spirit. At this stage it properly belongs to our being new-born disciples of Jesus Christ and is a sign of our resurrection with Him. At other times it occurs as Christians 'drink the new wine' of the Holy Spirit and find a new anointing. In our experience it is always part of other manifestations, such as conviction of sin, calling on Jesus to forgive and save, weeping and groaning, speaking in an unknown tongue of praise, liberated worship, removal of demons and healing of the sick.[17]

The Jesus Army found that laughter became hard to handle a few years ago, and so began gradually to discourage it, while other manifestations continued more frequently.[18]

Clive Calver, head of the Evangelical Alliance, expressed some concern to *The Sunday Telegraph* reporters that the experiences could divert people from their calling to be salt and light, preaching the gospel and providing practical help for those in need, taking the life and love of God into every area of society: 'What is important is that this internal transformation is accompanied by a new social action – such as care for the poor and the homeless.'

Sandy Millar, Holy Trinity Brompton, wrote an article in July 1994 to reassure those who were disturbed and others going home depressed from meetings because they had not been 'touched':

'Restrained? Quiet? Unobtrusive? My dear friends, why not listen to the evidence? This is the kind of thing that happens when the Spirit "comes" upon man: "Even the building was shaken."'

So said the Doctor – Dr Martyn Lloyd-Jones. We haven't seen the building shaken yet, but, as most of you know, we have seen some very remarkable things. Some of the more obvious signs are the loud and prolonged laughter that comes over some people and the spontaneous weeping and crying out in repentance and sorrow for the past. Along with all this and much else besides is the apparently effortless way in which people fall backwards (or, sometimes, forwards) and lie on the floor.

At some point in the 19th century, this phenomenon came to be described as being 'slain in the Spirit'. In the 18th-century accounts it is 'being overcome' or 'fainting'. In the Bible it is 'fell at his feet as though dead' (Revelation 1:17); 'drew back and fell to the ground' (John 18:6) and 'fell on my face' (Daniel 10:9).

In many cases a person may experience any or all of these experiences by turns. In some cases the experience of 'resting in the Spirit', which is probably what we would call it today, may simply be accompanied by a deep sense of peace – a silent activity of God in the heart, spirit or soul leading to radical changes in people's lives.

Is there anything that we can say about all this, even at this early stage? I think there is.

1. It is of God. It is a season of blessing and we would be wise to make the most of it while God is willing to continue to pour out his Spirit in this way. All the signs of the fruit of it that we have seen so far are consistent only with the activity of God by his Spirit.

People are experiencing a tremendous new love for Jesus Christ, for the Bible as God's word and for the things that God loves. Whilst we thought at the beginning of all this that it was God's way of blessing his church (presumably with a view to that overflowing out into the world outside in due course), there are already the most encouraging signs that people are being brought to repentance and faith in Christ through it all. There is a new joy, a new freedom in faith, a new love. That sounds like God's activity, doesn't it?

2. I think it is God's way of calling his church at this time to the desire of his heart for relationship.

It is no surprise surely that when Jesus was asked to set out the priorities for his followers he did so in terms of love: 'Love the Lord your God' (with basically everything you've got) and 'love your neighbour as yourself'. Love is key – more important even than truth (though dependent on it). I think too that with that recovery of relationship with his church, God is providing seasons (and this is one) of great joy.

Most of us, most of the time, take ourselves too seriously. See some of the things printed in the press in recent weeks! Of course there are seasons of sadness for most Christians, and others, at some times. But the experience of the early church, at a time of intense persecution incidentally when they never knew who would still be alive from one week to the next, was described as 'joy inexpressible' (1 Peter 1).

That's quite a lot of joy! And how we need that joy today! And God is giving it to us. Let's drink all we can, as often as we can!

3. Because it is God loving his church, let us not worry about whether we experience more or less of what others seem to experience, or of what we would like to experience. It really doesn't matter whether you fall over or not, or how long you lie on the floor! God loves you – that's what matters and if you will surrender totally to him you will know what Corrie Ten Boom once called 'the joy of total surrender'.

What matters is that you have the relationship with God that Jesus Christ died to make possible and that you allow him to change you into what he cares enough for you to want you to be! The stories we are hearing at this time of radically changed lives are phenomenal. What a thrilling time to be alive!

I know that some of the things we are seeing are difficult to understand and I appreciate all the hesitations that are being expressed from time to time. I would only encourage us all to keep praying – and keep coming! Keep sharing experiences and keep receiving.[19]

On Friday night, 1st July, Ruth Gledhill from *The Times* turned up at the Vineyard church in Putney, South London.

She described how the first person she saw was a young man who looked like he had a hangover, but it became clear that the intoxication had been a result of the previous night's meeting. She said that over the next two hours, she saw several hundred more become 'drunk in the Spirit, laughing, weeping and crying out, many shaking as if in delirium tremens, others simply fainting on the floor'.

The first to raise her hands in the air and begin swaying was Eleanor Mumford, wife of the Putney church's senior pastor, John Mumford. It was Mrs Mumford who visited the Toronto church because she felt 'spiritually bankrupt'. She claimed a 'fantastic' experience and returned to England to pray with her colleagues. She appears to have caused an almost instant ripple effect.

By the second number people were dancing in the aisles, and the back of the young man in front of me had begun vibrating as the beginning of a progression to spiritual drunkenness that was to end in rigid, on-the-spot shaking and leaping.

After his sermon, Mr Mumford prayed for 'the tornado to visit the church'. The band struck up with the song 'Pour out Your Spirit'. Outside it was calm, but suddenly the curtains shielding an open door blew in and over my face and a huge wind rushed in, scattering service sheets and papers.

Alarmed, I started singing along with the band, while nearly everyone else fell over, stood rigid or shaking, sobbing, clutching at their faces or waving their hands before them. I looked back beyond the empty chairs and bodies strewn over the floor, to see many who were not affected were chatting calmly over coffee as if nothing was happening, while bodies lay splayed at their feet, bearing beatific smiles and looks of tremendous peace.

I clambered over a couple of prostrate bodies for tea and coffee, and found myself giggling uncontrollably. Turning to look back at the band, the hall took on a bizarrely infinite perspective. I felt dizzy, grasped a chair in order not to collapse, and recalled that I still had a day's work to do at the office.[20]

Ruth Gledhill is describing here a classic case of someone on the edge of an altered state of consciousness (ASC) in a group setting – something we will examine more closely in chapter 5. Changes in consciousness are common in historic Christian experience. They are the key perhaps to understanding many of these manifestations, and explain why these experiences are often so helpful and intensely pleasurable; a gateway for many to a new depth of spiritual awareness or an expression of it.

Such changes in mental functioning are experienced by the Christian mystic who withdraws from the world, and by the charismatic who may often experience them with others. Christians who have enjoyed such a state of altered awareness regard it as a gift from God. Those with a more 'down-to-earth' view of faith can look on these things as unhelpful, meaningless, a waste of time, unhealthy or dangerous.

Three days later (Monday 4th July) Stuart Bell, church leader from New Life Christian Fellowship in Lincoln, described his own experience to thirty other leaders from Pioneer, meeting at Fairmile Court in Surrey. One or two others shared their accounts of a new happening in their own churches. Those sharing then offered to pray for people one by one if they wanted. The room was silent at first, but after a few minutes it gradually filled with laughter as people became touched by a profound sense of the presence of God.

After about half an hour, those praying and those receiving began to stagger around in small groups, trying hard to prop each other up until, laughing away, they fell over each other and tumbled helplessly to the ground, overcome with mirth. Some laughed until it seemed their sides would burst, to the point of agony – and still they laughed. Many reported afterwards that it had been highly enjoyable, relaxing and therapeutic, and that they felt very aware of God's love.[21]

This all continued for about forty minutes, much to the concern of Gerald Coates who was anxiously looking at his watch, awaiting the Queen of Romania, who was shortly due to arrive to address the disordered gathering!

When he saw her car arrive outside just a few feet away, there were so many bodies piled up against the door of the room that the only way in or out was through the French windows. The room was a scene of noisy pandemonium, with bodies everywhere and some of those still standing looking distinctly unsteady, others propping themselves up dazed and disorientated on the floor. For most in the room it was the first time they had seen or heard anything like it before, although some had heard reports.

The Queen, meanwhile, was swiftly and discreetly ushered into another room and then into lunch, by which time the dishevelled company had got themselves into some kind of order and staggered into the dining room.

Some weeks later Stuart Bell described to a smaller number of Pioneer leaders how things had progressed in Lincoln since. One local leader had heard about what was going on in the church and rang up Stuart to give his views, which were quite negative. They arranged to meet. As the leader entered Stuart's office he fell over. A woman in the Lincoln church also wrote to protest: 'I can't cope with all this.' She also fell on the floor in the church office as she walked in to talk face to face.

The church in Lincoln began to hold special meetings midweek, with an open invitation to other leaders to turn up. On Monday 12th September a meeting was arranged in a small venue with a capacity of around fifty but 100 turned up. The noise was great during the meeting and spread down the street. After the meeting the people overflowed onto the pavement, where some fell, unable to get up. Curious passers-by stepped gingerly between the bodies, with typical British reserve.

Meanwhile, churches in other European countries were becoming affected: France, for example. The Revd Charlie Cleverley is an Anglican vicar who planted three rapidly-growing churches in East London before moving in 1991 to Paris with his family to begin a similar work there. In June 1994 he wrote in the family prayer letter:

> As I have recently written to friends, it sometimes seems as if people are falling over themselves for God's attention.
>
> Some are coming out of the desert experience; some are coming to know God for the first time and some are finding an unprecedented refreshment and restoration in God's presence. This latter is not unconnected with recent events in the church in England which have found their way into the newspapers.

Later that September he described to me how French Christians had been affected by falling and laughter, perhaps as early as 1993. The phenomena had not been connected to Toronto or the USA. One example was in Pierre Cranga's church at Macon, two hours east of Paris. The church of 100 people had been overcome by laughter and falling over. Pierre had tried to make sense of it all, and his thoughts are recorded in a book he is writing called *New Wine*.

David Berly is the leader of a church at Lille, a large mining town north of Paris. His work among drug addicts is well respected, and he has no fewer than forty government-funded workers. His mission helped around 1,500 homeless people in 1993 alone. While he is no advocate of these new experiences, they have affected some in his church for some time. From 9th-11th September, Charlie Cleverley was at their church weekend conference where many prayed for were filled with laughter and some crashed to the floor, especially those recently converted from 'tough' backgrounds.

Charlie's own church in Paris became affected by what had happened in England when several members went over to London in June 1994. They returned convinced that what they had seen was of God and prayed for Charlie.

In June 1994 reports from Germany also began to reach my own church in Brentford of a new move of God in Frankfurt, with 'people falling all over the place and uncontrollable laughter'. Other reports began to trickle in. It seemed as if churches scattered across the whole Western world were beginning to see similar things.

On 6th July several hundred church leaders in London gathered together, as they had every three months over the last year, to pray for a revival in the city and the nation. Their newsletter 'Capital Calling' reported in July:

As Capital Calling went to press, the much-publicised outbreaks of hysterical laughter, speaking in tongues, weeping and being unable to stand were continuing to spread among London churches. Bob Cheeseman, pastor of Putney Community Church and a member of the London Leaders' Steering Group, was among the first British church leaders to visit the Toronto church where the 'revival' began.

'We are seeing a manifestation of the coming of the Holy Spirit. It results in an increased love for Jesus, a new hunger to pray and read Scripture, a heightened sense of adoration and worship, and a desire for holiness.' Mr Cheeseman believes it important to evaluate people's experience by the changes in their lives. 'The manifestations are unusual, but we know from the Bible that it is by their fruit that we shall know them.

This move of the Holy Spirit is certainly changing lives.'

At the meeting on 6th July, Sandy Millar of Holy Trinity Brompton and Norman Moss of Queen's Road Baptist Church were invited to explain what was happening, and then to pray for those who wanted ministry. Many fell to the floor, laughed or were affected in other ways, while some were unmoved and left disturbed.

An example of the confusion over how to handle these manifestations occurred in July at a big youth event for several hundred teenagers (INTERFACE) in Surrey. A counsellor called Andy was confronted by a young man who was bouncing up and down after a time of worship and ministry. 'Please pray for me to stop bouncing!' the man exclaimed. Andy escorted him down the corridor as he continued to bounce, but was uncertain whether to pray against what might in fact be a part of the working of the Holy Spirit.[22]

At around the same time Nicky Gumbel, Curate of Holy Trinity Brompton, received a letter from John Darling, Minister of Trowbridge Evangelical Church, who had attended an Alpha training course in Birmingham a few weeks previously. (The Alpha induction programme for enquirers and new believers was developed at Holy Trinity.)

> The evening started with a time of worship, and while we were singing one of our members shot out of the room. I followed her, thinking she was upset, to find her doubled up with laughter. She had fled the room, thinking that it was the polite thing to do.
>
> I had planned to explain what God is doing in this release of joy in the talk, but as we had not reached that point I explained briefly to her and encouraged her to rejoin the others. As we came back it was obvious that others were being touched, all

before any mention of the experience. It soon became very clear that no more teaching was appropriate and I invited the Holy Spirit to increase the joy and then one then another exploded in spiritual laughter.

I know it was an anointing because I have known these people for a very long time and have never heard them laugh like that. As it progressed I explained what was happening and when after 20 minutes it subsided I began the talk that I had heard you give at Birmingham.

It was such fun. One lady whose husband had explained to her what had happened in Birmingham said, 'Well, don't expect me to get involved in that.' She was one of the first to receive and she howled with lovely laughter.

We finally finished and met again the next day for worship. You can imagine the anticipation, and sure enough at several points it sprang up again during the worship and talk, and I simply had no choice but to let the Holy Spirit do his work while I shut up.

There were two crowning glories to the weekend. One lady on Saturday who had laughed herself to the limit, stood up and said she had received a miraculous healing of something she had been in constant pain with for months and the doctors feared it was a malignant growth. We also had a new family come along and as a direct result of the joy she witnessed and felt is joining. So it is both for healing and evangelism.

It is not uncommon for people initially opposed to what is happening to experience it in their bodies – before they are aware that they have changed their minds.

On Sunday 17th July I returned from speaking at a conference of Christian doctors in Norway to find a church worker living in our home had returned from a Sunday meeting at Holy Trinity Brompton. He was bemused to find that his left arm and hand were periodically shaking – something that was causing him some puzzlement and mild inconvenience. He was unstoppable as he talked of God's love, God's power, God's holiness, and of his love for Jesus.

On the Tuesday morning (19th July), my wife and I went to a meeting of leaders in Teddington organised by Thames Community Church and the Twickenham Vineyard. Over twenty different churches were represented across the denominations, few of whom had personally seen or experienced any of the so-called Toronto phenomena. After a short talk, a time of prayer began, during which most of the thirty or so present were affected, some by loud wailings with an acute awareness of sin, others with a sense of lifted burdens and worries with joy and infectious laughter, others feeling so weak that they fell down, or got down on the floor, or sat down quietly.

The next Sunday (24th July) Dr William Atkinson was having trouble leading the 5pm meeting at Kensington Temple (KT). Over 1,000 had crammed in for one of the two evening services. At one point in the worship spontaneous applause broke out, much longer than he had ever seen before (at the church clapping was common previously).

> Each time it began to die down, a fresh wave of applause would seem to break in with cheering, stamping of feet, etc. I had considerable difficulty stopping it to move the meeting on in the programme and was left wondering how long it would have continued if I had not had to move the meeting on.

Just four days previously I had myself spoken briefly at the KT church prayer meeting (700 people) to explain about the need for volunteers to care for those dying with AIDS in London. After further worship, a short talk by one of the leaders and a time of prayer, I observed a number overcome by laughter, or broken down in tears, prostrate before God, or shaken rhythmically by an unseen force. Earlier in the month the leaders of KT had felt such a sense of a mighty wave about to break that the whole of the church programme for the autumn was suspended to allow meetings almost every night in the church from September.

Many other nations were newly affected. By July 1994, churches from countries as far away as New Zealand were preparing to send members on a round trip of over 20,000 miles to the Toronto church. The New Zealand Christian Advance Ministries organised two trips. One of the leaders said: 'The key characteristic of the renewal is that it is spread by those who have experienced it. If this move of the Holy Spirit truly is of God we have a unique opportunity to help spread the fire.'[23]

However, by the beginning of August the manifestations had already broken out throughout New Zealand. There were reports by 10th August that Christchurch Celebration Centre had doubled the size of its congregation as a result. The Huntley Assembly of God, Tauranga's Faith Bible College, a church in Hawkes Bay and others also reported an 'increased awareness of the presence of the Holy Spirit' during worship. The 'Toronto Blessing' had been covered sympathetically by *The New Zealand Herald*, *The Dominian* in Wellington, the capital, and by *The Sunday Star Times*.[24]

Not surprisingly, by August the move of God had also spread from England to hit Scotland – it was already present some weeks before. It was further accelerated by a series of tent meetings at Blair Castle in the Highlands, north of Perth, organised by Covenant Life Church in Glasgow as part of 'Scotland Aflame'. John Price reported in *The Independent* on 12th August:

Airport Church Lands Converts

For each of the past five evenings Scotland has been witnessing mass religious hysteria manifested in the 'charismata' visited on the apostles at Pentecost. Hundreds of men, women and children line up before the stage of a large white marquee as the evangelism builds to a climax and, at a signal, as the Spirit apparently swoops on the tent, they start to drop. Caught as they fall, laid gently on the wet grass, they lie shaking and shouting, either riven with gusts of laughter or weeping uncontrollably. Some have begun talking in tongues.

These are the first signs north of the border of an apparent global 'awakening' of religious conviction, begun earlier this year in the bizarre setting of Toronto's Airport Church. The world's more radical evangelicals are now convinced they are witnessing a spiritual phenomenon, likened in scale to the Wesleyan movement that swept the land early last century.[25]

A common feature has been the way in which many different denominations and groups have been affected, the absence of individuals associated prominently with the phenomena, and the breaking down of traditional sectarian barriers in a new sense of fellowship and understanding. The overwhelmingly positive reception among both traditional church hierarchies and the secular media has also been remarkable.

The phenomena have not been confined to Protestant churches: the charismatic wing of the Catholic Church was also quickly affected by the new wave of enthusiasm among believers. In August 1994 *The Daily Telegraph* reported that a group of 300 charismatic Catholics in Guildford, Surrey were having similar experiences to those in many Protestant churches, with spread to other Catholic groups in the UK.[26]

The leader of the Catholic group Cor Lumen Christi, Damian Stayne, was reported as saying: 'We have had young people, and those in their 40s and 50s, crying or rolling around the floor laughing. Some felt refreshed, others emboldened, while one man said he had "entered into a deep love relationship with Jesus."

Meanwhile, The Upper Room, a mainly Catholic community in St Albans, Herts, saw similar things throughout August following a visit by a pastor from a Vineyard Fellowship.

Throughout August, many different Bible weeks held across Britain were reporting new phenomena. For example, at the Stoneleigh week (30th July – 4th August) organised by New Frontiers, large numbers of the 14,000 people were affected by manifestations. Some of the speakers visiting from the US were also newly affected and took what was happening back to their own churches on their return. Many of the 150 churches represented at Stoneleigh began to experience the new phenomena when members went home.

At another week, several thousand people of all ages pitched camp on the Shepton Mallet Showground in England at the New Wine Bible week. David Gardner, Minister of Burwell Baptist Church, Cambridgeshire described afterwards what happened to the children, as the *Baptist Times* reported on 25th August.

Mallet crew members were back on duty again at 6.30 for prayer; doors opened at 7.00 and 1000 children rushed in once again. The evening session was more singing, teaching, fun, team competitions, etc., sitting in groups and encouraging the children to pray for each other, and giving the children opportunity to respond to what God might be doing – including what might be regarded as 'Toronto' blessings (horrible name).

Similar things were happening when John Wimber came to this country in 1984 …

But give Alan Price his due. He does not work up enthusiasm, he does not play on the emotions of children, and he is aware of the dangers. In addition, the Cross of Jesus Christ is central to his teaching. ...

Later in the week, after the teaching about the Cross, there was teaching about the Holy Spirit, and opportunity to respond to Christ.

This was done very sensitively, and as children waited on the Lord, some of the unusual phenomena began to happen. Some children began to cry (later on they said they were not sad or frightened but very happy); some began to shake and some began to laugh.

I know laughing and giggling are contagious, but I believe there was much that was of God. And children did fall on the floor resting in the Spirit. Some of them heard the voice of Jesus and saw pictures or visions.

Let me describe a series of 'pictures' that one 9-year-old in my group saw as he slumped to the ground each evening. The first time he saw lots of angels and heard a voice saying that they were there to protect him through his life. The second occasion he saw angels everywhere, and a much larger person above them all who was in charge of them. He was told that this larger person was Jesus.

On the third occasion he saw a picture of heaven, which he described as really beautiful, with nothing to spoil it. In this picture he saw the other members of our group who were wearing crowns like kings and queens, and Jesus was in the middle. He also saw a glimpse of hell, which he described as very dark, and there were voices that were trying to talk to each other, but they were not allowed to. On the fourth occasion, he said he heard no voices, and saw no pictures – he was just speaking in tongues.

On the fifth occasion, he saw a picture of Satan in a cage, and as Christians marched around singing praises to the Lord, Satan got smaller and smaller and when Satan was the size of an ant, he was stamped on, and disappeared. All this from a very normal lad of nine years who was also full of fun and mischief. I do not think he could have made it up, and I do not think it came from the devil, either.

At this time there were a growing number of stories circulating the country of angelic visitations and other remarkable experiences. Let me describe one, the source of which has proved impossible to trace, despite many enquiries and phone calls, and which should almost certainly be regarded as apocryphal. However, these stories shaped the atmosphere and expectations in the churches that heard them, and are part of the history of this movement.

There are a number of versions. Most of them go something like this: a couple were driving along the road when they saw a hitch-hiker and stopped to give him a lift. He got into the car. During conversation he told them that revival was coming to the nation. Shortly afterwards he disappeared. As they explained what had happened to someone else in the area later on, they were told that exactly the same thing had happened to several other motorists on the same stretch of road.

Another story that keeps going round many churches is one involving police flagging down a driver they thought was drunk following a church meeting. As the policemen talked to the driver, they too were overcome by laughter and fell to the ground. There are various accounts, ranging from police arriving at a restaurant in Toronto where many guests were rolling on the floor, but the police were Christians and were quickly affected too (relayed by John Wimber to Gerald Coates), to others where the police tried to breathalyse the driver, but were too incapacitated to be able to do so (apochryphal).

Of course, with so many intoxicated drivers on the roads following these meetings, it would hardly be surprising to find that a growing number have been stopped, cautioned or even breathalysed. Drivers need to be sensible, as do all people operating machinery or in situations where fine judgement and skilled co-ordination are needed. 'Holy Spirit drunkenness' takes more time than people think to wear off. If we are not careful, there may be another story circulating soon where several people were killed in a terrible accident when driving home, or someone was injured with a power tool at home.

By mid-August, a weekly leaders' fraternal at Queen's Road Baptist, which started with only six leaders some weeks previously, had grown to around 200 people, with a number of leaders attending from non-charismatic backgrounds, or travelling long distances to be there.

From 20th-27th August 1,500 people took part in the Ichthus 'Revival Camp' at Ashburnham. Again extraordinary scenes were witnessed. On the first night of the Grapevine Bible week in Lincoln at the end of August, around 400 out of 3,000 began laughing during the talk. On the final evening, however, the preaching was totally disrupted as a number of those on the platform began convulsing with laughter. After a number of attempts to finish on a sober and serious subject, the speaker was forced finally to cut his address short and return to his seat.[27]

These effects on Bible weeks were being monitored with interest and possibly alarm by some involved in planning the Spring Harvest weeks for April 1995, expected to draw 70,000 from across all evangelical traditions – both pro- and anti-charismatic. The question was whether Spring Harvest's broad base of fellowship would survive if there were major disruptions. At a planning meeting of the worship leaders in September 1994 it was agreed that room would be made for what God was doing, while alternatives were provided on site for those wishing to worship in a more restrained atmosphere.[28]

By the end of August 1994 all the Bible weeks were now memories, but the effects on individual churches were continuing to accelerate. Ichthus made a decision to run extra 'receiving meetings' twice every week until the end of the year. Kensington Temple was committed to doing the same throughout September, while Pioneer People in Surrey pitched a huge tent in the grounds of a local school for two weeks, for meetings almost every day at which people like John Wimber spoke.

Martin Wroe of *The Observer* turned up at Queen's Road Baptist Church on Wednesday evening, 31st August, to see how things were developing. He wrote:

The congregation was rolling in the aisles. Rolling and weeping and laughing and sometimes just lying there, moaning, wailing but in no pain. In other churches, they are occasionally barking, crowing like cockerels, mooing like cows, pawing the ground like bulls and, more commonly, roaring like lions. But mainly they are on the church floor, laughing.

Hundreds of congregations of normally staid churchgoers are left shaking uncontrollably, to all appearances revelling in some killer joke that only their fellow charismatics have been let in on.

To the consternation of traditionalists and sceptics, a primitive Pentecostalism is breaking out in sophisticated Anglican churches throughout the country.

Tens of thousands of British churchgoers are experiencing the 'Toronto Blessing'. At Holy Trinity Brompton, more than 2,000 people – including recent celebrity converts, such as the former topless model and singer Samantha Fox – now attend services on a Sunday, including 1,200 for the evening service. The church is jammed to the rafters. Doors open at 5.45 for the 6.30 opening chorus, but there are queues of 500 outside by 5.30.

Converts are split on whether Britain is on the brink of an authentic religious revival – other revivals, such as that in Wales during 1904, began with ecstasy in the pews and ended with emptying of the pubs as the Holy Spirit fell on the unholy drinkers.

Mainstream Anglicans are horrified by the enthusiasm and unsophisticated antics of adherents, while others dismiss it as PMT – pre-millennial tension – or mass hysteria. But the official line of the Church of England is cautious approval.

Believers in Holy Ghost power, whether laughing like hyenas or roaring like lions, dismiss the ridicule, pointing to the 'drunken' antics of the first disciples in the Book of Acts, mocked for 'taking too much wine'.[29]

Many people have been drawn to what is happening by intense feelings of spiritual emptiness, particularly those in leadership who have been giving out for many years. A great desire for more of God, an overwhelming hunger, often comes before the experience – but when things happen, they can often surprise even those who feel they are prepared.

Mary Pytches is married to David Pytches, a retired Anglican bishop at St Andrew's Chorleywood, who has been an influential figurehead in the charismatic renewal movement for many years. In the 14th August issue of *HTB Focus* she wrote:

I went to Toronto with one or two things on my mind. One was that I wanted more anointing in my life. I felt I was so dry and so thirsty. I needed some anointing. I was standing up there praying, 'More anointing! More anointing!' And as I stood banging on the doors of heaven for more anointing, they were singing 'Holy and Anointed One'. Suddenly I thought, 'How stupid I am! Why don't I just ask for more of Jesus? That is the answer. If you have more of Jesus you have more of everything. You have more anointing, more gifting, more fruit, more righteousness and holiness – the lot.'

And so then I changed my prayer and I kept praying, 'Lord, I want more of Jesus' – and that's what I got.   But, secretly, I also had another desire. I didn't tell anyone about this because I was a bit ashamed of wanting it. But actually I wanted some of the laughter. Some people are laughing right deep down and I've never done that. I have a tendency to be a little bit serious. 'Oh Lord, that would be nice.' So on the first evening I went down in the Spirit in an 'OK' sort of way. I didn't flap around too much. But what I did do was start to wail and this really did disturb me. This was not what I went for.

Later on she began to laugh too. Meanwhile, David began to roar.

People were anointed in all sorts of ways out there. It was just incredible. They were jerking and shaking and doing all sorts of things – and there was this incredible roaring.

Some people were very nervous about it. Some people felt, 'It's OK to cry but it's not OK to roar; it's OK to cry but not to laugh.' It's funny how we box God in and say, 'He can do this but he can't do that.'

Mary describes how the roaring felt like a lion, reminding her of Hosea 11:10-11 '"They will follow the Lord; he will roar like a lion. When he roars, his children will come trembling from the west. They will come trembling like birds from Egypt, like doves from Assyria. I will settle them in their homes," declares the Lord.'

Roger Stephenson has pioneered a new church at Fairlight in Tooting, which has since planted again in Wandsworth and again in Balham, and is working with another similar project in Putney. The church is linked to Pioneer and is also a Shaftesbury mission. Affected very early by what was happening in the Putney Vineyard church just a mile or two down the road, he decided to take what they were experiencing onto the streets.

First he went with thirty people onto Wandsworth Common. There they prayed and worshipped. Some fell down and others laughed, attracting curious onlookers and a number of conversations. They did the same in a car park near some shops, with the same results. He came to the conclusion that it was no more or less effective than the well-oiled street performance work or questionnaires they had been doing in the area for years.

However, several people became Christians in very lively meetings on Sundays, including a doctor who had walked in as an unbeliever and was so struck by what was happening that he became a Christian there and then.

Jackie Oliver leads a church called Generation in Ewell, Surrey which is also linked to Pioneer. She describes how 'the Holy Spirit broke out' one night in August so that they were unsure whether to adjust a very tightly-timed programme. In one evening meeting they delayed the preaching until the last part of the service, at the end of which several literally ran to the place where counsellors were waiting to help them pray a prayer of commitment.

Andrew Walker, considered an authority by many on the history of the charismatic movement and of new churches in particular, was quoted in the *Daily Mail* as saying:

> We're counting up to the year 2000 and there's a strong apocalyptic anxiety. People want something. Remember even vicars nowadays are proclaiming there is no God. It is not possible (yet) to judge its effect. After all, we do not know how big it will become. We may be suspicious of it but so far it hasn't done anything wrong. When people pick themselves up off the floor they seem to be happy.[30]

On Thursday 8th September, 800 leaders, mainly from Anglican churches, came to St Andrew's Chorleywood to hear a leader from Toronto Airport Vineyard speak. The attendance was twice that of any previous leaders' conference there. Many of the leaders were not from charismatic backgrounds, but were curious. Laughter, shaking, groaning and falling were seen, as well as tears.

Two days later in Cardiff (10th September), another conference for leaders on 'times of refreshing' was expected to be attended by around eighty, but almost 300 turned up. Meanwhile an Elim church in Sunderland had become a magnet for many in the North of England.

On 12th September a group of around 400 church leaders representing Pioneer churches around London and the Home Counties, gathered to worship, hear news and listen to Gerald Coates speak at Holy Trinity Brompton. HTB senior leaders were elsewhere at a team meeting in the crypt.

Gerald described remarkable scenes at his own church, Pioneer People in Surrey, and elsewhere across the nation. He also told of a new hunger for God he had found, and an openness to the Holy Spirit in other groups such as the Salvation Army, where strange things had also happened when he spoke at a national conference for evangelists a few weeks before.

After the address, those who wished to be prayed for were invited to come forward. Up to this point there had been no manifestations of any kind, apart from one man seen to be shaking violently for ten minutes during worship, but who had been left alone in a corner. As thirty or forty people were prayed for, there was perhaps an expectation after all the things people had heard and experienced that things might happen rather quickly. They did not.

As the ministry team quietly and unobtrusively moved among the people, laying on hands in prayer, gradually over the next twenty minutes those at the crowded meeting became aware of one, and then another in the church who were now on the floor, or becoming very unsteady. One or two pockets of laughter developed, rose and faded, just discernible above the quietly playing musicians. Many of the chairs were stacked away as people began to fall.

Within forty minutes, the whole of the floor space had become so littered with bodies that it was almost impossible for the ministry team to walk from one place to another without treading on people. Those getting up received further prayer as they wished and were often soon on the floor again.

Not everyone was so affected. Some did not fall but shook, others laughed and for a good many there were no external manifestations at all, only a sense of God's goodness, his presence and his love. For some there was thoughtful reflection and questioning: 'Why not me? Why have I not experienced anything like this? Is there something wrong with me, or is it just the variety of what God wants to do?'

Questions of a more general nature were growing among some people. For example, by the end of September 1994 the consensus among Ichthus leaders was that what was happening was remarkable, but still very different from the experience of revival in Argentina seen almost a year before. Surely this move of God was not just to refresh people over and over again? The hope was that it would result in a new desire to pray for the world, and in many conversions.

In the early stages Ichthus saw some find faith – three, for example, in one of the receiving meetings. However, large numbers of Christians were transformed. 'Incredible changes' were seen. Some were 'amazingly restored'; others who had been Christians for years, faithfully serving God, felt personally renewed in their love for Jesus.

Gerald Coates remarked at the end of two weeks of special tent meetings in Cobham, where remarkable things had taken place, the like of which on the last night he said he had never seen before: 'We do have to be careful that these times of refreshing don't knacker us completely.' If the move of God is sustained and grows, then churches will need to pace themselves for the long haul.

There is no doubt that we are seeing the early stages of a transnational move of God, linked to the whole unfolding process of world revival, in which is inevitably mixed a number of other elements which are not of God.

This is no 'flash in the pan', no unexpected visitation. Historians looking back in future decades will say there was a sense in which the timing was almost inevitable, without in any way denying the absolute sovereignty of God.

To understand why this was the case in Britain at least, we need to wind back the clock through fifteen critical years. But first we need to listen to a few individuals report back on the 'fruit' of what has happened in their own words.

The witnesses

There is always a major problem in assessing the early stages of a fresh move of God: the true test is the long-term effects on people's lives, yet at that time we only have access to the immediate. However, we know from previous revivals, whether of individuals, churches or areas, that the pattern and nature of the immediate fruit is likely to be a reasonable indicator of what may survive the passage of time.

In every age there are those who make a quick response, then relapse just as quickly into their old ways, but there are also many who continue, especially where their encounter with God has been profound, where there has been genuine repentance, and where there has been mature and wise biblical teaching. So what are the early signs today? Is a healthy framework in place? Are these manifestations the immediate emotional reactions of the ignorant – or are they responses to God by those who know and love the Scriptures and have mature common sense?

Here are just a selection of the hundreds of personal accounts I could have presented, but a representative sample of those whose bodies have been affected as they worshipped. They are inspiring and encouraging to read, because they indicate an increased love for Jesus, an awareness of God's holiness and love, of compassion for the lost, of the need to pray for others, and of a hunger for Scripture.

I make no apology for their repetitiveness, if only to emphasise the consistency, not of the experience or of any manifestations (both ultimately of little relevance), but the consistency of the effects on their lives.

There are several striking differences from the accounts of, say, the Welsh revival, or other similar times. Then the work of God happened among those completely unused to the power of the Holy Spirit and completely inexperienced in discernment or in handling meetings where manifestations were taking place. Most of the signs happened in those on the edge of faith, or in new converts who had little or no understanding of the Bible.

The situation could hardly be more different today, where such things are happening at present primarily among believers in churches well used to the movement of the Holy Spirit in visible ways. By 1994, half of all Evangelicals worldwide and in countries like Britain were enthusiastic charismatics, positively promoting ecstatic experience of the power of God as a normal part of daily Christian living. It is partly a reflection perhaps of the culture in which we live.

The culture of many previous ages may have greatly

despised religious enthusiasm. However, we live today in the 'age of experience'. While technology, mass communications and large anonymous cities have often eroded individual identity and 'significance', there has been an ever greater hunger for new insights, experience, feelings and spiritual knowledge.

Today's Western world is increasingly influenced by the recreational use of mind-altering drugs, by Eastern mysticism and by New Age beliefs. We live in an age of psychotherapy, counselling, group therapy, self-help groups, self-discovery, self-awareness, self-realisation and stress reduction techniques.

Feelings are very fashionable in many circles – except perhaps in those of an older generation where a 'stiff upper lip' is still seen as a virtue; a noble strength linked to courage, character, achievement, honour and self-discipline. However, a 'stiff upper lip' or 'repression of emotion' is increasingly seen by the rest of society as something to be pitied or even despised: a serious emotional handicap which could be a recipe for future emotional and physical ill health. The culture clash continues and its effects are seen in the debate within the church at the moment over manifestations.

Despite these tensions, the growth of charismatic faith fits well with the prevailing attitudes of our times, and perhaps explains why the media have been so positive in describing even what may be its worst excesses. In a world hungry for new experience, these manifestations of religious ecstasy or trance-like states are fascinating to many people and make compulsive reading.

In our pluralist Western societies at the end of the second millennium, the attitude is that 'anything goes', however strange, 'if it is all right for you'. The idea of Absolute Truth has been discarded and all experience is therefore seen as equally valid. The secular attitude to charismatic Christianity is therefore surprisingly tolerant, so long as it is something confined to the Christian ghetto – but there is often a strong reaction when we challenge the values of society, insisting that faith in Jesus is the only way to God our heavenly Father, and that he is also the Truth and the Life.[31]

This positive response by many unbelievers in the media to the bizarre has been a surprise to many charismatic Christians, who are still trying to present the gospel to yesterday's culture, playing down emotion or experience which they fear will put others off.

Clearly one cannot generalise too much, and every person is unique with his or her own attitudes and background. But it is true to say that in the last years of the twentieth century there is a great openness to a form of enthusiastic Christianity which is heart- and mind-changing, radically affecting all of life, personal, real, and which gives people first-hand experience of the power of God in their lives.

However, the great challenge is to turn people around from a quest for self-realisation which may make them curious about the gospel, to the point where they accept the authority of Jesus Christ, turn away from the old life, deny themselves and, as Jesus commanded, take up the cross daily and follow him, being prepared to lose their lives for his sake in order to find their true selves (Lk 9:23). There is no other route to revival.

The other challenge in an experiential age is to keep charismatic Christians focused on Jesus himself, and not on some new personal manifestation or experience of God's presence or power for its own sake, however rewarding that experience might be. Spiritual tourism or consumerism can become another form of idolatry, and lead to disaster in excess. Times of refreshing are to equip us for service.

Despite the popular mythology in some traditional circles about 'brainless' charismatics, the base of Bible teaching is far stronger than it has been in the past. Knowledge of the Scriptures among believers in some congregations may well be better than in many non-charismatic churches. There is also a healthy realism among many charismatics and a common-sense questioning of unusual experience, particularly at the moment. However, there is also a determination not to reject what is clearly of God just because other things not of God are inevitably mixed in with it.

The oft-repeated jibe 'I want to be a cabbage for Jesus' is a slur on charismatic worship and theology, and a very sad reflection on the limited contact those who say such things have had with others outside of their own circles. It is also a hazardous position to take, given the tendency God has to choose 'the foolish things of the world to shame the wise' (1 Cor 1:27). The fact is that many with charismatic experience are intellectuals of the first order, yet have been, in the words of C. S. Lewis, 'surprised by joy'.

There may not be the same admiration of the cerebral in charismatic churches (where is there in Scripture?), nor the same level of academic brilliance in personal, domestic Bible study that there might be in some more upper-middle-class traditional churches, but then Jesus did not come only to those with first-class honours university degrees. He came for all, including the simplest, and children too. He also came to humble us.

Those who are only prepared to believe what they fully understand put God in a box the size of their own brains, literally creating God in their own mental image. If God is God, then by definition we as finite human beings, limited in a time-space world, will only be capable of 'knowing in part' (1 Cor 13:9).

The charismatic takes a humble view of human brain capacity, willing to embrace the mystery of God, willing to accept what is biblical but hard to understand, but confident that God's word is to be trusted when properly understood in context, and that it has greater authority than human reason alone. The aim is not to 'kiss our brains goodbye'. After all, intellect and reason are God-given and we are made in his image. We are to use our minds to bring understanding. However, ultimately we are called to bring our minds under the lordship of Christ, subject to him.

The accounts that follow have been checked either by me or by other church leaders known to me personally.

Ken

The first is from a friend of mine who is church warden of an Anglican church and also a merchant banker in the City of London. It would be hard to imagine a profession more likely to be level headed and pragmatic in approach to faith, less prone to be affected by emotional manifestations or bizarre behaviour, and my friend is no exception.

He describes how he had heard of a strange 'giddiness' affecting a number of people at his church, which had resulted in them falling over and laughing. He decided it was probably just 'a passing phase' in a church discovering afresh the power of the Holy Spirit.

He felt rather detached from it all and slightly sceptical: 'If they wanted to lie about giggling, let them lie about giggling. I came to the conclusion at first that it sounded like a mild dose of emotionalism and expected it to pass over.' However he was due to speak that Sunday at another church not far away where similar things were happening.

While informal worship was continuing, he turned to the curate and spoke to him briefly with some words of encouragement. He put his hand on the curate's shoulder to pray for him. What happened next took them both by surprise.

Well, blow me, he sort of crashes out and lies down with a soporific smile. Meanwhile the worship leader was playing songs, waiting for the chap who was lying on the ground to come and introduce me to the people.

I eventually decided we couldn't wait any longer, so I thought I would start. But as I got up I had only just prayed, 'Father, in the name of Jesus we pray your Spirit would come upon us,' when I broke down in absolutely uncontrollable laughter.

Meanwhile, the curate was still lying down, and I thought I had to try to make the best of it. But, try as I may, stuff a handkerchief in my mouth as I could, turn round as I tried to, I could not get going. Eventually I pulled myself together, gritted my teeth and I said, 'Would you please turn with me to the letter to the Ephesians, and crashed out laughing yet again.

I thought this was all extremely odd. I'd neither desired it nor did I want to be in this strange position but I realised that something was happening and I needed to find out a little more about what was going on.

Deeply challenged by his own experience, a couple of weeks later he had the opportunity to fly to the US via Toronto and went to the Vineyard church at the airport. He continues:

I listened to the worship which was indifferent, saw people shrieking and roaring and falling over and once again found myself dismissing it as a mild outbreak of giddiness associated with emotion and faith. I was convinced it would end in due course.

However, the next morning I was sitting down when suddenly I started shaking in every part of my body, to the point where much to my surprise I was actually bouncing up and down like a pogo-stick.

He was very puzzled and more than slightly embarrassed by what had happened to him. The shaking returned two or three times on other occasions. However, after prayerful reflection and discussion with others he came to the conclusion that the experience had been positive, indeed more than that, deeply significant as part of God's dealings with him. He commented some time later:

> I had come from a position of some scepticism. But I have now been, in those words of C. S. Lewis, 'surprised by joy'.
>
> Why does God allow this sort of shaking? I think he does it to draw attention to himself. I suspect this is in a way similar to a prophecy, a picture if you like, of God shaking me – my life, my control, my vested interests, my determination to run my life by what I understand.
>
> We've tried might and power and organisation of the church but now God seems to be moving in this prophetic way with a trumpet call to all of us. I do not believe that he will abandon us to experiences not of him. He won't allow us to be deceived.
>
> We have men and women of faith who have gone on ahead of us helping us evaluate it. We have the Scriptures. We have experience over the ages and we have the witness in our own hearts that this is God at work.[32]

Ruth

'As Sandy prayed for people and they fell on the floor, I found it quite funny and couldn't believe how calm I was … I had an incredible sense of God holding me and saying that he is my Father, and no man, no organisation, no church is going to be able to break that bond. I didn't understand what was going on, but that didn't matter. I had never been so close to God. I had also never been so happy. I had a passion for God like I've never known. And instead of being angry with old friends, I found myself weeping for them to find out what I have. Later I sat with Emmy praying through some of my past ... I would give anything to be free of those memories and pain....

'Then came last Sunday. I spent over an hour rolling on the floor, hysterically laughing and crying. When I left I was so drunk! I couldn't get into the car. I had to be put in.

'I am free! ... the pain has gone. My life will never be the same again.'[33]

Ashley

'When the Spirit first came on me, I had a sense that there was some dirt inside me, and that the Lord's presence was here and he wanted to clear it out.... There was a lot of pain and tears. I began to cry. After that I experienced this incredible peace.

'A month later ... I was very tired ... a couple of guys (close friends) started to laugh. I very naturally laughed at their laughter. And that grew. Then I just felt the Lord pour it out on me and the tiredness just went. It was as if I'd taken laughing gas. It was almost like Jesus telling me jokes. It was just like Jesus was in the room and he just wanted to have some laughter and we started to laugh.'[34]

Juliet

'Since I became a Christian two years ago I haven't felt like I've known God at all. I've known him in the Bible, but I've not had a relationship.

'I was really angry because everyone was getting touched

and I was sure that I wasn't going to get touched ... And she started praying for me and I just started crying ... I'd been standing there for quite a while crying, feeling healed, feeling good, but crying. And she said: "Do you want to sit down?" And so I went to sit down and suddenly I was on the floor and I thought consciously "Wow!"

'I was trying to analyse what was going on and I tried to wipe the tears away, but I couldn't move my arms to my face. It was just amazing. I felt really drunk and I cried for about an hour and a half ... That has happened to me loads of times now. The second time, I got knocked over with laughter ... And there I was on the floor for about two hours, laughing. The funniest thing is that I could not stop laughing and I had a big picture of Jesus with his head thrown back and he was laughing his head off at me laughing!

'I've never experienced God before. I've always had to rely on the word of the Bible and other people's experience. Now I *know* he exists and I *know* he loves me – which was a major, major thing for me.'[35]

Sarah

'There have been times when I have felt the power of God very powerfully on me, but not to the depths and the degree that it has been recently. I'm just desperate to read more and pray more. I feel different inside me and I feel beautiful. It is as if the Lord is blessing me and affirming me. I feel his pleasure in me and that makes me feel good.'[36]

Stephen

'As I was prayed for my hands began to shake and I fell to the floor. I lay there for a few minutes thinking, "What do I do next?" I was about to get up, but someone praying for me said, "I believe God wants to touch you some more," so I stayed where I was.

'Then each time someone prayed for me I had a different manifestation. Someone prayed that I would tell people about the goodness of God. My teeth started to chatter uncontrollably. A little later someone prayed that I would return to my first love for Jesus. My hands were shaking and my feet were tingling, and I felt a power surging through my fingertips into my chest.

'I must have lain like this for at least half an hour. When I got up it was difficult to walk for at least five minutes as I was still shaky.

'Before these experiences I had been in a rut spiritually and quite uninterested in getting out of it. I also felt quite unaccepted by God because of my spiritual state.

'It has totally changed my worship. I now find it difficult to sing songs about Jesus without crying. I now want to spend time with God and he has given me a new hunger for his word.

'I feel accepted by God. God has really taken me out of the rut I was in. I have not slept well since these experiences because I have been so excited at what God is doing in the church and in me. I have been a Christian for twenty years, but have never known a time like this in my life.'[37]

Mary

'Whenever the Holy Spirit came upon me I cried and cried, like a well that would never dry up. One evening God came in such power that I felt I might not survive. I fell over and the Holy Spirit came through my feet like a tingling electric current and up my body to my chest, where I felt a resistance.

'I remember moaning, and then a huge crying came out

from deep inside me like waves sweeping over me. This experience gave me a fear of God I hadn't known before – it was awesome and took away any doubts I may have had at times about his existence.

'During a prayer meeting we started to pray for one another and the Holy Spirit came and I had my first taste of joy. I always wondered what the joy of the Lord was like and had never experienced anything like this. After a while it turned into tears.

'The following week tears came as usual, and then I asked a friend to pray for my spine, which was painful. I fell over instantly and began to laugh and laugh as deeply as I had cried. It came right from deep inside and I shouted out and praised God and clapped unashamedly without inhibition.

'My daughter was quite disconcerted, as I couldn't stop giggling on the way out and was calling out to people I didn't know, completely uninhibited, in a way she knew I would never normally be.'[38]

Roger (church leader)

'Five non-Christians were in one meeting where all these sorts of things were happening. They all walked out before the talk, but two came back and were saved. Many people's lives are being profoundly changed. Many of our leaders have been almost permanently twitching. Our leaders' meetings have often been suspended because all the team were on the floor. Then gradually they would all settle down, until another leader turned up, and then they would all start manifesting again. There are people in the church who, whenever they hear the name Jesus, start twitching. They are Christians. They love God.

'Three months ago my view was that as Paul says in 1 Corinthians "the spirit of the prophet is subject to the control of the prophet". However, we have had to ask ourselves whether this can be applied to all other aspects of the work of the Holy Spirit in people's lives. What about Paul struck blind on the road to Damascus, and falling to the ground?

'Three months ago I would have said that some of the things we are seeing now are clearly demonic, because in the past, people needing deliverance used to manifest in similar ways. However, we are needing to rethink. Many of these people are not demonised, yet their bodies are being affected in strange ways.

'I have seen nothing but good come out of what is happening. Issues in people's lives that would previously have taken months to work through are being dealt with in a few days. Relatively young believers are growing very quickly in faith and maturity. In every area it seems as though God's work has been accelerated.

'We have had some "wild" meetings. One person got trodden on and bruised, another had a sprained wrist following a fall. But such injuries are very unusual. Marriages are being restored, some (not floods of people yet) are finding faith, people are being encouraged.'[39]

Jeff

Jeff Lucas is the Vice-President of the Evangelical Alliance in Britain and an internationally renowned Bible teacher. One evening he and his wife Kay were so intoxicated at a meeting that they were completely incapacitated. Unable to drive or even walk to the car, they were carried bodily by friends to the car and later into the house. This was difficult because their bodies were violently jerking. They were unable to sleep in the same bed that night because the jerking had 'the same effect on the bedclothes as the action of a washing machine'. Eventually Jeff slept on the couch. Jeff writes of an earlier episode:

'My wife Kay, who is a fairly quiet and sensible person, came home from a meeting with three other pastoral leaders. Upon my return home I noticed that the car was parked some two-and-a-half feet from the kerb, as if parked by a drunk. During the meeting earlier she had been laughing so much that she was rolling around on the floor. Now with my parents in the room above (asleep) she was laughing so hard at 1.30am that she was pushing a pillow into her face and loudly singing, "We're all going on a summer holiday."

'Recently I spoke to a small group in a public park in Cowes on the Isle of Wight. Quite a number of the fifty to seventy-five people were sprawled out on the grass for quite some time.'[40]

So why was Jeff's wife singing the old pop song 'Summer Holiday'? What has that got to do with a so-called touch of the Holy Spirit? One obvious explanation is that she was intoxicated, disinhibited and euphoric.

Here is a selection of the many accounts sent to me by leaders in Kensington Temple, from people in their church. One could repeat these a hundred times over no doubt in most parts of London and the Home Counties, as well as in many other towns and cities across the UK. I have left them in note form, exactly as I received them.

Linda had been praying with the woman. Later in the hotel the woman broke into holy laughter in the lobby of the hotel, and was against the wall. People were asking if she was OK. They thought she was probably drunk....

Tanya had left Christianity (backslider). Gave her life back to Jesus (31st July 5pm).

Sarah says: 'I was a witness to a girl on 31st July. She was thrusting the upper part of her body backwards and forwards like a clockwork doll for over half an hour. I saw her after the service. She was radiant.... '

Jules at various times has been crying in the Spirit – more aware of her own sinfulness.

Mark was prayed for on 10th July and received new joy, freedom, cleansing of personal hurts, unity with brothers and sisters, loss of inhibition....

Graham (throughout July) experienced shrieking, screaming, laughing, crying. This became joy, deliverance from anger, felt like a polishing, a diamond glistening....

Isobela prayed for at a meeting for mission: joy released, felt empowered to go out. Many were slain in the Spirit.

Eddie – last few months has felt call to holiness, to worship God in Spirit and in truth. Dissatisfaction with situation, uncomfortable. God has been working deeply in his life, then bringing him joy and laughter....

Alistair has felt a call to holiness. Before he was unfulfilled. Now he has a new and glorious vision, began looking at God for himself, not for his blessings. He has a new sense of his goodness, sees reasons to give.

There are many first-hand accounts of reconciliation between church leaders who have been distanced for years. I have a number of remarkable accounts before me which I cannot publish, for reasons of confidentiality. These are people who are very senior within their denominations. There have also been big shifts in the views of some leaders well known for their indifference or even suspicion of the charismatic movement, who became far more positive during the critical five months from May to September 1994.

However, I now want to take us back to the revolution in British church life over the fifteen years up to 1994, to explain why what has happened was, looking back, so predictable. Over the last few years it has seemed utterly inevitable to me that a new wave of enthusiastic faith was going to sweep the nation, and I have said so on many public platforms.

I remain convinced that recent events may well turn out to be early signs of a significant revival, which may fade and rise again several times perhaps, before there is an awakening in the nation as a whole. How can the current global revival race ahead unchecked for a further decade or two and not profoundly affect nations like Britain? The lesson of history is that the pendulum swings – and the pendulum of faith and values is swinging again in a profound way, which I believe will ultimately affect every aspect of Britain and many other Western nations.

However, the number of manifestations seen in churches could rapidly decline in some places. It is perhaps unrealistic to expect people every week to need or want to be lying on the floor. After a time, those well refreshed are likely to want to get on with the business of living.

As history shows, such things are more likely to be sustained on a large scale in churches where publicity continues to draw new people each week, experiencing these things for the first time, as in Toronto or Holy Trinity Brompton. Manifestations can be an indicator of a revival, but are never the cause: the unseen changes within people's lives are what count.

2

Background to Events in 1994

The apparent jump 'out of the blue' from Toronto to Britain is no surprise when we look back at the way the country has been prepared for such a thing. Indeed, many over the last few years have been expecting revival in one form or another, although mocked by the cynics who maintained they were deluded.

The charismatic movement had a profound effect on church life throughout the 1970s and 1980s. It took classical pentecostal experience into every denomination – speaking in tongues, prophecy, healing and strange bodily sensations. Tens of thousands had a crisis experience which they called 'being baptised in the Holy Spirit' and then had varying degrees of problems fitting into existing church structures. Hundreds left their denominations to form breakaway groups which became known as 'house churches'.

Many became so preoccupied by a new discovery of fellowship and of God's love that the heat went out of the call to evangelise, and a large number of new churches became very inward looking in the 1970s and 1980s, expecting that as we loved each other, Jesus would be seen. As we experienced the Holy Spirit, miracles would happen and people would come rushing to our door. No need to go out: the world would come to us.

While some groups remained introspective and died, others soon began reproducing themselves through conversions and restoration of the lapsed, growing so big that the term 'house' became replaced by 'New'. While links between these churches developed, by 1994 a significant number were still isolated.

The historic denominations were also affected by what became known as a process of renewal, a rediscovery of gifts of the Holy Spirit. Evangelical churches, especially charismatic ones, grew at the expense of liberal churches, some of which even doubted the deity of Christ, and denied the supernatural work of God today. Throughout the 1980s, the New churches continued to be an engine of change, a rich and unending source of new songs which became adopted as replacements for hymns throughout hundreds of evangelical churches, whether charismatically inclined or not.

But still the hunger grew for more of God's power to be revealed. Nothing would satisfy a growing number of Evangelicals except seeing a mighty revival – a spiritual awakening that would shake the nation to its knees. It was widely believed among charismatics, who by now made up almost half of all Evangelicals in the country, that such a revival would only come as a result of a mighty visitation of God's power, with repentance and mass conversions linked to signs and wonders (miracles), as happened in the early church. In the meantime, it was believed that we should prepare ourselves by seeking God with holy lives open to his power in us.

However, the charismatic movement was heading for trouble over the issue of physical healing. By 1980 many charismatic churches were beginning to experience their first deaths of members from illness since embracing a theology of supernatural healing. Many people were devastated when their first 'prayers of faith' for miracles went apparently unanswered. This was especially the case if they believed strongly that God had indicated to them in some way that physical healing would happen. Some became confused and uncertain about understanding what God was saying for the future, with serious questions about the use of specific prophetic words.

Sometimes the finger was pointed not at our lack of understanding or God's sovereignty, but at the lack of faith of a person or group, or at the failings of leadership, or sin in the church. Therefore serious sickness often resulted in conflict and distress. As a doctor caring for the dying, this is something I became acutely aware of. Stories were circulating of spectacular healings, but they were few and far between, unless of minor complaints, and some were hard to verify. God clearly has the power to heal, and I am convinced as a doctor that he does so today, but he does not seem to do it nearly as often as we might wish – in Western countries at least.

There was also the realisation that pastoral problems often continued despite an emotional spiritual experience. Gerald Coates, leader of the Pioneer network of churches, talks in a recent book of 'charismatic depression' which grew through the 1980s, with many church leaders feeling demoralised, burned out and lacking vision for the future.[41]

There was intense speculation about the right ingredients for successful prayer for healing, and anyone with what appeared to be a track record of 'success' in this area drew great crowds to hear their explanations, sometimes poorly rooted in Scripture. Different approaches, theologies and techniques were tried, but it has to be said that success rates for medically verified long-term chronic or terminal illness remained low in most people's experience.

It was into that context that John Wimber first began visiting Britain in 1981, with an established healing ministry and a theology that seemed to many in the established denominations to be unusually well-balanced and biblical, emphasising the fact that any Christian can pray for anyone to be healed. John and his team held a major conference at Harrogate in the autumn of 1986 which was attended by 2,470, and he became an increasingly influential figure among British charismatics across the denominations.

He held 'Signs and Wonders' conferences on the work of the Holy Spirit which were attended by hundreds, with many affected by similar manifestations to the ones later seen in such numbers in 1994 – apart from the laughter. However, these effects seemed to die out relatively quickly once these large gatherings were over.

Incidentally, John Wimber's style, and that of many other leaders from Vineyard churches, is relaxed, low key, matter of fact, non-sensational and gentle. His preaching is often lengthy, conversational and slightly rambling, almost in a lecture style. He is certainly not a tub-thumping, emotional, manipulative, crowd-controlling, charismatic showman.

In my limited observations the Vineyard worship styles are often relaxed, gentle and soothing, constant and relatively unvarying in tempo, changing almost imperceptibly from one song into another, rather than with a heavy fast beat. When manifestations break out they often do so in a hall that is silent, apart from people quietly praying.

By the end of the 1980s there was a growing recognition in many charismatic churches that power is given not for nice meetings, but for service. Part of service was obedience to the command to reach every nation; to be involved in every level of society as 'salt and light', impacting politics, caring for the oppressed, the vulnerable, poor, sick and marginalised.

But always at the root was a heart-cry to God across the nation for nothing less than revival. That cry brought 13,000 believers together in 1993 to pray at Birmingham National Conference Centre, with larger numbers meeting across the country in many smaller groups as part of other prayer initiatives. Annual Prayer Breakfasts became established nationally at Westminster and in the City of London, while Members of Parliament also began to meet for informal fellowship and prayer.

It was that cry to God for something to change in our cities and in our nation that is the key to understanding another phenomenon of a different kind: March for Jesus. In 1987, a couple of thousand people met on a cold, wet day in the City of London to pray for the capital. The open-air meeting was the start of a colourful march through the streets with banners and songs especially written for 'prayer marching'. The following year thousands more met on London Embankment and marched through Westminster to Hyde Park.

By 1990 the annual marches had such a momentum that on 15th September *The Independent* reported that up to 250,000 were expected to march in various places around the country. Marching had become decentralised, with hundreds of local groups joining in smaller and larger marches around Britain. In the event, far fewer took part, but it was still a very significant occasion.

Meanwhile, groups in the United States began organising marches of their own, using the same music, the same format, and having the same vision. In some years, various groups in the UK were attending two marches a year, 'declaring God's praises and his authority over the earth'.

Cohesion for this rapidly-growing movement came primarily from the music of the prolific song-writer Graham Kendrick, who at one stage was completing almost an entire album of new worship music each year for the marchers. It also came from a tiny office in Surrey, formed out of the relationship between Graham Kendrick, Roger Forster of Ichthus, Gerald Coates of Pioneer and Lynn Green of Youth With A Mission (YWAM). These four shaped the vision, strategy and direction of the movement.

Dozens of other countries began to wake up to what was happening. It must be stressed that while the initiative came primarily out of British New churches with an informal charismatic theology, a grass-roots, faith-filled enthusiasm across the country and beyond swept March for Jesus into an international, global event.

On 25th June 1994 came the first global march – 'A Day to Change the World'. We will never know how many took part in the marches that day, which stretched from Tonga beyond New Zealand to Alaska and involved 177 nations. Estimates range from 10 to 12 million.

A million took part in a prayer rally in Seoul, Korea, 250,000 marched in Australia, 1.5 million in the United States, 700,000 in the Philippines, 17,000 in Kenya, 4,000 in Hungary, 10,000 in Norway, 850,000 in Brazil, 200,000 in Costa Rica, 58,000 in Venezuala, while in countries where marches were banned, believers walked silently praying through the streets. Something was stirring in our world.

On Sunday 11th September 1994, BBC television broadcast a one-hour special programme, using footage from many nations collected on that day. There could hardly have been a more dramatic and visible demonstration that something was happening worldwide.

This movement needed little leadership and hardly any central machinery to keep it going, but it sparked a vision among millions, uniting them in a common, worldwide, simple prayer: 'Your kingdom come, your will be done.' It is but a symptom of a global trend towards radical, life-changing, lively faith which is increasingly confident and assertive in proclamation, and has a big vision to reach every person in every nation with the gospel.

And as would be expected, while millions of believers have taken part in the largest act of corporate prayer this world has ever known, and experienced a new sense of solidarity and fellowship together, crossing all language, time and space boundaries, unfortunately some church leaders in places like Britain have carped on, complaining about the theology, complaining about banners, complaining about open-air meetings, complaining about marches.[42] And often these complaints have been aired first to journalists in the secular media rather than face to face, by people who have never been on a march and never discussed their objections with those involved. Thus the history of different moves of God repeats itself today.

But there was some bad news too, especially about big groups of media-loving charismatics. The moral fall of televangelist Jim Bakker, sentenced to forty-five years in prison on 24th October 1989, cast a huge shadow over the work of evangelists in general in the United States, and was also widely reported in countries like Britain.

The Praise the Lord organisation (PTL), started in 1974, had quickly grown to become one of America's largest and most influential television ministries. Jimmy and his wife Tammy Faye reached up to 13 million homes every day. In 1979 the Inland Revenue Department began to investigate alleged irregularities in the use of funds and tax avoidance, but before the enquiry was complete he resigned, in March 1987, after admitting an affair in 1980 with a church secretary who later sold her story.[43]

Bakker's disgrace had less impact in other countries, although confirming people's worst fears about the excesses of manipulation and corruption of God's purposes through media ministries. Others with television programmes, such as Pat Robertson, had firmly distanced themselves from Bakker's unorthodox approaches to finance and fundraising some years previously, but their image was tarnished too by his fall. There was an added cynicism in Britain about 'manipulation', 'emotionalism' and 'excesses'.

Meanwhile, John Wimber's influence in Britain continued to grow, and an increasing number of churches formed links with the Vineyard, a group of churches closely associated with John's work in the US.

In 1990 there was a series of John Wimber meetings in Britain on the nature and use of prophecy. One prophecy at one of these meetings was by Paul Cain, who came over with John Wimber from the US, and suggested that a major revival was going to break out in Britain soon. He mentioned the autumn of 1990 as the time he felt God was saying something was going to begin. There is debate about exactly what he said, but in my view it is unimportant. He felt God was showing him that revival was far closer than we thought and that the start was imminent (however you define revival – church growth, restoring the lapsed, spread of enthusiastic faith, national awakening). But something was already underway even before he spoke, as we have seen.

As a result of this prophecy, many people began to pray with a new sense of expectancy, while others were alarmed at such apparently dogmatic pronouncements about the future. In view of the prophecy, John Wimber returned in

October 1990 to hold mass meetings at the huge new arena in the Docklands, East London, and at Harrogate.

Although attended by 6,000, the numbers were fewer than hoped for and the pressure was on, because although there were very encouraging signs of change in the spiritual climate, there was little that could be pointed to as a definite indication of imminent revival.[44] Having said that, many people present were affected by spiritual experiences of one kind or another, some falling down, others aware of unusual sensations in their bodies.

I have often said over the years that perhaps one of many signs of revival is not when Christians are saying revival is here, but when unbelievers sit up and take notice; when the media start saying a revival is beginning to hit the nation. That is exactly what happened just twelve weeks later.

In January 1991 a big survey showed that many churches were struggling or closing, while charismatic churches were booming. The *Independent on Sunday* ran a big feature on the growth of charismatic faith, also pointing out that traditional churches were losing thousands of members a year, and all this just days after the launch of the Decade of Evangelism by all the major denominations.[45]

The *Independent on Sunday* carried an account of a lively 'Jesus Praise Day' at Wembley Conference Centre, led by Noel Stanton, ending with the startling conclusion that despite the massive loss of church members over the previous decade, 'a religious revival is definitely underway'. I know they were using the term in a different way from some others, but it was still a strong statement. The journalist had seen a picture of a future widespread movement full of manifestations, and he was right:

Then, stamping his feet to add emphasis to his repeated

supplication: 'Lord, I want to thank you – these people are going to be cleansed of all sin. Demons are going to be cast out. Lord, I want to thank you – they are going to receive the Holy Spirit.'

And, on cue, hundreds poured forward to be saved. Within two minutes the stage was overflowing with swaying figures, bodies prone on the floor, some held down, groaning, shaking, crying, shrieking, howling, retching and babbling – all manifestations, Noel Stanton said, of the demons that were being cast out.

Little knots of people stood out, a lost soul surrounded by three or four Jesus Army members, each with a hand on the head, praying fervently or in a trance, murmuring and chanting, 'Jesus is Lord, Jesus is Lord.'

Hundreds of such gatherings took place last year, as like-minded Christians met at rallies, marches, festivals and jamborees, in towns and cities across the United Kingdom, from Edinburgh to Brighton. Many more are scheduled for this year.

Although modern Britain is still predominantly a secular society, in which less than 15 per cent of the population regularly attends church (compared to 40 per cent in the US and 36 per cent in Italy), figures indicate that a religious revival is undoubtedly under way – part of a worldwide evangelical movement, fuelled by something known as the 'charismatic renewal'.

Leaders from traditional churches (not present at the meeting) were then quoted condemning the 'dangerous' emotionalism.

The Decade of Evangelism was greeted with mixed feelings, as the *Economist* reported in 1991:

The Church of England has declared the 1990s to be the Decade of Evangelism; but some people think evangelism is already doing too well. Attendance at traditional churches declined by 9% between 1979 and 1989, but the guitar-strummers' numbers are swelling. Not only is fundamentalism growing fast outside the Church of England – attendance at the independent churches that practise this sort of Christianity increased from 44,000 in 1979 to 108,000 in 1989 – but there is also a boom inside the Church of England itself, at places like Holy Trinity (Brompton).[46]

In fact the term 'fundamentalist' is very unpopular with Evangelicals, because it implies to them an image of intolerance and literal adherence to the Bible, when many are quite comfortable with the notion that the Bible contains poetic language where the meaning is figurative rather than literal.

The year 1991 was a depressing one for many in traditional churches. In March 1991 the press carried reports that half a million people stopped going to church over the previous ten years – that is 1,000 people every week, of which 750 were Catholics. The English Church Census showed, however, that one in ten still went to church on Sunday and the fall in numbers was slowing down, partly because it was increasingly offset by the rapid rise of charismatic Evangelicals, particularly in the house or New churches as they came to be called, which grew from 44,400 to 108,000 in the same period. The census collected information from 27,000 churches on Sunday 15th October 1989.[47]

In April 1991 Clifford Longley wrote in *The Times* of widespread concerns about a new dominant style emerging in the church; a noisy and offensive, trite revolution, supported perhaps by a new Archbishop?

Nothing offends the Anglican sense of 'seemliness' in worship as much as laughter in church, or dance, pop music, hand-clapping, or any other new-fangled innovation. There is even talk, horror of horrors, of having an electronic synthesiser [at the Archbishop's induction].

Modern charismatic Evangelicals fancy a more American style of Christianity, more open, friendly and direct. English reserve does not long survive the heavy emotionalism of their services, the singing with hands waving in the air, the uncontrolled outburst called speaking in tongues and the open displays of religious fervour. 'Jesus loves you' is the message of their hymns and of the provocative slogans outside their churches.

In the past the more staid parts of the Church of England have been prepared to put up with such odd activity provided it remained on the fringe. Only one or two bishops had much sympathy with it. Until now, that is.

The charismatics are 'enthusiasts', in the sense defined in a famous demolition job by the late Ronald Knox, which added the word to the vocabulary of ecclesiastical put-downs. The Church of England now has to come to terms with an enthusiast, in the Knoxious sense, as its primate.[48]

A huge question being debated was whether the Anglican Church could survive without major change, yet such change might split the church. The issue was not at root that of women in leadership, although that was to flare up in an ugly way two years later. The issue in 1991 was whether traditional forms of worship would survive, and if they did, who would still be attending as an older generation died off?

Then came the startling appointment of the new Archbishop, who was not only a serious Evangelical, shocking enough, but also a charismatic who had promoted prophecy and speaking in tongues, and who had ecstatic experience of his own in the past. To many his appointment was seen almost as a scandal and potentially divisive.[49] For others it merely symbolised a rite of passage: a change from a church dominated by liberal thinking such as that represented by the Bishop of Durham at that time and a catastrophic decline in membership, to a church where most of the growth was among Evangelicals of whom almost half were charismatic.

In May 1992 the Anglican Church continued the debate by publishing a four-year report into music in church, encouraging modern musical styles alongside traditional worship. Robin Sheldon, a director of the evangelical Music and Worship Foundation, said: 'You have to recognise that the fastest-growing part of the church is the charismatic movement. You can't just be toffee-nosed about it. You have to ask what music in church is for. You have to decide whether your standpoint is musical or spiritual.'[50]

However, Professor David Martin, vice-president of the Prayer Book Society and an organist, expressed the views of many when he said: 'I cannot respond to third-rate jigs and I don't think it's worshipful. One is a kind of evocation of the sacred, the other is a form of jollification.'

The Decade of Evangelism was widely mocked as ineffectual, a concept that could never work because so many churches were 'dying on their feet' and because they would never work together for fear of being overrun by Evangelicals and charismatics. However, the reality has been a gathering momentum, with probably more evangelistic initiatives taking place in 1994 alone than in all of the previous three years.

In February 1992 a remarkable history-making event took place. Some 400 senior leaders, representing all the major denominations and other groups such as New churches, assembled to discuss and agree a master plan to plant hundreds of new churches across the country, by sending small teams from growing churches to new areas.

This might seem strange given the vast number of empty church buildings and dying congregations in many places. The project was called Challenge 2000. It was prompted by the extraordinary success of the Dawn 2000 movement, mainly in developing countries as part of the growing revival they were experiencing. Different denominations in these countries had set targets and strategies for establishing New churches, and found not only were churches started very quickly, but also a new dynamic of faith and vision was released which enabled these fledgling groups to seed more churches themselves.

The British church leaders took a giant step of faith in the face of decline, and committed themselves on behalf of their denominations to planting no fewer than 20,000 New churches in areas of little or no evangelistic witness over the following ten years. They also agreed to review progress annually and to mobilise their own denominations to do this.

Many, when they heard what had been decided, were deeply sceptical. Yet by the following year it was reported that already at least 300 New churches had been established by different denominations and groups since they last met, and possibly as many as 600 (records were very incomplete, especially of planting by New churches and other independent groups).[51]

However, the new fashion for church growth through planting new congregations began to cause major tensions within the Anglican Church, where church planting was 'illegal' outside a church's own parish boundaries, unless the other parish agreed. In practice the growing parishes tended to be lively Evangelicals, while those parishes needing an injection of life and numbers tended to be more traditional and often liberal and were in serious decline.

Permission was often very hard to obtain, raising the spectre of a new kind of Methodism, with young, energetic, Anglican converts striking out on their own into new areas, forced outside the Anglican Church by a rigid and authoritarian structure, yet forming groups otherwise Anglican in belief and practice.

By the end of 1991 the problem looked so serious that in January 1992 two charismatic bishops founded a rebel 'Federation of Independent Anglican Churches'. The Revd David Pytches and the Revd Brian Skinner, former bishops of the Anglican Church in South America, now Vicar and Curate of St Andrew's, Chorleywood, Hertfordshire, had the aim of 'linking together congregations which are not able to be part of the parish structure of the Church of England, but which seek to be Anglican in ethos, belief and worship'.[52]

As the British nation was seen to become steadily more atheistic and secular, and as the evangelical movement grew, parental pressures also grew for separation from state education, leading to churches starting their own schools. These parents were fed up with poor standards and the corrosive influence of many state schools on the faith of young people from Christian families.[53]

Some have tried to make out that the remarkable growth of lively emotional faith in Britain has been American in origin, powered by televangelists and others. Hence there were great anxieties during 1992 over plans by US evangelist Morris Cerullo for a UK satellite TV channel.[54] However, the reality is that each country has its own indigenous faith, shaped and moulded by the culture of its own people, although also influenced from outside.

Morris has conducted no fewer than three major 'healing missions' each August in Earls Court, London up to 1994, with major publicity. His support base in the UK for this was mainly from pentecostal churches and some of the Black independent churches – groups that had been growing with an exuberant, lively faith, expecting the miraculous power of the Holy Spirit to be seen today. Manifestations have been very common, with mass swoonings, swaying, trembling, shouting, shaking, tears and other phenomena, as well as many accounts from people saying that they have been physically healed.

When he spoke of television channels, the response among many in Britain was suspicious or hostile. The familiar arguments over brain-washing of individuals, or the accusations of auto-suggestion have been trotted out. We consider these more fully later. If only it were that easy to transform the behaviour of a person, a group, a network, a town, a denomination or a nation.

The human spirit is hard to control, as all parents with teenagers will testify. A television programme is unlikely to change a nation any more than another programme is likely to corrupt it. These things have a small but additive effect in shaping the culture of people's lives. However, controversial fundraising methods are a more serious issue.

The whole culture of the Church of England has been challenged, not only by the charismatic movement, but also by pioneers such as Canon Robert Warren, National Officer for Evangelism. His own church grew from 150 to over 1,000 from 1972 to 1993, and is home to the 'Nine O'clock Service' – a radical, noisy, experimental service using multi-media techniques.[55]

In October 1993 he said:

> There is a very profound transition for the Church of England from being the established church in a predominantly Christian culture to being a missionary church in a multi-faith culture. The substance of establishment has already gone. The church as we know it is not going to survive in rural and Urban Priority areas without massive change.

Another sign of a new dynamism in British church life has

been the remarkable growth of Spring Harvest. This started as an Easter week of Bible teaching in 1979 at Prestatyn, North Wales, with 3,000 people. It grew rapidly under the visionary leadership of Clive Calver and Pete Meadows of the Evangelical Alliance. By 1993 the annual event was drawing around 70,000 people. There was no site big enough, so the same programme ran across four sites, repeated simultaneously in different parts of the country. Even then, the event was running one week after another on several sites in a grand total of up to nine separate weeks of repeated programme in order to get everyone through.

This is a major movement. The Christian community in 1993 spent up to £2 million, and gave up 70,000 weeks of holiday to be together. So what was the big attraction? For some there was the excitement of being part of something bigger than a single congregation. For others the attraction was a first-class line-up of many of the country's most gifted Christian communicators, the children's work, the late-night chat shows on ethical issues, the time spent with others in the same group, going along together.

The worship styles vary within each site, but are often revolutionary compared to what people experience at home, with contemporary music, an absence of set liturgy and a charismatic flavour, but usually in a relatively modest, 'safe' and controlled way.

Spring Harvest is the largest Christian conference in Europe and almost unique among industrialised countries in size and breadth. It has had an immeasurably large impact on the culture of the church, breaking down sectarian barriers and fostering understanding. While encouraging new worship styles and informality across the church, it has also encouraged social and political activism. Pete Meadows said to *The Times* in April 1993:

In the 1970s, there was a rediscovering of the evangelical social conscience, blending the word and works. Evangelicals like Wilberforce (who led the campaign to abolish the slave trade) were the forerunners of social change but, with the attack on biblical authority that followed, evangelicals lost their nerve and fled from social involvement.

In the past few years, we have been recapturing our social roots. The evangelical church today is unrecognisable from that of 15 years ago in terms of its worship, thinking and relevance.[56]

Spring Harvest is only a part of the booming Christian conference scene, however. The New Frontiers network of New churches, headed up by Terry Virgo, was drawing up to 14,000 people a year to Stoneleigh Showground by the early 1990s, while other smaller events throughout the country were also attended by perhaps a further 15,000 a year, not including Greenbelt Christian music festival with up to 40,000 (Christians and others) over the August Bank Holiday weekend.

Overall the picture of faith in Britain by 1993 was of a nation hungry for God, yet unsure where to find him. On 13th March 1994 a Gallup poll found that three out of four people said they believed in God, while mainstream denominational attendance continued to plummet.[57]

Only one in five of regular churchgoers was Anglican, while even the Anglicans and Catholics combined formed only four out of ten regular worshippers. More people believed in the devil than in John Major as the Prime Minister (30% against 28%)! Meanwhile, half the new batch of Anglican clergy were Evangelicals.

Bridge Church in West London carried out a survey of shoppers in two West London communities from 1991 to 1993. Up to six out of ten in some samples said that if it were possible to know God personally, that is what they would like.[58]

With the collapse of idealism among the young, the end of communism and of traditional socialism, then the destruction of the Thatcher ideal of material growth, there was a malaise, a depression, an emptiness among many that led directly to a growing search for the spiritual.

Religion became big business in the High Street during the early 1990s. You only had to look at the growing section on religions and the paranormal in bookshops and other outlets such as WH Smith. Even 'intellectual' papers like *The Sunday Times* were giving large pages over to horoscope readings for an increasingly credulous readership. New Age beliefs in other dimensions to life became very widespread. The tinder was dry, just waiting for that spark.

One worry was whether such a spark could come from a cult or from a group of dangerous extremists. The Waco Branch Davidian Cult in Texas ended in the deaths of many followers in 1993, leading to much soul-searching in Britain and other countries where David Koresh recruited his members. Although the charismatics of the New church movement in Britain had a strong defender in the Archbishop of Canterbury, George Carey, others expressed worry that emotionalism could lead to emotional disorder and manipulation.[59]

On 20th April 1993, the Bishop of Leicester, the Rt Revd Thomas Butler, highlighted the danger of all marginal religious groups: 'There is a great lust for certainty now, and any group that offers certainty, an instant family and intoxicating worship will find people who will follow.'

The approaching millennium is also thought by many to be a significant factor in the recent phenomena. Andrew Walker talks of PMT, pre-millennial tension, similar in some ways to the focus of attention 1,000 years ago.

In early 1994 it seemed to many that the church was becoming more polarised. Now we had atheistic clergy in the pulpit and we also had tambourine-waving charismatics.[60] But who wants to hear from an atheist when they have enough doubts of their own? What people were searching for was certainty, confidence, faith, meaning and purpose.

Major new evangelistic initiatives took place in the first few months of 1994, the scale of which had never been seen before in all of British history. In April 1994 the pentecostal churches launched a £2 million national advertising campaign called JIM (Jesus In Me), supported by many other denominations, linked to an intensive programme of mission run by hundreds of different congregations. The climax of the campaign was a television advertisement on Good Friday, repeated on Easter Sunday.

A poster and press campaign began in mid-February and 10 million copies of the colour JIM magazine were delivered by local Christians in each area.[61] Although the style of the campaign was criticised by some inside and outside the church, it succeeded in mobilising a very large number of outreach events over eight weeks, attended by tens of thousands across the country. The organisers estimated that around 20,000 had made new commitments as a result.[62] That is a lot of people. If they had all been in one town or city, what would Wesley have said? 'Signs of revival' would no doubt have been his response. So is it any less a sign of revival when instead of a massive concentration of new converts in one area with nothing anywhere else, we have a massive number of new converts spread over a wide area?

In today's mobile, techno-age the location of converts may be more spread in the early stages of revival than has ever happened before. A prime example of this was seen the same week in another history-making national initiative.

Over Easter 1994, just weeks before the new manifestations described in the previous chapter hit British churches, the fifty-year-old German evangelist Reinhard Bonnke targeted 23 million homes with a thirty-two-page colour booklet on how to become a Christian, entitled *Minus-to-Plus*.[63] Over 30,000 responded by signing a name and address coupon saying that they had prayed the prayer of commitment.[64] Signs of revival? Early signs, perhaps, but still very little that was visible.

People may criticise and ask, 'How many of those responding were established as church members two years later?' However, the same criticism could be applied to one of Wesley's meetings where he preached to 20,000, saw perhaps a thousand make an instant response, of which only 100-200 formed the basis of a new worshipping group, and perhaps only a hundred remained a year-and-a-half later.

Reinhard had conducted many huge missions across Africa, drawing crowds of over 250,000. He had also held a number of meetings in Britain, with an emphasis on simple life-changing faith in Jesus and on the power of the Holy Spirit to work miracles today. Manifestations were common in his meetings.

There were few protests about the massive literature distribution – except from hundreds complaining that their homes had been missed by the distribution contractors. This shows just how much the climate in the country had changed in five years. In 1989 questions were asked in Parliament after Southend bookseller Paul Slennett raised £50,000 to have letters passing through sixty sorting offices stamped with the slogan 'Jesus is Alive'. Dr Robert Runcie, then Archbishop of Canterbury, criticised the gesture at the time. However, on this occasion Reinhard Bonnke's initiative had warm support from across the churches, as well as from 7,000 individuals who support his work regularly.

Then came the 'On Fire' initiative in the week leading up to 24th May 1994. Over a year previously a group of church leaders from many different church backgrounds met to plan a national celebration of the church's birthday, timed to coincide with Pentecost. The initiative was spear-headed by Oasis Trust and the work of Baptist minister and GMTV personality Steve Chalke.

Over 2,000 churches took part in 'On Fire' events, with street parties, celebrations, special services and firework displays. There was a recognition that the churches always celebrated the birth of Jesus (Christmas) and his resurrection (Easter), but largely ignored the start of the church and the coming of the Holy Spirit (Whitsun). By 24th May, of course, the events described in Chapter 1 of this book were well underway. 'On Fire' was so successful that a decision was made almost immediately to repeat it.

During 1993 and 1994 many Christians prominent in the media began to detect a gradual but profound change in attitude to Evangelicals among programme-makers and journalists. While the Conservative Party was rapidly exposed to scandals following John Major's Back to Basics campaign, the media were becoming increasingly open and sympathetic to evangelical points of view. This was due in part to a remarkable effort by Clive Calver, General Director of the Evangelical Alliance, and to Keith Ewing, the press officer, who at one point was receiving up to seventy press calls a week on issues ranging from women in leadership to abortion, Sunday trading, euthanasia, racialism and social action. The stage was being set for the remarkably positive coverage of manifestations that was to come.

Yet as the numbers of Christians with confident Bible-based faith grew, so did the numbers of atheist clergy. In July 1994 *The Sunday Times* reported that at least 100 Church of England priests did not believe in an external supernatural God. At a conference of 'Christian atheists', part of the 'Sea of Faith' movement, one priest said, 'You don't have to believe in God to be a Christian.' However, the climate was changing in a world looking for faith, not doubt. Clergy with public doubts were nothing new. I remember over twenty years ago the parish priest of the Anglican church I went to saying in his Easter Sunday sermon that he no longer believed in the resurrection. Many in the church were scandalised, but his job was not in question.

Times had changed by 1994. On 31st July one vicar conducted his last service in West Sussex after being told that his lack of faith meant he could no longer fulfil his role properly. His dismissal caused a country-wide debate.[65]

Fashions change as faith and culture change. Gospel music sales soared in Britain through 1990 to 1994, together with sales of classical religious music, such as Gregorian chants or Handel's *Messiah*. In 1994 it was not unusual to listen to the top twenty and hear overtly spiritual lyrics, or even ones that seemed as though they could have been composed by a Christian. In most cases these were sung by artists with no particular faith of their own, but who wanted a gospel sound and spiritual content – new gospel styles were fused with jazz, reggae and others.[66]

Meanwhile, in September 1994, a live recording of the Pope singing the rosary, broadcast originally by Vatican radio, became number one in the Spanish charts – and stayed there for several weeks.[67] Was this all a part of an increasing hunger for new values in other parts of Europe too?

Another sign of tremendous new British energy in evangelism in 1993 and early 1994 was the explosive spread of Alpha courses across the country. The first course for new believers and enquirers was started at Holy Trinity Brompton (HTB) some years ago in a large house. More recently it has been developed by Nicky Gumbel, and attendance on these courses has grown so that now a conference centre is needed for the residential weekends that form part of the course.

Each course consists of a series of lectures on the Christian faith, followed by small group discussion. Towards the end of the course everyone goes away for two days together to be taught about the workings of the Holy Spirit, and to experience this in their own lives. Conversions are common, as are recommitments, while those already firm believers have found their faith strengthened and encouraged.

By September 1994 there were around 500 other churches across the denominations that had registered similar courses, with probably as many again running them without registering at HTB. This all followed on from heavily subscribed training days, where church leaders were provided with tapes, videos and books. Meanwhile, the courses at HTB itself and neighbouring churches continued to grow until at one point in June 1994 there were almost 1,000 attending one course or another at the same time.

As I said earlier about Kensington Temple's remarkable growth, 150 years ago a church like Holy Trinity Brompton would have been described as in the middle of revival. It started to grow from a tiny congregation some fifteen years ago, and it now has four packed services every Sunday in a church holding 1,200, and has had around 1,000 new Christians or enquirers going through a three-month course at one time. It has also sent large numbers of church members to fill several other redundant churches in London, all of which are now filling fast with people whose lives have been changed. What has happened to our sense of history? If that is not a sign of revival, what is?

And then, of course, there has been the latest outbreak of manifestations and enthusiasm.

In September 1994, Bryn Jones of Covenant Ministries (formerly known as Harvestime), a national network of New churches in Britain, began to advertise 'Revival 1995', the name for the August Bible week the following year. Many church leaders were beginning to speculate quietly that it would not take much more to see the wind of refreshment turn into a mighty revival, although the key would be intense hunger for God, linked to repentance, intercessory prayer and a turning to God on a massive scale.

Every day the story extends and further history is being made. Too much is happening to be able to record it all, but perhaps this brief glimpse carries something of the sense of expectation that had built up by the end of 1994. The outcome could be that the new momentum fades, and then hits the churches with greater force than ever before, breaking into every community, town and city, heralding revival of the church and a national spiritual awakening – or it could fade away altogether for another generation or more. However, as many are praying, this new move of God could yet be sustained by faithful prayer and obedience until the whole nation is aflame.

So then the changes in the British picture of church life over the last fifteen years have been dramatic, with a catastrophic decline of liberal faith more than offset by the rapid growth of a radical new evangelical Christianity, thoroughly influenced by charismatic experience. At the beginning of 1980 such experience remained deeply suspect and 'fringe', but by April 1994 it had become 'mainstream' and well accepted as a normal variant of denominational church life. Thus the context for revival today is entirely different from the church situation, say, in the time of Edwards in the US, or Wesley in Britain.

World revival

Of course, what has been happening in Britain is just a part of the global picture. According to the *World Christian Encyclopaedia*, 372 million Christians were charismatics in the early 1990s, or about one in four of the total number in the world. The fact is that there has been an almost continuous process of revival in many parts of the world over the last thirty or more years.

Here are some recent examples. In September 1989 a gathering of 20,000 Evangelicals in Brasilia created a big storm in what had been a traditionally Catholic country. On 14th September 1989 the Latin America report described how people were just waking up to the explosive growth of charismatic Evangelicals in Brazil.

From 1950 to the present day, membership of these [evangelical] churches had increased from 1.7m to 7.9m, or from 3% to 6% of the population, while membership of the Roman Catholic Church had declined from 93% to 89% of the population.

As in other parts of Latin America, the Assemblies of God are among the fastest growing. They now have more than 30,000 places of worship throughout Brazil, 'only overtaken in numbers, in the interior, by the kiosks selling tickets for the Viacao Itapirim bus line'.

In fact, the growth of the evangelical Churches and the parallel decline of Roman Catholic membership are more dramatic than suggested by the statistics. Whereas the latter count as members all those baptised into the Church, infants and adults alike, whether or not they practice their religion, most evangelical denominations count only adults who are full and active members of their congregations.

Another report dated April 1993 is typical:

Take a bus through Brazil these days, and you will probably encounter a polite young man or woman who will spend the journey engrossed in the Bible. Go to the main square in Santiago, in Chile, on Sunday evening, and you may see a smartly dressed man preaching excitedly to an enthusiastic congregation. They are part of an explosion of evangelical Protestantism in Latin America.

The Protestant churches that Latin Americans flock to join are not traditional denominations like the Methodists or Baptists. Some, like the Assemblies of God, are large churches represented in several countries. Others are tiny local splinters. What they have in common is the ability to attract poor people, and – often – a strongly pentecostal flavour that draws on Latin American traditions of folk-religion: adherents go in for ecstatic worship, faith-healing and speaking in tongues.

The new churches seem fresh, modern and direct. They use television and radio, broadcasting their services literally into the street. They offer the certainties of the Bible and the promise of personal salvation, combined with an emphasis on a sober, hard-working way of life that appeals to migrant people desperate to succeed in the big city.[68]

Revival – or a taste of it – has also hit Hungary, along with many other East European nations, where lively faith has flourished under the brutality of the former communist regimes. The *Financial Times* reported in December 1990:

It is Saturday night in suburban Budapest and three trendy teenage girls stand with their eyes closed and rapture on their faces as a bearded man in a suit babbles at them. One of the girls falls away from the preacher's hand pressed against her forehead and collapses to the floor. She gets up, blinks in the light and then drifts off in the arms of her friends, dazed but still smiling.

Another Hungarian soul has been baptised in the Holy Spirit and harvested by the Faith Church. Only a part of the religious revival is fad. Opinion polls have shown an increase in religiosity since the late 1970s, fuelled largely by conversion among the young. Now that official constraints have gone, the pace appears to be accelerating. Nowhere in Hungary is this more evident than at the Faith Church's marathon five-hour sermons at a bleakly functional sports hall in the Buda hills.[69]

The pentecostal revival is also very much alive in Southern Africa. For example, Ray McCauley started a small prayer group in his home a few years ago. Now he heads up Rhema Ministries, a charismatic church in Johannesburg with 15,000 born-again Christian members. This was also the home of Rodney Howard-Browne through whose ministry so many began to laugh in the US from 1989 to 1994. Reuters reported of Ray McCauley in 1991:

He speaks in tongues, cures the sick by laying on hands, and calls de Klerk with advice at 10 o'clock at night. McCauley, 41, helped broker peace talks between Inkatha, Nelson Mandela's African National Congress, and de Klerk's government. It was the first time that the three major players in the South African political arena had got round the table together.

Rhema's 5,500-seat church in northern Johannesburg, built at a cost of seven million rand (2.3 million dollars), has to hold three sessions every Sunday to meet demand.

Quiet dignity is not McCauley's style – the louder his services, the better. Enraptured members of the congregation clap, wave their hands in the air and yell hallelujah.[70]

Then there is the rest of Africa. In May 1988 Gerald Coates, worship leader Noel Richards and I went with several others to Uganda at the invitation of Robert Kayanga of the Miracle Centre in Kampala, to see the AIDS situation for ourselves, and discuss with government officials and church leaders the ways in which a new Christian AIDS initiative based in the UK might be able to help.

The night we arrived we were driven straight to a meeting of several thousand people, some of whom had travelled up to 200 miles, either on foot or by hitching lifts from lorries. This was the monthly all-night prayer meeting – and it did go on all night.

The church structure was little more than a vast roofed area suspended on metal poles, with open sides. Thousands crammed into every available inch of space around the compound area. They worshipped and prayed without interruption for about ten hours, starting at around eight in the evening. That night we witnessed hundreds of people shaking, moaning, shrieking, crying out, writhing, groaning and falling down. At the time, from where we were standing on the platform, we concluded that some were not so much filled with the Spirit of God, as either exhibiting human copying behaviour or bordering on the hysterical, or were possessed of another spirit altogether – witchcraft was very active as a religion among some of the people there.

Robert Kayanga had had perhaps a couple of hundred church members about eight years before. Hundreds were making decisions each year. Many were not continuing in the faith, but a number were. We visited and spoke in a number of other churches during the two weeks. It was clear that the scenes at the Miracle Centre were not uncommon in the area, although they were shocking to many other African church leaders from traditional, formal denominations. Meanwhile, other British leaders returning from visiting other African nations also reported similar manifestations and rapid church growth.

Then there is China, representing perhaps one in four of the entire population of the world. On 16th April 1994, John Gittings sent a report to *The Guardian* in London of 'Christian fever' sweeping China, with evangelical house churches springing up to fill a massive vacuum left by the end of the pseudo-religious personality cult of Chairman Mao. After enjoying a relaxation of severe repression, the unofficial churches became illegal in February 1994, as did missionaries working among them, unless they were willing to register officially, which many feared to do because of decades of persecution.

The bare earth courtyard with mud walls all around is packed with Chinese peasants squatting on the ground, praying, weeping, or doing both. The meeting takes place in an unofficial 'house church' outside the authority of the government-recognised 'patriotic' church movement.

Official statistics concede that there are well over 1 million converts in Henan province – which has a total population of 51 million, mostly poor peasants. Those with fairly long experience of modern China can only rub their eyes in amazement.

These scenes of worship are infused with an enthusiasm verging on hysteria. There are mass meetings at night on hilltops, with tears and prostrations. Mass baptisms take place, again by night, in cold mountain waters. Hands are laid on sick children and crippled elders: miracles are attested. Young women speak in tongues, others interpret in Standard Chinese. Lay preachers emphasise their sermons with a skipping motion.

Those who belong to the more extreme sect called 'the

Yellers', they say, are far more noisy. All this is taking place in the same Chinese countryside where 90 years ago foreign missionaries were taunted, stoned and – in the Boxer rebellion of 1900 – murdered for seeking to proselytise. Now their reception is very different.

Pastor Dennis Balcombe, of the Revival Christian Church, is almost breathless with the work of bringing the Lord's word to China. 'Going to South Henan,' he says, 'is akin to stepping back into the pages of the Acts of the Apostles and first-century Christianity. Almost every village is aflame with revival fires.'

Hundreds are up for prayer by 5am. Thousands, predominantly young people, are converting to the faith. Many will tell you about answers to prayer, miracles, deliverance. It is revival in every sense of the word.

Patrick Johnstone has written a unique resource called *Operation World*, charting the progress of world revival, and people groups still unreached by the gospel.[71] Here are some figures.

Evangelicals in the industrialised West grew from 57.7 million in 1960 to 95.9 million in 1990. In the rest of the world the number of Evangelicals rose from 29 million to no fewer than 208 million in the same period – an average annual growth rate of 6.8%. Now 70% of all Evangelicals live in developing countries.

Pentecostals are charismatic Evangelicals. Ignoring all charismatic individuals or small groups within non-pentecostal denominations, the growth has been spectacular. In 1960 there were 11 million Pentecostals. By 1990 there were no fewer than 93 million – nearly 31% of all Evangelicals – but over half of all other charismatics are found within the other denominations. Four out of ten of the world's Pentecostals are in Latin America, where the greatest growth has been.

Patrick Johnstone remarks: 'We are living in the time of the largest ingathering of people into the Kingdom of God that the world has ever seen … astonishing growth in Africa and Asia today.' In Asia alone the number of Protestants rose from 58 million to 127 million in the ten years from 1980 to 1990. In China 1.5 million Protestants in 1949 had become an estimated 63 million by 1992, while the Catholics had quadrupled from 3 million to 12 million in the same period. 'The world has never known a turning on such a scale before.' Korea is now home to the twenty largest churches in the world. One joint meeting in 1980 drew 2.7 million people.

So then, there is a global spiritual awakening taking place, and while we may not say yet that such an awakening has hit the UK, there has been a revolution of renewal in church life before the recent events of 1994. There are now definite signs of revival in some churches, affecting increasing numbers of unbelievers, and there is a greater openness to the gospel in the nation than most Christians alive today can ever remember.

We have seen these things before, those of us trawling through the histories of the past. Revival of the church could well be far nearer than we think, and through it a national awakening in which hundreds of thousands find faith, with an impact on every aspect of life in Britain. In turn this could trigger a massive new missionary movement across the world, perhaps targeted primarily at the rest of Europe which, in comparison with other sub-continents, is still a vast spiritual desert.

3

The History of Emotional Faith

The history of emotional Christian faith can be traced back to the Day of Pentecost when the disciples had their first experience of being filled with the Holy Spirit – an occasion on which they became so intoxicated that the effect on their bodies seems to have been similar outwardly to that of alcohol.

The crowd who looked on made their own diagnosis of alcohol abuse – drunkenness – presumably because of what they could see and hear. 'Some, however, made fun of them and said, "They have had too much wine" (Acts 2:13). Luke records that a crowd gathered when they heard the disciples speaking fluently in the languages of different nations represented. That is not a description of drunkenness, but a description of extraordinary miraculous mental powers.

It is reasonable to assume these men were staggering about. This is hardly surprising in the light of what they had just experienced in the Upper Room. Their experience was essentially indescribable. All they could say afterwards was that they heard a sound like a wind blowing around them, and saw what seemed like tongues of fire that separated and came to rest on each of them.

Nothing is recorded by the doctor (Luke) who wrote the

Acts of the Apostles of what it *felt* like inside. Did they feel hot, cold, trembly, shaky, peaceful? Can we really believe that they sat there praying, they heard a strange noise, saw light (that is all fire is to the eye), and quietly got up and walked outside, finding they could now speak several more languages each?

Surely not. Luke describes an explosive event, a life-changing crisis experience, a moment of transformation in which they turned from being cowards afraid of martyrdom into fearless evangelists. I have no doubt that if we could talk to them today they would say that they came out of that Upper Room in a daze. They were overwhelmed by an extraordinary experience, impossible to put into words fully. They were spaced out, inebriated and euphoric. Luke wastes little space describing the manifestations in detail because they were of little ultimate importance. It was the result which was vital, pointing to the reality of the resurrection of Jesus.

The accusation of drunkenness was difficult to deal with, precisely because the appearances of drunkenness were so very convincing. The first thing Peter had to do when he got up to make a speech was to deal with the drunkenness issue. He said: 'These men are not drunk, as you suppose. It's only nine in the morning!' (Acts 2:15).

The apostle Paul also made a strong parallel between alcohol intoxication and an overwhelming experience of the Holy Spirit when he told the Ephesians: 'Do not get drunk on wine, which leads to debauchery. Instead, be filled with the Spirit' (Eph 5:18). We might have written: 'Do not get drunk with wine, which leads to debauchery, but exercise self-control in all things.' Paul's point is different: he is saying that if you have been used to getting drunk, and do so because you enjoy being inebriated, seek to enjoy being filled by the Holy Spirit instead.

He knew himself what it was like to experience an altered state of consciousness, intoxicated in God's presence. For example, he says that he was 'caught up to the third heaven. Whether it was in the body or out of the body I do not know … caught up to paradise … heard inexpressible things' (2 Cor 12:2,4).

Christians were called *tarsa* or 'shakers' by the Persians in the first centuries, presumably because unusual manifestations were known in that period too.[72]

However, the history of enthusiasm goes back far further than the time of Jesus to David, commanding God's people to sing and dance, and beyond. We look later at some of the scriptures that have been used to justify the experiences people are having today.

To some extent it is probably true that reactions to the manifestations seen in 1994 and beyond will be shaped to a large extent by opinions on the charismatic movement or pentecostalism. The arguments for and against become very similar.

George Jeffreys was the founder of today's pentecostal Elim movement, which has its roots in the (re-)discovery of the power of the Holy Spirit. In 1935, shortly after the two thousandth anniversary of the first Pentecost, he wrote *Pentecostal Rays*, a powerful justification from Scripture and church history of the use of spiritual gifts, in particular the use of tongues. Many of the arguments he used are particularly relevant to us today as we debate emotional faith, enthusiasm and manifestations associated with previous revivals. We consider them in the next chapter.

At the turn of the century the main controversy was over the use of tongues as part of ecstatic Christian experience. Today the very phrase 'speaking in tongues' has become so much a part of our culture that it is used freely in advertising and copy-writing, in different contexts. A strong argument Jeffreys used was the evidence of history since Pentecost. He showed that tongues and other manifestations could be traced down the centuries, so could not have died out, as some argued, when the first apostles died.

Jeffreys based much of his work on research by Stanley Frodsham in *With Signs Following*. Many of the quotations below are from Jeffreys, unless otherwise stated. I have also interwoven in chronological order many other historical sources regarding manifestations in general.

I have also drawn extensively from the work of John Gillies, a friend of George Whitefield. In 1754 he wrote a long and detailed account of the history of revival.[73] It is over 650,000 words long, almost seven times the size of this book you are holding now, packed with eyewitness accounts, letters, documents and other records of revival in every age. There are so many accounts of enthusiasm and manifestations of various kinds from these and other sources that it is hard to know what to leave in and what to leave out.

This is a brief sample of just a few of the manifestations seen in the church over the centuries, and some glimpses at what revival feels like for those swept up in it – a complete record would no doubt be as long as several volumes of *Encyclopedia Britannica*. Of course, history is only a partial record. Most of what happens to people is never recorded.

As we will see in a later chapter, there are two different but not entirely separate strands of historic Christian experience. One is mystical, with (usually) gradual alterations in conscious state through meditation and contemplation, seen in many over the centuries such as St Francis of Assisi. The other is charismatic, with (usually) more rapid alterations in conscious state associated with tongues, sudden loss of strength, unusual body movements and other outward manifestations. Let us start then with George Jeffreys.

160-225

'Tertullian lived from 160 to 225 and described spiritual gifts still in current use among the montanists to whom he belonged.'

347-407

Chrysostom lived from 347 to 407 and wrote: 'Whosoever was baptised in apostolic days, he straightway spake with tongues; for since on their coming over from idols, without any clear knowledge or training in the ancient Scriptures, they at once received the Spirit; not that they saw the Spirit, for He is invisible, but God's grace bestowed some sensible proof of His energy; and one straightway spake in the Persian language, another in the Roman, another in the Indian, another in some other tongue; and this made manifest to them that were without that it was the Spirit in the very person speaking. Wherefore the Apostle calls it "the manifestation of the Spirit which is given to every man to profit withal".'

Spurgeon also says that there was clapping of hands, stamping of feet and shouting for joy.

354-430

Augustine wrote in the fourth century: 'We still do what the apostles did when they laid hands on the Samaritans, and called down the Holy Spirit on them, in the laying on of hands. It is expected that converts should speak with new tongues.'

1100-1400

Even in the Dark Ages God gave some gracious revivals. From the twelfth to the fifteenth century there were revivals in Southern Europe in which many spoke in other tongues. Foremost among these revivalists were the Waldenses (12th century in southern France and northern Italy) and Albigenses.

The *Encyclopedia Britannica* states that the glossolalia (or speaking in tongues) 'recurs in Christian revivals of every age, e.g., among the friars of the thirteenth century, among the Jansenists and early Quakers, the persecuted Protestants of the Cevennes, and the Irvingites'.

1419

'This church history says of Vincent Ferrar, who died in 1419: "Spondamus and many others by this saint was honoured with the gift of tongues."'

1536

Erasmus was the most well-known writer on church history in his time, and helped pave the way for the reformation. Before he died in 1536 he wrote: 'Sometimes the Spirit of Christ can be seen to be present in the hearers. Some sigh, some burst into tears, the faces of some grow happy. In short you could say they had all been transfigured.'[74]

1552

Jeffreys also tells of Francis Xavier, who died in 1552, that he 'is said to have made himself understood by the Hindus without knowing their language'. The *Catholic Encyclopedia* also speaks of him preaching in tongues unknown to him. Xavier was a truly converted man, and a most remarkable missionary.

1596

Moving on from Jeffreys' accounts, on Tuesday 30th March 1596 John Gillies records a meeting in Edinburgh which was interrupted 'by sighs and groans and with shedding of tears among the most, everyone provoking another by their example, and the teacher himself by this so the very church resounded'. This was the time of Robert Bruce's ministry in the same city.

1625

There was a great Scottish revival in 1625. William Blair, Minister of Dunblane Presbyterian Church, wrote in 1859:

The remarkable work of God in Ayrshire, from 1625 to 1630, was attended by physical symptoms identically one with those of recent times. 'Under the ministry of Rev. Mr Dickson,' says the author of *The Fulfilling of the Scriptures*, 'few Sabbaths did pass without some eminently converted, and some convincing proof of the power of God accompanying His Word, yea, that many were so choked and taken by the heart, that, through terror, they have been made to fall over, and thus carried out of the church, who afterward proved most solid and lively christians.' The malignants called those affections the 'Stewarton sickness'.[75]

1628

In 1628, Gillies records a great revival in Ireland:

One of the largest manifestations of the Spirit, and of the most solemn times of the down-pouring thereof, that almost since the days of the apostles hath seen; where the power of God did sensibly accompany the word with an unusual motion upon the hearers, and a very great tack [old Scottish word for catch of fish] as to the conversion of souls to Christ.

Just eight years before, on 6th September, the first of the religious refugees set sail from Plymouth, England across the Atlantic to land at Cape Cod after nine weeks at sea.

1650

In 1650 Justice Bennett called George Fox a 'Quaker' because he bade the justice tremble at the word of the Lord. The word, however, was already in use three years previously and stayed with the movement because of the way in which members shook at their meetings.[76] The Quaker movement swiftly abandoned many aspects of orthodox Christian faith, but in the early days they are an example of a group which experienced manifestations.

1685-1714

Jeffreys again:

Writing of the revivals among the Huguenots, Canon A. A. Boddy states: 'When Louis XIV of France in 1685 revoked the Edict of Nantes, which had given religious liberty, he strove by dragonnades to drive Protestants into the Roman Catholic Church. The Huguenots were led by John Cavalier, a farmer, into inaccessible mountains. Among the persecuted people were those who spoke in tongues. There are records both by enemies and by friends as to their prophetic gifts. '

1714

Miraculous Gifts came from the Cevennes to Holland, and on to Germany. At that time, among professors and students, there was great receptivity to God's power. In 1714 they brought the gift of tongues and prophecy to Wetterau, near Frankfurt-on-Main. Their leaders were an ejected Wurtemburg pastor, named Gruber, and a Brother Rock, a saddler. They and their 'gifted' followers were called 'the inspired ones of the Wetterau'.

1739

On New Year's Day, 1739 Charles and John Wesley, Ingham and Whitefield were present at a love-feast in Fetter Lane, London. Wesley had spent time in the US preaching, which had been a near disaster as far as he was concerned. He was feeling low and disheartened: 'About three in the morning, as we were continuing constant in prayer, the power of God came mightily upon us, insomuch that many cried out for exceeding joy, and many fell to the ground.'

Three weeks later, as John Wesley preached, 'A well-dressed, middle-aged woman suddenly cried out as in the agonies of death. She continued to do so for some time, with all the signs of the sharpest agony of spirit. When she was a little recovered, I desired her to call upon me the next day.'

In April 1739, Wesley began preaching in Bristol in Baldwin Street. To his astonishment: 'One that stood cried out aloud with the utmost vehemence, even as in the agonies of death.' Several others also cried out, before finding relief and beginning to praise God. These disturbing scenes became more frequent, affecting large numbers of people, usually women at first. At the end of April Wesley visited

Newgate Prison in Bristol. Wesley records that as he was preaching,

> one, and another, and another sunk to the earth: they dropped on every side as thunderstruck. One of them cried aloud. We besought God on her behalf and He turned her heaviness into joy. A second being in the same agony, we called upon God for her also; and He spoke peace unto her soul. In the evening, I was again pressed in spirit to declare that Christ was Himself a ransom for all. And almost before we called upon Him, to set to His seal, He answered. One was so wounded by the sword of the Spirit, that you would have imagined she could not live a moment. But immediately His abundant kindness was showed, and she loudly sung of His righteousness.

The same happened the next day and the news spread across Bristol like wildfire. There was a big reaction, with accusations of fraud, trickery or demon possession. A doctor went to see for himself. He closely observed a woman who

> broke out into strong cries and tears. He went and stood close to her, and observed every symptom, till great drops of sweat ran down her face, and all her bones shook. He then knew not what to think, being clearly convinced it was not fraud, nor yet any natural disorder. But when both her soul and body were healed in a moment, he acknowledged the finger of God.

Another fierce critic changed his mind on 1st May. A Quaker came to Baldwin Street to investigate. Wesley recalls that the meeting was so noisy that he could hardly make himself heard, bellowing above the din of cries and groanings:

> A Quaker who stood by was not a little displeased at the

dissimulation of those creatures, and was biting his lips and knitting his brows, when he dropped down as thunderstruck. The agony he was in was terrible to behold. We besought God not to lay folly to his charge; he soon lifted up his heart and cried aloud, 'Now I know thou art a prophet of the Lord.'

This is just one of many examples of believers who were affected. This was not something limited to unbelievers finding faith. Some have correctly pointed out that most of the manifestations seen by Wesley were associated with conversion. However, Wesley himself was a believer when his own heart was 'strangely warmed', and he continued to have strange experiences afterwards – for example, in the following year. It is incorrect to say that the only people affected in these meetings were unbelievers.

It is certainly true that the revival of faith in people like Wesley and his followers led to a national spiritual awakening. My purpose here is not to distinguish between people becoming Christians who fall over or have other physical manifestations, and those who have believed for a while with varying degrees of commitment and understanding, but to examine the history of manifestations in general.

Yet another example of a believer affected was John Haydon, who was also at Baldwin Street that night. A local weaver who was a regular churchgoer, he had come out of curiosity. He was appalled by what he saw going on and left with friends, with whom he argued till one in the morning, trying to persuade them that the whole thing was 'a delusion of the devil'.

Wesley, meanwhile, had said goodbye to others and was walking home to his lodgings in the early hours. He was met in the street by some people who told him, 'John Haydon was fallen raving mad,' and he rushed to his house. John had decided not to have dinner until he had finished reading a sermon he had borrowed on salvation by faith. 'In reading the last page he changed colour, and began screaming horribly, and beating himself against the ground.' Wesley continues the story:

> Between one and two I came in, and found him on the floor, the room being full of people, whom his wife would have kept without; but he cried aloud, 'No; let them all come; let all the world see the judgment of God.' Two or three men were holding him as well as they could. He immediately fixed his eyes on me, and stretching out his hand, cried, 'Aye, this is he, who I said was a deceiver of the people. But God has overtaken me. I said it was all a delusion. But this is no delusion.'
>
> He then roared out, 'O thou devil! thou cursed devil! yea, thou legion of devils! thou canst not stay. Christ will cast thee out. I know His work is begun. Tear me in pieces if thou wilt; but thou canst not hurt me.' He then beat himself against the ground again; his breast heaving at the same time as in the pangs of death, and great drops of sweat trickling down his face. We all betook ourselves to prayer. His pangs ceased, and both his body and soul were set at liberty.

C. E. Vulliamy records:

> Many of the lay preachers of Wesley experienced the most violent forms of conversion. Thomas Maxfield was converted during the Bristol revival in 1739. He was listening to Wesley at a meeting in Nicholas Street, when he saw a young man and then little boy fall into convulsions. Maxfield fixed his eyes on the child, and 'sunk down himself as one dead'. He roared and beat himself on the ground, so that six men were hardly able to

hold him. 'Except John Haydon,' said Wesley, 'I never saw one so torn of the evil one.'[77]

Today many charismatic leaders would make a diagnosis of demonic oppression in such a situation – as did Wesley then. Wesley was puzzled by these sudden events in Bristol and later wrote: 'Perhaps it might be because of the hardness of our hearts, unready to receive anything unless we see it with our eyes and hear it with our ears, that God, in tender condescension to our weakness, suffered so many outward signs … yet many would not believe.'

Here Wesley is clearly saying that he felt most of what was happening was the direct effect of the Holy Spirit on people's lives. He would change his mind later on.

1740

In 1740 Wesley was overcome with laughter and was uncertain what to make of the experience. It had happened to him for the first time as early as 1729. We pick up the story from his diary in May 1740:

Friday May 9: I was a little surprised at some, who were buffeted of Satan in an unusual manner, by such a spirit of laughter as they could in no wise resist though it was pain and grief to them. I could scarce have believed the account they gave me had I not known the same thing ten or eleven years ago. Part of Sunday my brother and I then used to spend in walking in the meadows and singing psalms. But one day, just as we were beginning to sing, he burst out in a loud laughter. I asked him if he were distracted; and [I] began to be very angry and presently after to laugh as loud as he. Nor could we possibly refrain, though we were ready to tear ourselves in pieces, but we were forced to go home without singing another line.

It is hard to be certain what Wesley made of the experience in 1729, but by 1740 he was clearly convinced that laughter was so unhelpful that presumably it was demonic.

> Wednesday May 21: In the evening such a spirit of laughter was among us that many were much offended. But all the attention was fixed on poor L.S. whom we all knew to be no dissembler. One so violently and variously torn of the evil one did I never see before. At last she faintly called on Christ to help her. And the violence of her pangs eased.
>
> Most of our brethren were now convinced that those who were under this strange temptation could not help it. Only E.B. and Anne H. were of another mind; being still sure anyone might help laughing if he would. This they declared to many on Thursday, but on…

> Friday May 23: God suffered Satan to teach them better. Both of them were suddenly seized in the same manner as the rest, and laughed whether they would or no, almost without ceasing. This they continued for two days, a spectacle to all; and were then, upon prayer made for them, delivered in a moment.

It is clear from the account that Wesley found the experience of laughter very hard to cope with. Even when he found himself laughing uncontrollably he was very uncomfortable about seeing it as anything other than some kind of trial or temptation. I have no doubt that if he had been alive in 1994 he might well have seen it differently.

1741

Whenever people in 1994 write of manifestations they often seem to quote Jonathan Edwards and his accounts of the revival in Northampton, America, the traces of which began in 1734, peaked in 1735, were accelerated by George Whitefield's arrival in 1740 and was still growing strongly in 1741 when they both met at Northampton. The town had been started eighty-two years previously and had grown to a mere 200 households,[78] yet it was a significant element in the New England revival, which saw 50,000 of the 250,000 population added to the church.[79]

One of the things that is striking when one reads about this revival, or later ones in Wales and Los Angeles in 1904-7, is how quickly news spread. We tend to think that in a world without telephones, faxes or airmail letters, people must have been very isolated.

While news may have taken longer to travel a great distance, it spread like wildfire across small neighbouring communities. In a world without radio or television, the biggest entertainment industry was gossiped news. One person in a village could get the message of war or revival to every inhabitant in an hour or two through networks of families and households. These were very small groups of people.

This affected the pattern of revival which nearly always affected a large proportion of the people in a small area. If we are expecting revival to come again in a similar way in developed countries in the 1990s, we may miss the first signs, because in a mobile age it is far more likely that revival will affect large numbers but across far wider areas, so the visible effect at first may seem far more diffused and hard to measure.

Transatlantic travel was quite common even in Wesley's day. Wesley, Whitefield and others made huge journeys, carrying reports with them of what God was doing elsewhere. These revivals were happening simultaneously and affected each other greatly. Every boat that landed brought more news.

Edwards notes that in Northampton, America:

> There has before now been both crying out and falling down in this town, under awakenings of conscience and in the pangs of the new birth, and also in some of the neighboring towns. In one of them, more than seven years ago, was a great number together that cried out and fell down under convictions; in most of which, by good information, was a hopeful and abiding good issue.

Many of the manifestations were at least as extreme as anything seen under Wesley's ministry. And they were not confined to conversion experiences either. For example, his wife was intermittently overcome by emotion, falling down or losing her strength or crying out for almost two weeks. Edwards wrote extensively on the nature of revival. He said: 'A great deal of noise and tumult, confusion and uproar, and darkness mixed with light, and evil with good, is always to be expected in the beginning of something very extraordinary, and very glorious in the state of things in human society, or the church of God.'

Edwards received severe criticism for the emotional excesses seen in some of the churches associated with him during the revival. In reply he wrote *Distinguishing Marks of a Work of the Spirit of God* in 1741. Some of his phrasing is tortuous, so I've simplified it here. Within the explanations are clear descriptions of the manifestations:

> There is a great aptness to doubt things that are strange; especially it is difficult for elderly persons, those that have lived a great while in the world, to think that to be right which they have been never used to, and have not heard of.

A work is not to be judged by any effects on the bodies of men; such as tears, trembling, groans, loud outcries, agonies of body, or the failing of bodily strength. The influence the minds of persons are under, is not to be judged one way or the other, whether it be from the Spirit of God or not by such effects on the body. The reason is because the Scripture nowhere gives us any such rule.

We can't conclude that persons *are* under the influence of the true Spirit, because we see such effects upon their bodies, because this is not given as a mark of the true Spirit. Nor on the other hand have we any reason to conclude, from any such outward appearances, that persons are *not* under the influence of the Spirit of God, because there is no rule of Scripture given us to judge spirits by that expressly or indirectly excludes such effects on the body; nor does reason exclude them.

If we consider human nature, we need not wonder that when persons have a very great sense of that which is so amazingly dreadful, and also have a great view of their own wickedness and God's anger, that things seem to them to forebode speedy and immediate destruction.

'Tis no sign that a work is not from the Spirit of God, that many that seem to be the subjects of it, are guilty of great imprudences and irregularities in their conduct. We are to consider that the end for which God pours out his Spirit, is to make men holy, and not to make them politicians.

'Tis no wonder at all, that in a mixed multitude of all sorts, wise and unwise, young and old, of weak and strong natural abilities, there are many that behave themselves imprudently. Few know how to conduct themselves under vehement affections of any kind, whether they be of a temporal or spiritual nature: to do so requires a great deal of discretion, strength and steadiness of mind.

A thousand imprudences won't prove a work not to be the work of the Spirit of God. That it should be thus may be well accounted for from the exceeding weakness of human nature, together with the remaining darkness and corruption of those that are yet the subjects of the saving influences of God's Spirit, and have a real zeal for God.

We have a remarkable instance in the New Testament, of a people that partook largely of that great effusion of the Spirit there was in the apostles' days, among whom there nevertheless abounded imprudences and great irregularities; and that is the church of the Corinthians.

There is scarce any church more celebrated in the New Testament for being blessed with large measures of the Spirit of God, both in his ordinary influences, in convincing and converting sinners and also in his extraordinary and miraculous gifts.

Yet what manifold imprudences and great and sinful irregularities, and strange confusion did they run into, at the Lord's Supper, and in the exercise of church discipline, and their indecent manner of attending other parts of public worship, and in jarring and contention about their teachers, and even in the exercise of their extraordinary gifts of prophecy, speaking with tongues, and the like, wherein they spake and acted by the immediate inspiration of the Spirit of God?

1742

Back in England, Whitefield was preaching at Cambuslang in Lanarkshire in 1742 where he saw violent conversions on a large scale. Whitefield spoke of people seeming to be 'slain in scores', and being carried off like casualties. However, these scenes became unusual in Whitefield's experience, while many still continued to find faith over the next few years.

In the same year Wesley 'carefully examined those who had lately cried out in the congregation' at Tanfield. He came to the conclusion that most of the manifestations had been genuine in people with 'a piercing sense of their sins'.

1743

Vulliamy writes regarding charges of emotionalism against
Wesley's work:

> Charles, [Wesley] who was invariably repelled by emotional
> scenes ... always suspected the presence of these fraudulent
> cases. The outward affections, he said, could be readily
> imitated. By 1743 he took up an attitude that was almost hostile
> in regard to what he brusquely called 'the fits'. He had detected
> many counterfeits, and many rogueries.
>
> On a certain day, 'One who came from the ale-house, drunk,
> was pleased to fall into a fit for my entertainment, and beat
> himself heartily. I thought it a pity to hinder him,' said Charles
> drily; 'so, instead of singing over him ... we left him to recover
> at his leisure. Another, a girl, as she began her cry, I ordered to
> be carried out. Her convulsion was so violent as to take away
> the use of her limbs, till they left her without the door. Then
> immediately she found her legs, and walked off.'
>
> He announced that anyone who cried out so as to drown the
> preacher's voice would be gently carried to the farthest corner
> of the room, and left there. After this, he was rarely troubled
> with such disturbances.
>
> Yet, in the earlier days of his preaching, he appears to have
> been convinced that such things proved 'the power of the Lord'.
> On the 12th of March 1739 he recorded how 'A woman cried
> out as in an agony – another sunk down overpowered – all were
> moved and melted as wax before the fire.'
>
> Again, in September of the same year (at Bristol): 'The
> breath of God attended His word. A man sunk down under it. A
> woman screamed for mercy... Never did I see the like power
> among us.' On the other hand, his earliest impulse was to
> repudiate energetically the idea of sudden conversion. He noted
> in his journal a meeting which took place at five in the morning.
>
> 'We fell into a dispute whether conversion was gradual or
> instantaneous. My brother was very positive for the latter, and

very shocking... I was much offended at his worse than unedifying discourse. Mrs. Delamotte left us abruptly.'

The quotation is of importance as it shows the original beliefs of both John and Charles.

While Wesley's brother Charles began clamping down on all disturbances in his meetings, Wesley continued to take a different approach, cautiously welcoming signs of change in people's lives, but examining people afterwards to check that what had happened to them was genuine.

In 1743, after examining cases in Newcastle, he said: 'These symptoms I can no more impute to any natural cause, than to the Spirit of God. I can make no doubt but it was Satan tearing them as they were coming to Christ.' Here, perhaps influenced by Charles, he no longer saw the power of God operating in people's lives, but the power of the devil.

It was clearly just as confusing then as it is today, 250 years later.

1745

Back to the colonies again, and there was also a remarkable revival among the American Indians in 1745, with people bending over or falling. Arthur Wallis comments:

David Brainerd recorded the beginning of the wonderful movement among the American indians in 1745 thus: 'The power of God seemed to descend on the assembly "like a rushing mighty wind" and with an astonishing energy bore down all before it. I stood amazed at the evidence that seized the audience almost universally, and could compare it to nothing more aptly than the irresistible force of a mighty torrent.... Almost all persons of all ages were bowed down with concern together, and scarce one was able to withstand the shock of this surprising operation.'[80]

1750

Jeffreys reports that tongues were experienced in Wesley's time: 'In the diary of Thomas Walsh, one of Wesley's foremost preachers, March 8, 1750, the record stands: "This morning the Lord gave me language that I knew not of, raising my soul to Him in a wonderful manner."'

1758

Manifestations became very uncommon from 1745 to 1757.
Wesley first met Berridge in November 1758 at Everton, shortly before the climax of the Everton revival. By November there had already been 'the same violent outward symptoms' which had occurred under Wesley's own preaching nearly twenty years before. Berridge and Wesley travelled to Wrestlingworth, five miles away, where Wesley preached in the church that night and the following morning. He wrote: 'In the middle of the sermon, a woman before me dropped down as dead, as one had done the night before.'

Later at Everton 'some were struck just as at Wrestlingworth'. On the evening of 18th December, he again preached at Everton. 'God gave me great liberty of speech, and applied his word to the hearts of the hearers; many of whom were not able to contain themselves, but cried aloud for mercy.'

1759

Wesley continued to agonise over the place of manifestations in the church. On the one hand he felt uncomfortable about some of them – and afraid they would bring his work into disrepute, but on the other hand he was concerned when they all seemed to fade away, which they had done for well over ten years.

After all, he had seen the fruit in people's lives and knew that the manifestations were often associated with lasting change. He also knew that manifestations were often a dramatic public sign of God's presence, power and authority, and were often used by God to draw many to meetings where they heard and responded to the gospel. He remarked:

> The danger was to regard extraordinary circumstances too much … as if these were essential to the inward work, so that it could not go on without them. Perhaps the danger now is to regard them too little, to condemn them altogether, to imagine they had nothing of God in them, and were a hindrance to His work. Whereas the truth is, God suddenly and strongly convinced many; the natural consequences whereof were sudden.

He returned again to Everton in March 1759 on his way to Norwich, but was not there eight weeks later when the full revival started. He returned to find out what had happened and includes in his journal a long, rambling but detailed account by one of the women in the church. The biographer, C. Vulliamy, summarises her letter and other records rather well when he writes that in the middle of May 1759:

> Inside the church at Everton, while Berridge was preaching or conducting his service, some of the people fainted and fell quietly on the floor, others roared and screamed, sinking down in horrible contortions; at one moment they felt themselves dropping into the blazing cavity of hell, and at the next, they were rising in ecstasies of joy and gratitude. Those who were

less affected stood on the seats of the pews in order to see the disturbed congregation.

The noise was incredible. Rustic boots hammered against the boards, broke the benches and split the sides of the pews. Children set up a shrill wailing. Women shrieked horribly, clapped their hands, or fell upon each other's necks. Some uttered short ejaculations of praise, and others shouted in wild triumph.

Below the louder sounds there was all the while a noise of hard breathing, as of men half strangled and gasping for life. And above all the appalling din could be heard the powerful voice of Berridge, praying and preaching and calling on sinners, louder and more unmelodious, and louder still, until no voice, no human head or heart, could bear the strain any longer, and he walked out through the stricken multitude.

Berridge walked from the church to the vicarage, and there the work was continued. People were carried into the house like casualties from the scene of some hideous disaster. Children raved and struggled in the passages. It was observed by a witness that 'almost all on whom God laid His hand turned either very red or almost black'.

Some laughed foolishly 'with extreme joy', tears of inexpressible emotion running down their pale, radiant faces. In some instances, the process of conversion was rapid, in others it was most painfully prolonged. While some were singing praises in the vicarage parlour, others were lying with closed eyes, with chattering teeth, and heels drumming on the floor-boards.

Strangers, after looking on placidly all at once staggered down on their knees, or ran against the wall, roaring for mercy. Careless young women, cool and curious at first, broke out all together in 'a loud and bitter cry'.

Some of the congregation, tottering from the church towards the house, fell on the side of the road, or under the shrubs in the vicarage garden, where they were found lying like dead bodies. Some, unmoved by the service, had gone away stolidly enough, and were overcome and stricken down before they could reach their own cottages.

A stranger coming to Everton, and knowing nothing about the 'spiritual influenza', would have thought he had come to a place where every other man was a lunatic or a drunkard.[81]

I find it impossible to accept that all the people affected in the Everton church were atheists, agnostics or lapsed believers coming to faith. It seems to me far more likely that the whole congregation became affected to one degree or another. The trouble with so many of Wesley's descriptions is that, by his own definition, even someone with faith in Christ who had given up years of his life and taken huge personal risks to preach the gospel might not be truly saved. That, after all, was Wesley's own verdict on himself, before he realised that he was saved by faith not by works in 1739. His definition of people being saved is therefore quite wide. Of course there are huge differences between what happened in Wesley's day and what has been happening in many countries in 1994, but not perhaps quite as absolute in character as might at first appear.

Vulliamy continues:

The same thing, but with rather less violence, was going on at Wrestlingworth. The 'arrows of the Lord' flew among the congregation of Mr. Hicks. 'While he was preaching, fifteen or sixteen persons dropped down. A few of these cried out with the utmost violence, and little intermission, for some hours; while the rest made no great noise, but continued struggling, as in the pangs of death.' Here, as at Everton, the more desperate cases were carried, or made their way, to the parsonage. 'Their cries increased beyond measure, so that the loudest singing could scarce be heard.'

It is remarkable that such things were brought about by Mr. Hicks, who, only a short time previously, had not only scoffed at the doings of Berridge, but had actually refused the Communion to those of his parishioners who went to hear the Everton preaching.

It is to be observed that preaching in the open air very rarely, if ever, produced the extraordinary scenes which occurred in churches and chapels. Berridge went on to Shelford, about four miles south of Cambridge: a table was set up on the common, and about ten thousand people came to hear the preaching. 'The audience,' he said, 'behaved with great decency.' We hear nothing of loud outcries or sudden conversions.

During the months of June and July 1759, many astonishing scenes took place at or near Everton, and among the villages to the south of Cambridge. Jane Thorn and Patty Jenkins of Potton had trances and saw visions of ineffable glory. Redeemed souls walked together in the lanes or through the fields, chanting hymns of praise.

Still, the more notable conversions took place among men, and it was the men who fell into ugly fits, with dreadful sweating and awful heavings, groanings and violent bodily disturbances. Symptoms of this kind were rare among the women.

At Grantchester, seventeen people were 'broken down' more or less spontaneously by the mere singing of hymns, and an innocent child of seven saw many visions.

At Everton, powerful men were seized by the hand of the Lord, shaken like clothes drying in the wind, or flung to the ground as though by the blow of a giant, or they stood gaping and staring, full of a huge dismay.

In the churchyard, women fell among the graves, plucking at the turf and grass with convulsed fingers. Others burst into peals of hideous laughter.

Emotions quickly fade – and manifestations can quickly disappear. All would have vanished by November. On Sunday 5th August, John Wesley returned to Everton to find out about the revival. He preached at Everton and Wrestlingworth, but the meetings were fairly quiet. The following day he talked to two women who had apparently been in 'trances'. Berridge also asked him to go and see Alice Miller who was still affected. Wesley writes:

> I found her sitting on a stool and leaning against the wall, with her eyes open and fixed upward. I made a motion as if going to strike; but they continued immovable. Her face showed an unspeakable mixture of reverence and love, while silent tears stole down her cheeks.... Her pulse was quite regular.
>
> In about half an hour I observed her countenance change into the form of fear, pity and distress. Then she burst into a flood of tears, and cried out, 'Dear Lord, they will go to hell! the world will go to hell!' Soon after she said, 'Cry aloud! Spare not!' And in a few moments her look was composed again, and spoke a mixture of reverence, joy and love. Then she said aloud, 'Give God the glory.'
>
> About seven her senses returned. I asked her, 'Where have you been?' 'I have been with my Saviour.' 'In heaven or on earth?' 'I cannot tell; but I was in glory!'

The example above is clearly not one of an unbeliever. It is of someone with faith who is concerned for others who are lost. Once again the simplistic image we have of manifestations only affecting those being converted is seen to be false. Wesley himself had great problems justifying manifestations of any kind in an 'age of reason', which was the climate in which he lived. Perhaps it is not surprising therefore that conversion manifestations are reported so prominently.

Wesley continued to keep in close touch with what was going on at Everton. He came back a few weeks later to preach. Many sank down 'in agonies of prayer', and a young man and woman had to be carried out of the church to the vicarage – with great difficulty because they were 'in violent agonies both of body and soul'. In other words, they were thrashing about, crying and shouting.

When Wesley returned in November he found the climax of the Everton revival was over. Berridge had gone to the University of Cambridge to preach. Wesley said: 'I observed a remarkable difference since I was here before, as to the manner of the work. None now were in trances, none cried out; none fell down or were convulsed. Only some trembled exceedingly; a low murmur was heard, and many were refreshed with "the multitude of peace".'

Wesley came to the conclusion that some of the people at Everton imitated the cries and convulsions of those who really had been overpowered by the Spirit of God. However, even if some of what had been seen was just contagious human emotion, he was anxious that people should not minimise what God had done in the area. However, within three years, the Everton revival was over.

1762

Vulliamy continues:

> In January 1762, less than three years after the revival, Wesley paid two visits to Everton. He found the people not only 'more settled', but in danger of running to another extreme – that of disparaging the least appearance of religious enthusiasm. On Sunday, the 10th of January, he took the morning and afternoon services in the church, observing before him a grave, seemly and pious congregation, attentive though not openly moved. There were no more fits, visions or trances.

1761-65

Wesley once commented that phenomena often seem to 'attend the beginning of general work of God ... but after a time they gradually decrease, and the work goes on more quietly and silently'.

After the first Bristol revival of 1739-40, manifestations of sudden overwhelming emotion during Wesley's preaching became less and less common. It seems that in some years none was seen at all. There were a few in 1758, shortly before the big revival at Everton, but they were isolated instances. In 1761 there was just one case, with three in 1765, of young men falling into convulsions.

1772

In 1772, a revival took place at Weardale in Durham, but only some of the manifestations seen happened while Wesley was there.

1780-86

There were more cases in Warrington in 1780, and again in Newcastle and at Chapel-in-le-Frith in 1786, when Wesley was eighty-three years old. In 1786, five years before his death, Wesley speaks of Satan pushing the 'lively people' of Chapel-in-le-Frith to extravagance: 'Just so, did the French Prophets, and very lately the Jumpers in Wales, bring the real work into contempt. Yet whenever we reprove them, it should be in the most mild and gentle manner possible.'

However, what happened at Chapel-in-le-Frith in 1786 hardly seems that different from what took place almost half a century before in Bristol. They cried out, dropped as though dead, and then loudly proclaimed their salvation. But this was now looked on as 'extravagance', begotten of the Father of Lies.

Wesley's attitude therefore seems to have changed as he aged, with a greater recognition of the value of gradual conversion, and increasing caution about emotion. But in the early days it is clear from his journal that such experiences were a dominant part of his thinking about mission. Even at the very end of his life he held to the view that just because something can be imitated it does not follow that it is never real.

Wesley died in 1791, having travelled 250,000 miles, preached at 40,000 different meetings, and having seen 140,000 become Christians (Methodist members).[82]

1801

Hugh Bourne was a powerful Methodist preacher through whom another more limited revival began in 1801. At Congleton he said: 'The Holy Spirit descended on us to such a degree that we began again and again, and for some time could scarce stand or speak, so great was the power of God on us.' Bourne was expelled by the Methodists in 1809 for having unauthorised and 'improper' meetings (they did not like the emotion), and began a separate group which became the Primitive Methodists. By 1842 they had grown to more than 85,000 members.[83]

1824

From 1824 onwards there was a new experience of the Holy Spirit in America. George Jeffreys records:

From 1824 down to the present time, from Maine to Connecticut, quite a goodly number of the Adventist people (known as Gift Adventists) have had more or less talking in tongues, and also the interpretation of tongues. Some gifted men of their ministry have been thus exercised. The most talking in tongues has been by Wm. H. Doughty, a minister for over forty years. (Since 1895 ed.) He was the leader among the Gift Adventists. The writer knew him well. He was a very sweet-spirited, humble Christian, of great power in prayer.

1831-59

The gift of tongues was also found in France, Sweden and Ireland in the nineteenth century. Jeffreys notes:

In the *History of the Christian Church*, by Philip Schaff, Vol. I, page 237, of the edition of 1882, this author shews that the phenomenon of speaking in tongues reappeared from time to time in seasons of special religious revival, as among the Camisards and the prophets of the Cevennes in France, among the early Quakers and Methodists, the Readers (followers of Lasare) in Sweden in 1841-1843, in the Irish revivals of 1859, and especially in the 'Catholic Apostolic Church', commonly called Irvingites, from 1831-1833, and even to this day.

1840

There was also a revival in Dundee, Scotland (1840), with many manifestations, which also caused reactions and questions. The Revd Murray McCheyne was asked by the Presbytery in Aberdeen to investigate. He wrote:

I have been fully convinced that the outpouring of the Holy Spirit at the Kirk of Shotts, and again, a century after, at Cambuslang etc., in Scotland, and under the ministry of President Edwards in America, was attended by the very same appearances as the work in our own day.

Indeed, so completely do they agree, both in their nature and in circumstances that attended them, that I have not heard a single objection brought against the work of God now which was not urged against it in former times, and that has not been most scripturally and triumphantly removed by Dr James Robe of Kilsyth in his narrative... of 1742, and by President Edwards in his invaluable 'Thoughts on Revival'.[84]

1857

'Mr. O. P. Simmons of Frost Proof, Florida, writing in "A Call to Faith" in November, 1909, states: "While I have been a church member for sixty-two years, I have associated with those who talk in tongues for fifty-two years."'

1858

From 1858 to 1859 a revival swept America, with the revival of perhaps a million nominal church members and the addition of a further million new converts.[85] However, considering the size of what happened there were few manifestations of any kind.

There were many Irish settlers in America, and news of what was happening spread rapidly to Ireland. But it would be true to say that early signs of revival can also be traced to prayer meetings which started more or less simultaneously on both sides of the Atlantic in 1857.

1859

In 1859 a huge revival broke out in the north of Ireland that immediately became extremely controversial, with writers in the medical press condemning the manifestations, accusing the church of driving people insane. In August 1859, William Blair, Minister of Dunblane Presbyterian Church, went to Belfast to see the revival for himself.

I have reproduced his comments at length because the manifestations included people losing speech, sight and other faculties for days at a time. There have been occasional reports of similar things in 1994 in Britain, so the precedent is important. Also, the accusations were some of the fiercest fired at any revival. They came from doctors, and the same could happen again in the mid- to late 1990s. He wrote:

> I shall ever recall the scenes I witnessed, during a short visit to the north of Ireland, in August 1859, with lively satisfaction. I thank God I was enabled to mingle for a very short season with those who were there visited by the effusion of the Holy Ghost.
>
> Too little as well as too much has been made of the singular physical features of this great revival. By some they are regarded as mere excrescences. I do not think so. They have accompanied all revivals.
>
> The same kind of effects were seen in the revivals in New England under Edwards, in Cambuslang under McCulloch, and in Kilsyth under Robe.
>
> I shall not occupy much space in my remarks on the physical phenomena. I saw no cases of prostration, or what was commonly called 'striking down'. But I met with many who had been so affected, and saw several that had not rallied from the consequences, who were either deaf, or dumb, or both. I know that deceivers have tried to simulate these bodily manifestations, and even to pretend to have their persons marked with certain stigmata, which they alleged were

supernatural. But I know for certain that the cases I investigated were thoroughly genuine.

One young woman was lying in a helpless state, as incapable of expressing her wants as one born deaf and dumb. Her face bore every token of conscious intelligence; but the ear was closed, 'the string of the tongue was tied', and the teeth fast clenched together. She had continued in this state for several days.

Another had been blind and mute, and, on recovering her vision, lost her hearing and speech. She communicated with us in writing. She had been five times under this deprivation. She said she was very happy in Jesus Christ for a fortnight before she was struck down deaf and dumb. She was stricken the first time the large prayer meeting was held in the Royal Botanic Gardens.

She did not know what was going on around her when she was deprived of sight and hearing; but when she was asleep, she heard all the prayers that were offered up in her behalf. She had mentioned the day and hour when she would recover on several occasions, and had always awakened at the time specified.

What was very remarkable in her case was a kind of vision she had of balls of fire that came down from heaven, to which two men were witnesses. And I know from one of the parties – the travelling agent of the London City Mission – that the phenomenon was seen by him before his footsteps were directed to the house of that woman. She is a member of Mr Hanna's church, and is now rejoicing in the recovered possession of her physical and mental powers.

Another case was that of a young woman in Ballymena, who had been similarly deprived of her senses but had recovered them. She attended a prayer meeting in a church, where I had the pleasure of witnessing the mighty power of God. Before the service was closed, she was carried into the vestry. I saw her there after the dismissal. Her limbs were rigid. Her face wore a lovely hue, as if transfigured by the light of heaven. Her eyes were open, and lifted heavenward. She seemed neither to see nor hear aught that was transpiring around her.

It was a most solemn spectacle, as if we had gazed in upon the face of a Saint worshipping before the throne. All were deeply impressed. Her minister knelt, and we all joined in prayer for her. When we rose from our knees, she was restored. I care not what sceptics may say or little-faith Christians, who have no confidence in the extraordinary influences of the Spirit. I believe, as firmly as I believe my own existence, that the Holy Ghost would never have permitted His work to be entangled with such perplexing and seemingly incredible phenomena, had He not had a most important end to serve by them.[86]

There are of course strong precedents in the Bible for people losing speech or sight temporarily as an 'act of God'. For example, John the Baptist's father, Zechariah (Lk 1:20), and the apostle Paul (Acts 9:8). A psychiatrist who does not believe God exists is forced to an explanation of hysteria, because he has no other explanation. A Christian has a range of possibilities to consider in every recent case.

Another minister describes scenes at his church in Carrickfergus at about the same time:

In many instances bodily agony and suffering accompanied the conviction and conversion of the sinner. These bodily affections were very slight in some, but in others so severe as to weaken the person for some days, and in a few cases even affected the health.

There were about four hundred awakened or revived in my congregation of whom I was cognisant, and of these, about two hundred were accompanied with bodily symptoms and prostration. In some instances the individual would be smitten instantaneously with a sense of conviction of sin, would fall prostrate, and in some cases nearly powerless, screaming for mercy and pardon, would writhe in the agony of despair, in fear of the Divine wrath, and continue in this state for a day or two.

And in one or two cases the persons continued so for more than a week. One person was nineteen days under conviction of sin before finding peace, but the most of them found peace in a day or two. Some few, but they were very few, had those bodily manifestations more than once. It was very touching, when they were stricken with the conviction of sin, to hear them cry for mercy.

The eyes of the understanding, that had been formerly closed, were then opened. They saw as it were the gulf into which they were falling. They felt the burden of sin very weightily upon their soul. All their sins appeared before them black and terrible. The fear of the wrath of God, and of the torment of hell was excruciating. It was then you would have heard them pray fervently and exclaim, 'Oh, my sins, my sins, how great! O Jesus, have mercy on me. Pardon my sins.'

One evening during prayer, or shortly afterwards, three prostrations took place; two of these were overpowered with an overwhelming anxiety about relatives. Their prayers for their friends were incessant and affecting. The other was a case of deep personal concern, which has ended hopefully.[86]

In the same year (1859) the Revd Samuel Moore also travelled to Belfast to see for himself what God was doing. He observed that as in the previous century, the manifestations were largely associated with terrible feelings of unworthiness and imminent judgement. His descriptions are very important for us today:

Prominent characteristics of revival

The soul is felt to be guilty and lost. Sin is seen to be loathsome and deadly, and it is generally felt to be an intolerable burden, crushing the body and soul to hell. Horror unutterable overwhelms the heart, especially of those who feel that the devil is persuading or dragging them to perdition. With some this conviction has reference to particular besetting sins – with others, the greater number, to the general sinful state of the soul … unworthiness.

The physical features

When the conviction as to its mental process reaches its crisis, the person, through weakness, is unable to sit or stand, and either kneels or lies down. A great number of convicted persons in this town and neighbourhood, and now I believe in all directions in the north where the revival prevails, are 'smitten down' as suddenly, and they fall as nerveless and paralysed, and powerless, as if killed instantly by a gun-shot.

They fall with a deep groan – some with a wild cry of horror – the greater number with the intensely earnest plea, 'Lord Jesus, have mercy on my soul!' The whole frame trembles like an aspen leaf, an intolerable weight is felt upon the chest, a choking sensation is experienced, and relief from this found only in the loud, urgent prayer for deliverance.

Usually the bodily distress and mental anguish continue till some degree of confidence in Christ is found. Then the look, the tone, the gestures instantly change. The aspect of anguish and despair is changed for that of gratitude, and triumph, and adoration.

The language and the looks, and the terrible struggles and loud desperate deprecations, tell convincingly, as the parties themselves afterwards declare, that they are in deadly conflict with the old serpent.

The perspiration rolls off the anguished victims; their very hair is moistened. Some pass through this exhausting conflict several times; others but once. There is no appetite for food; many will eat nothing for a number of days. They do not sleep, though they may lie down with their eyes shut.

When partially recovered they cannot use the requisite quantity of food, and hence, I presume, the continued weakness and incapacity, and consequent indisposition to work on the part of some, complained of by parents and employers. Surely, in the meantime, these should be satisfied with somewhat less than the usual task, in the assurance that wherever genuine conversion is the issue children will be better children and servants better servants.

One person I have seen quite speechless about three hours on one occasion, and about six on another occasion.   Yesterday I saw a girl just recovered from being dumb exactly twenty-four hours. To-day I visited a third party, who had been entirely dumb these last twenty days.

There are great varieties in these physical afflictions. These I cannot now enumerate. To me many of them are quite mysterious. We may call them hysteria, and know as little of their cause as before.

Will strong overwhelming emotion account for many of the phenomena? Do these emotions, whether gentle or confounding, result from a consideration of sin issuing in the soul's everlasting destruction, and of the long, unseen, and slighted Saviour – His love, His charms, His power to save to the uttermost – to save me?

And is this consideration produced by witnessing these agonies in others, by hearing their wild cries for mercy, their supernatural prayers – by reading or hearing the awful and glorious Gospel truths, and especially by hearing a lately redeemed one tell tearfully, urgently, adoringly, what Jesus did for his own soul?

Or may not God, as in ordinary times, send the affliction of body to rouse to consideration, to fear, to prayer to Christ for pardon and life? Cannot God work by means or without them? Is it not the glorious number, not the nature, of the cases that puzzles?

There are many cases of quickening and revival without this physical prostration. So it has been in the present American revival, and so it was in the Connor district (a few miles from here) for about eighteen months. May not the free sovereign Spirit work as He pleases?

Oh, Spirit of God, lead poor sinners to consideration, to conviction, to conviction, to conversion, to Christ by hysteria, by cholera, by fever, by war, by famine, by sympathy, by the truth, read or talked, or sung, or preached by prelate or by priest, by minister or by mechanic; only let souls be saved and the Saviour Jesus glorified, and all's well![87]

The mental features he describes are particularly important, as we will see in a later chapter when we look at altered conscious states and their significance. Note the changes in general perception during these experiences.

The mental features.

There is not merely an illumination, so that sin is seen in its true colours, and truth in its beauty, and error in its deformity; but there is an impulse given to the memory and imagination, elevating these powers inconceivably beyond their ordinary range. Sins long forgotten are remembered with the freshness of yesterday; and religious instructions, and divine promises, and other passages of the Word which may have been read or heard in youth.

In some cases the conflict with the enemy is fearful – agonising to both mind and body – and when deliverance is felt the triumph is ecstatic. The minds of some three poor creatures have given way, whether from predisposition or fright, or the long continued apprehension of hell without any feeling or hope of deliverance, or whether from injudicious treatment or cruel restraint from the society and sympathy of kindred spirits, or from want of food and sleep, or from several of these causes combining I am unable to determine.

The first of these is now quite well and spiritually happy, the second is in the asylum slowly improving, the third died. I visited the second in these cases, and amid all her frenzy and wild maniac wanderings at intervals she held firm by Christ.[87]

This and other accounts which follow clearly show that a small number of those caught up in the Irish revival later found themselves in a mental hospital. We will look further at the debate between doctors at the time over this. Does extreme emotion induce a mental breakdown, and if so should there be a warning for us today?

First, we need to realise that the understanding of mental illness in 1859 was very different from today. Modern psychiatry was non-existent. Sigmund Freud was only a three-year-old toddler, and Carl Jung was not born until seventeen years after the revival started. People with mental instability were confined to lunatic asylums where, in places like Bethlehem Hospital in London (Bedlam), they were shackled with chains to the walls of dark cellars and they were paraded for public viewing and entertainment on Sundays.

Secondly, some of them may well have had existing mental illness, made more apparent by their new experiences. Thirdly, at such a time (as perhaps today) it is worth remembering that both the apostle Paul and Zechariah would have been in danger of being diagnosed as hysterical as well.

The Lancet medical journal carried a vitriolic editorial on 23rd July 1859, just four weeks before William Blair arrived:

The violent physical 'manifestations' which have accompanied the 'revivals' in the north of Ireland are morbid and injurious phenomena, which are comparable with similar conditions seen in hospitals where hysteria is prevalent, and witnessed in all female communities in crises of excitement and agitation. The insensibility, the relaxation of muscle power, the prolonged convulsions, the foaming at the mouth, the rolling of the eyeballs, the fixed and glassy stare, the wild dreams, the incoherent ravings, which are viewed by the friends of these 'revivals' as signs of regeneration that should be encouraged and propagated, are well known to be indicia of hysterical and epileptiform seizures, consequent upon an overwrought condition of mind and an enfeeblement of body due to prolonged abstinence and to great mental excitement. This statement has met with great disfavour amongst a small portion of the Irish press and *The Lancet* has been warmly abused for taking such a view of these phenomena.

Two years later, another editorial appeared, this time in the *British Medical Journal* on 2nd November 1861:

The annual report of the Irish Lunatic Asylum Inspectors states that more cases of insanity occurred in Ulster in two months during the late revival movement than had taken place in the year. 'Religious excitement' is described as the cause of insanity in 87 males and 86 females, but it is observable that, though religious excitement was the cause of the breaking down of the mind, the mania is not generally religious. The patient does not rave about religious matters but about matters totally different.

It is fascinating to browse through copies of the weekly *Revival* newspaper, published in 1859 and 1860. On every page there are first-hand accounts of remarkable events taking place across Britain and in Europe. It had a circulation of 30,000.

As if in answer to the scathing criticisms in *The Lancet* and the later issue of the *British Medical Journal*, alleging that the Irish revival was driving people mad, Dr James Carson wrote an open letter from Coleraine, Ireland, dated 20th September 1859. He took the view that God was at work, but there were other factors as well. His words are in many ways as relevant today:

Without doubt there is a physical agent as well as a spiritual one abroad. The one is, as it were, the handmaid to the other. They are both specially from God and are most admirably calculated to work out his great design. It would be difficult to imagine a plan more perfect for the salvation of sinners.

[However] it would be as well for those parties who look on the physical manifestations as an evil which should be avoided and repressed to re-consider their ways. It is an awful thing to be found fighting against God! How dreadful is the presumption which will dare to dictate to the Almighty the way in which he should save sinners!

They look for a Revival, but will not accept it unless it tallies with their own pre-conceived opinions. Their conduct reminds me of the Jews who expected a Saviour, but refused to acknowledge him when he came, because he was not exactly according to their fancy.

They are not satisfied to take things as he sends them. They must have a new, improved and corrected edition. All must be brought to the level of their fancy. If God sends physical manifestations, these must be repressed with a holy zeal. Meetings must be dispersed long before the very unfashionable hour at which the Apostle Paul left off preaching, and public assemblies must be avoided for fear of prostrations.

I see a good deal of time and labour have been spent in asserting over and over again that the physical manifestations are nothing more or less than hysteria. There is no reason why the country should be free from hysterical cases now, any more than at any other time. On the contrary we should expect the number to be increased in consequence of the excitement that is abroad. Hence, as might be expected, some cases of hysteria are met in every district where the Revival has appeared.

But the man who will confine his observations to these cases, or confound them with the Revival manifestations, has but a poor capacity for the observation of facts.

The fact is that the Revival and hysteria have scarcely any symptoms in common.

Here he lists a number of contrasting factors, particularly that all the classical descriptions of the day described what they diagnosed as hysteria as almost completely unknown in men, whereas many men were exhibiting manifestations.

I have seen and known of an immense number of instances in which the strongest, stoutest, most vigorous, healthy and lion-hearted men in the country have been struck down like children, and have called, with most agonising entreaties, for the salvation of their souls. How could all this be hysteria? Would any medical practitioner disgrace himself by saying it was?

Even if he were so very thoughtless as to do so, how could he account for the fact that more cases of Revival have occurred in the male subject in one town within three months than are cases of hysteria to be found among men in the whole records of medicine over the whole world since the days of Hippocrates?

We should never place the Book of Nature and the Book of Revelation in opposition to each other. They must be capable of reconciliation as they are both from the hand of God. Let us therefore never shrink from a full examination of the Revival in its scientific as well as its religious aspect.

There would have been Revival cases nearly every day, for ages past in some part of the world, if they were entirely owing to sudden conviction and conversion. There must be a physical agent concerned. This view ... is greatly strengthened by the way the Revival has travelled. It has not leaped from the north to the south, nor from the east to the west. On the contrary it has followed a steady, gradual, progressive, uninterrupted course from parish to parish and district to district. It has travelled like a wave. This is a factor which is patent to all and speaks of a physical agent.

Again it was observed that the most illiterate convert who had himself been physically affected had far more power in producing the manifestations than the most eloquent and touching speaker who could address them. It looked more like a physical effect produced by individual on individual than anything else.

Of course, many charismatics would say that the physical agent is the direct intervention of the Holy Spirit, dwelling as an 'anointing' on one person, and transmitted to others through the laying on of hands, prayer and other means. The doctor continues:

If we do not adopt this view [of two factors at work], what are we to do with those cases of deafness, dumbness, blindness, extraordinary visions and prophesying which have occurred in some of these localities?

Be the physical agent what it may, it is evidently sent by God for a special purpose. Why, simply to excite such a degree of attention to spiritual matters as humanly speaking could not be done by any other means. No person but the man who has witnessed them could have an idea of the awful effects produced on the public mind by a number of such Revival cases. A scene like the one … at the New Town Hall in Coleraine has perhaps never been equalled in the world.

Wherever the physical manifestations broke out in town or country they put terror into the heart of all who saw them, and at once convinced the on-looker that there was a great reality in them. Deception was considered to be out of the question. One case at either end of the Parish would set the whole Parish into excitement. The people all ran to see them. They could not avoid it.

Consequently I conclude that physical manifestations were a most important part of the work, as they entered into God's design, and were no mere accidents of the Revival. They were essential or God would not have sent them.

This Revival has taken more root in Coleraine than anywhere else, and I believe this has been greatly owing to the fact that the clergy of the different denominations have allowed the physical manifestations to progress without interruption. They seemed determined to make the best they could out of what God had sent and they had their reward.

The manifestations awakened the attention of the people in the highest degree, and the Spirit of God which was poured out at the time, effected the conversion of multitudes. It might safely be said that more people have been converted in this district during the last four months than during the previous fifty years.

1859

Wales was also affected by what happened in America. H. R. Jones returned to Wales from America with news of revival. David Morgan was greatly affected. He describes what happened in one town as an elder began to speak:

> 'Amen!' exclaimed a young girl in the highest notes of a lovely voice. 'Blessed be His name forever!' This cry might be compared to the touch of the electric button that shivers a quarry into a thousand hurtling fragments. Scores leaped from their seats, and, gathering in the vacant space in the centre, they gave vent to their pent-up emotion in cries which were almost agonising in their ardour and intensity.[88]

The effects of the revival were profound. Crime fell, for example, in 1860. It is estimated that 100,000 were added to the church out of a population of a million.

1860

In 1860 the revivals spreading around Britain hit London. Spurgeon said: 'The times of refreshing from the presence of the Lord have finally hit our land.' However, there were few manifestations in London.[89]

1872

Jeffreys again reports that tongues were received in America in 1872. 'In Southern New England, among the Second Adventists, 1875, I learned that some had for three years previously in their religious worship spoken in what is termed as "the unknown tongues".'

1875

Charles Finney saw an almost continuous revival in New York, starting in 1832 through to 1837. Before he died in 1875 he wrote (quoted by George Jeffreys):

> I received a mighty baptism of the Holy Ghost. Without any expectation of it, without ever having the thought in my mind that there was such a thing for me, without any recollection that I had ever heard the thing mentioned by any person in the world, the Holy Spirit descended upon me in a manner that seemed to go through me, body and soul. I could feel the impression like a wave of electricity, going through and through me. Indeed it seemed to come in waves of liquid love; for I could not express it in any other way. It seemed like the very breath of God.
>
> I can recollect distinctly that it seemed to fan me like immense wings. No words can express the wonderful love that was shed abroad in my heart. I wept aloud with joy and love; and I do not know but I should say, I literally bellowed out the unutterable gushings of my heart. These waves came over me, and over me, one after the other, until I recollect I cried out, 'I shall die if these waves continue to pass over me.' I said, 'Lord, I cannot bear any more.' Yet I had no fear of death....
>
> Thus I continued till late at night. I received some sound repose. When I awoke in the morning the sun had risen, and

was pouring a clear light into my room. Words cannot express the impression that this sunlight made on me. Instantly the baptism that I had received the night before returned upon me in the same manner. I arose upon my knees in the bed and wept aloud with joy, and remained for some time too much overwhelmed with the baptism of the Spirit to do anything but pour out my soul to God.

1878

The Salvation Army today is not perhaps associated with great displays of emotionalism. However, William Bramwell Booth (1856-1929) who succeeded his father William Booth as the second General in 1912, recalls the period in the 1870s when the Army first started.

All my life I have been interested in what are sometimes called bodily manifestations, though I have had a considerable degree of misgiving. From my earliest years of responsible work for God I have approached all such manifestations, if not with a hostile mind, certainly with a mind deliberately cautious. Nevertheless I have this feeling also – and with regard to the Army I have it particularly – that there is a place for these outward demonstrations which have undoubtedly been witnessed by us, and the like of which are recorded in various periods of religious history.

I have seen men in our meetings who were raving and blaspheming when the service began, suddenly broken down as though some physical power had laid them prostrate on the floor, and after a time of silence, weeping and penitence, they were confessing their sins and imploring the mercy of God. In many cases the whole of their subsequent life was changed and no question could arise as to the reality of their experience.[90]

He describes how one man who had been criticising the

work fell in the street 'like a piece of wood, apparently losing consciousness' when rebuked by a leader. Afterwards he became a devout Christian. Christians as well as those finding faith were both affected.

> Later on in the meetings of the Army we had more wonderful scenes of this nature … during the singing or the address of a particular speaker, here and there among the audience people would be observed to fall to the ground. At times they appeared to fall with such great violence, yet I have never known of anyone being really hurt. On some occasions there would be perhaps in a meeting of several hundreds of people only half a dozen such manifestations, although I have known as many as sixty in one gathering. Sometimes the younger people were in the majority but at other times those influenced were mainly from the older portions of the audience.

On 16th January 1878, Booth records that the leaders were affected:

> At night Corbridge led a hallelujah meeting till 10 o'clock. Then we commenced an All Night of Prayer. 250 people were present till 1am. 200 or so after. The power of the Holy Ghost fell on Robinson and prostrated him. He nearly fainted twice. The brother of the Blandys entered into full liberty and then he shouted, wept, clapped his hands, danced amid a scene of the most glorious and heavenly enthusiasm. Others meanwhile were lying prostrate on the floor. Some of them groaning aloud for deliverance.

> Not infrequently those who seemed most unlikely to be the subjects of these special influences – some of whom had indeed openly said 'I will take care that nothing of this kind happens to me' – had been overcome.

> My own course, and the course adopted by most of the leaders in the presence of these influences, was while never

opposing or deprecating them, to take care to have the subjects of them immediately or at any rate as soon as possible removed from the public gathering. They were usually led to adjoining rooms, the men separate from the women, and quietly laid down.

Wherever possible, especially in the early days when we were less accustomed to what afterwards became more common, we had a doctor within call lest some ill effects should follow these experiences; perhaps also sometimes with a view to confirming their genuineness.

The rapid removal from the open meeting was a wise thing. It effectually prevented any vain or neurotic persons from drawing attention to themselves. But it is important to remember that we had very few cases that were not entirely sincere. The number of cases in which it was the medical opinion that there was something 'put on' was exceedingly small, almost negligible.

What happened afterwards? The great majority of those who were unsaved sought the pardon of God and lived new lives, and the fact that their new lives dated from so extraordinary a beginning no doubt helped their faith. With regard to those who were already our people or who were Christians visiting our meetings the effects were of course varied. In the majority of cases an immediate desire was manifest to give themselves wholly to the will of God.

I must have heard hundreds of testimonies to the wonderful help received during or in consequence of these visitations. In a certain number of cases we had remarkable descriptions of visions or revelations occurring during the period of unconsciousness. The impression they gave was akin to that expressed by the Apostle when he spoke of having been caught up to the third heaven, and being uncertain whether he was in the body or out of the body, being, that is, in some kind of rapture or ecstasy which left him afterwards undecided as to where he was – and of hearing unspeakable words not again to be uttered.

Nor can I dwell on at any length equally well authenticated cases of divine healing ... the views and the experience of the Army itself that God should heal after this fashion.

All these manifestations of the unusual have been experienced also in the work of the Army in other lands. Holland ... Switzerland ... Scandinavian countries where indeed we have had trouble owing to manifestations called the 'Gift of Tongues'. While I believe that these things, as I have experienced them are divine in origin, I do not forget that in some instances they may have been mixed up with what is the very reverse.

Bramwell Booth describes a big difference between Europe and the US. In Europe the manifestations tended to be quite solemn. In America, they were accompanied usually by 'extreme, overpowering joy, exhibited in singing and sometimes in a disposition to dance, or to remain for long periods in a kind of ecstasy'. In 1994, over a hundred years later, Gerald Coates described how the Holy Spirit had broken out at a Salvation Army conference for evangelists after he spoke and prayed for people. There were other signs of great changes in the autumn of the same year, with a new openness to the supernatural in the Army not seen for several generations.

1885

Jeffreys records of 1885:

At an international conference held in England in 1885, Mrs. Michael Baxter, whose husband was the author of the well-known book, *Forty Future Wonders of Scripture Prophecy*, and the founder of the *Christian Herald* of London and the *Christian Herald* of New York, told of being able to preach for thirty-five minutes in German when she was almost entirely unfamiliar with the language.

She was well understood and one soul was converted. She stated, 'After that He led me to speak almost every day, and often twice a day to hundreds of people, although when I went into a shop I could not make myself understood, nor could I understand the people.'

1886-1904

What then of the great pentecostal revival at the start of the twentieth century? Some would say that since that time the experience of revival has been more or less continuous somewhere in the world, with many manifestations in each place. Donald Gee writes:

The Pentecostal Movement had its rise as a recognised entity during the early years of the twentieth century. The Movement does not owe its origin to any outstanding personality or religious leader, but was a spontaneous revival appearing almost simultaneously in various parts of the world. We instinctively connect the Reformation with Luther, Methodism with Wesley, the Plymouth Brethren with Darby and Groves, the Salvation Army with William Booth, and so on. But the outstanding leaders of the Pentecostal Movement are themselves the products of the Movement.

The last quarter of the nineteenth century was blessed on both sides of the Atlantic by the outstanding evangelistic movement associated with Moody and Sankey; and by the growth, within the Church, of what may broadly be called the Holiness Movement.

In England, beside the rise of the now world-famous Keswick Convention for the deepening of spiritual life, there were Conferences associated with such names as W. E. Boardman. The scriptural phrase the 'Baptism of the Holy Ghost' began to appear and become familiar in the sense of a spiritual crisis for the Christian subsequent to regeneration.[91]

1904

Then came the great Welsh revival of 1904. It is impossible, and would be historically incorrect, to dissociate the pentecostal movement from that remarkable visitation of God's Spirit.

> The profound impression which the Welsh Revival made upon the entire Christian world can scarcely be realised by those who were not living at the time. Visitors came from far and near. Newspapers sent special reporters, and published lengthy reports. Some mocked; some were converted, all were impressed. It seemed, for a time, like an irresistible torrent.

However, the Welsh revival had many critics because of the emotional scenes and manifestations. Evan Roberts was at the centre of the revival. In 1905 he wrote in response to fierce criticism by those opposed to displays of emotion in church:

> The Power of the revival in South Wales is not of men, but of God. God has 'made me glad', and I am showing others the great joy of serving Him, a joy so great and so wonderful that I shall never be able to express it in its completeness.
>
> I have been asked concerning my methods. I have none. I never prepare the words I shall speak. I leave all that to Him. I am not the source of this revival. I am only one agent in what is growing to be a multitude. I am not moving men's hearts and changing men's lives; not I, but 'God worketh in me'.
>
> His Spirit came to me one night, when upon my knees I asked Him for guidance, and five months later I was baptised with the Spirit. I know that the work which has been done through me is not due to any human ability that I possess. It is His work and to His Glory.[92]

As in 1994, the controversy and the massive media coverage

which happened – mostly very positive – helped fan the flames by spreading the news of what was happening. The same would occur in Los Angeles just a year or two later. Evan Roberts continues:

> Some things have been said about our meetings, and about me which are not true; but God's truth has not been hurt by these misstatements, and they, therefore, matter little. I believe, too, that He has put it into the hearts of those who have written of the revival to say helpful things, for some of the papers have carried our message to many whom we have not personally reached.
>
> I believe that the world is upon the threshold of a great religious revival, and I pray daily that I may be allowed to help bring this about. Wonderful things have happened in Wales in a few weeks, but these are only a beginning. The world will be swept by His Spirit as by a rushing, mighty wind.

In the same book is an eyewitness account from 1904 or early 1905 by Arthur Goodrich, a journalist from London. The Welsh revival had such a huge impact, which is still felt today, as a foundation stone of modern Pentecostalism, that I have reproduced the account of one of the meetings at length. The other reason is that the account gives us a warning of how great a change happens to whole communities when revival sweeps forward. We have seen in previous accounts how little close-knit communities have often been deeply affected by one meeting, five conversions or one supernatural event. Many manifestations occurred which are minimised in the following account by Goodrich, but which gave ammunition for savage attacks on Roberts (see later).

The Story of the Welsh Revival

All South Wales is aflame with the spirit of a great religious revival. In a few weeks the fire of it has run up and down the length of the Garw Valley and the Rhondda. They are talking of little else in the snug little stone cottages that line the ridges like low ramparts; in the tiny shops where the women come to buy the day's supplies; in the railway carriages, and at the street corners.

Every church community is stirred to the depths, and out on the edges rough miners are shaking their heads ponderingly, and are being drawn toward it until the power of it seizes them and they leave their work to attend the day meetings as well as those at night. Strong men are in tears of penitence; women are shaken with a new fervour, and in the streets small children at their play are humming revival hymns.

'And they do say that the publicans (saloon keepers) are closing,' says a bent little man with a black beard, in a train to Landore, and certainly many drinking places that were crowded are empty, the frequenters being led away either by the religious workers in person, as they were at Pontycymer, or by the irresistible spirit of the movement.

'Aye,' says another, 'there's something funny about it. They say you feel it as soon as you're inside the building where he's going to speak.'

He went home to Lougher immediately and opened his first meetings alone, and before the doubtful eyes of those who had always known him, and who wondered at his sudden change of plan – this leaving the school which he had left them to enter only a few weeks before.

He could scarcely have chosen a more difficult place to begin a difficult work. 'Where will you get the money?' asked someone. 'Money!' he cried, with that merry, boyish confidence that is part of his charm. 'Never mind about the money. Look above for the money. It'll come.'

At the beginning little happened. The people who came to his meetings, came out of friendliness or out of curiosity. Why should this young theological student open special meetings all unaided, and why should anyone go to hear him? And those who heard him wondered the more, for although he said little that they had not heard before, he said everything in a way that crowded conviction upon them. He told them frankly at the start that he had not prepared anything to say, but that he would only say what was put into his mind by the Holy Spirit.

Naturally, everyone talked about him, and, although few at first took him seriously, they came to hear him in gradually increasing numbers. And he seized them with a remarkable power that he had never shown before, and which he says frankly he had never felt before.

In a few days Lougher shops were closed early for the meetings; workmen hurried in late in their working clothes; evening meetings lasted far into the night; the chapel was crowded, and the road outside was lined with disappointed but waiting people. They came from miles around to hear him, and went away with old faith revived or new faith kindled. The papers began to talk of him as 'a wonderful preacher'; neighbouring churches heard of him, and asked him to come to them; ministers hurried to hear him, and came away mystified at the simple power of the young man, and with a new impulse in their hearts for harder effort.

And that is the way Evan Roberts began a work which is slowly stirring the whole religious world to action.

Here is no mystic with some weird mystery to draw the morbid instincts of weak men. It is a full-blooded, hearty, young man, who has worked in the coal mines and at the smithy, and who hammers his unambitious words home with an inspiriting vigour. Here is no dreaming sentimentalist making a sweeping appeal to the sympathetic hearts of women and children.

It is a deep-voiced, firm-jawed young man moving men hardened by rough toil. Here is no fiery, impassioned orator, stirring people by his rhetoric at night and being forgotten, along with his words, in the morning. It is a simple, straightforward speaker, who began alone, but who already has scores of active helpers, men and women, among those the whole course of whose lives have been changed.

Here is no exhorter terrifying his hearers into belief in God's love by threats of eternal punishment. It is a buoyant, happy man trying to show in a quiet, direct way how joyful a thing Christianity really is. Here is no pompous prelate who condescends to advise his congregation concerning their conduct. It is a frank, sincere man, who links his arm in yours, and means 'brother' without saying it.

Here is no narrow sectarian. An army of ministers of all the denominations in Wales are working with him, and his only desire is for results. Go into one of his meetings. Every seat is taken, there are people in the aisles, and more are crowding in. They are singing and there is no such stirring congregational singing in the world, I believe, as in Wales – a swinging Welsh hymn, martial and inspiring.

In the midst of a verse a tall, boyish-looking young fellow slips in almost unnoticed, and takes a seat at the front, never behind the high desk, but down upon the main floor. He sings a verse with them, and perhaps starts another, while only a few realise that this is Evan Roberts.

When the singing stops, he steps out quickly before the audience, his hands in his pockets, shoulders thrown back, eyes bright, and his mouth widened in a smile. A single sentence catches the attention of everyone in the building, for it is at once short, quiet, and vigorous. The tone is conversational, and the eyes are friendly. He begins to pace up and down, turning to the people with short, rapid phrases, and accentuating them with tense, earnest gestures as short and jerky as his speech.

He is seldom still, but when he is you can feel the restrained intensity. The movements are not those of high-strung, nervous force, but of superabundant vital energy.

Suddenly he stops short, and looks over the congregation, where every eye is upon him, and, uttering one quick sentence, laughs aloud. And such laughter as it is, boyish, joyous, confident. A moment later he is on his knees, leaning over the railing, his hands clasped, talking confidently with his audience as if it were one friend instead of many.

After a time he is on his feet again, and a Bible is in his large hands, and then he is again leaning over the railing and calling appealingly to the congregation, perhaps with tears in his eyes. Then suddenly it is over, and he sits down.

One of the girls who has come from Lougher or Pontycymer to help him, begins to sing, and sweet as her voice is, it is not long before the congregation joins in one by one until the room rings with the melody. He has talked less than half an hour. It has been entirely in Welsh, and yet without understanding a word he said you have felt the spirit of it.

The frankness, the downright earnestness, the militant sincerity have given you a feeling that you have seldom had in all ordinary church services, and through the spirit of his message, they are working in the hearts of all the people about you.

And yet those who know the language say that he has said nothing that is extraordinary; that there has been little brilliancy of phrase; that he has talked simply and cheerfully of his own experience, and has asked those who are not Christians to give themselves to God.

Certainly it has all been very quiet. There have been no loud rantings, nor spectacular displays, nor open appeals to the emotions. But what is happening? He tramps up and down the aisle, singing with the congregation, and perhaps leading them with inspiriting gestures.

Then suddenly he has disappeared. In the gallery is a powerful-looking man, whose head is hidden in his arms on the back of the seat in front of him. Evan Roberts is bending over him, helping him like a brother to make the right decision.

A moment later he stands straight, his eyes flashing with joy, and cries out with joyous fervour, and then the swinging, stirring cadences of that greatest of Welsh hymns, 'Diolch

Iddo', which is always sung after a conversion, begins and grows in volume until they sweep another man upon his feet with an avowal of his changed life.

Evan Roberts is once more before the people, and he breaks in upon the singing with a few half-spoken, half-whispered words. A wave of deep feeling dashes aside something of his self-control as he begs them to 'Come to Him! Come to Him!' and he sinks upon his knees in prayer, while one of the girls who have come with him sings a simple hymn in English.

Slowly the congregation has risen out of itself, out of its curiosity, out of its indifference. Something has caught them as in a rushing tide.

If you put a man into the midst of one of these meetings who knows nothing of the language of the Spirit, and nothing of the life of the Spirit, one of two things will happen to him. He will either pass out saying 'THESE MEN ARE DRUNK,' or he himself will be swept up by the fire into the Kingdom of God.

Whence has it come? You tell me that the revival originates with Roberts. I tell you that Roberts is a product of the revival. You tell me that it began in an Endeavour meeting where a dear girl bore testimony. I tell you that was part of the result of a revival breaking out.

Cynddylan Jones wrote at the time of the future of the move of God: 'Is the revival likely to continue? Yes, till it has done its work. We do not want it to last longer – the tension is too great. Will it extend? Through Wales, yes; through England, doubtful. However, it depends upon England itself. Given the necessary conditions, the Spirit will descend.'[93]

However, Evan Roberts found himself under severe attack from other church leaders:

An attack on his motives and methods by a Congregational minister, Peter Price. This appeared in the correspondence columns of the *Western Mail* on January 31st, and initiated a protracted and heated public debate, although Roberts himself took no part in it. Price claimed that there were two revivals, one true and the other false. The former had been in progress for as long as two years, his own church at Dowlais having been blessed with an increase of some hundreds in the previous five or six months. The Evan Roberts movement, on the other hand, was 'a sham, a mockery, a blasphemous travesty of the real thing'. The former, 'the gloriously real revival', was of the devil.[94]

Vyrnwy Morgan also wrote a scathing attack on the 'excesses' of the Welsh revival which was published just four years later in 1909. Here are some extracts:

The neighbourhood of Port Talbot was once noted as the place that could supply characters capable of working up these wondrous religious spectacles. These itinerant devotees were in the habit of attending various religious gatherings with the expectation of being 'touched'. The congregation knew beforehand what to expect and the special preacher for the occasion did not at all resent their appearance, and even shot his arrows with a view to the desired end.

There could be heard a deep wail, then a piercing cry; the next moment a woman would be casting off her bonnet, raising her arm, and throwing everything into disorder and confusion. Others would catch the infection; and there would be no attempt at checking such manifestations, for the common people took pleasure in them, and the preacher looked on with a complacent smile. Some of those who were affected during the Revival kept it on for months afterwards, giving way to violent emotions when the preacher reached a certain point.

Such characters have been known to interrupt preachers during the delivery of a sermon and to completely overcome them, to the annoyance of the congregation and detriment of the service. Such scenes have occurred repeatedly since the last

Welsh Revival. But there have been strong personalities in the pulpit, who have successfully resisted such interruptions, thus proving beyond a doubt that such paroxysms are largely a matter of encouragement.

On what principle are we to explain such violent bodily exercises? Have they any spiritual significance? Had they any Divine message? My belief is that they were purely physical. They did not possess any specific spiritual value, and did not convey any moral lesson.

True, there is much in the action of the Divine Spirit that eludes our grasp and which no philosophy can ever hope to fully explain. But those wild cries of horror which were so fearful in their violence during the Revival were undoubtedly due to mental action, to sympathy, to the power of suggestion and physical causes.

The press worked the sentimentality of the Revival for all that it was worth. It was a harvest-time for publishers and journalists. There was money in it, and unfortunately there has always been money in Welsh sentiment. There is more wealth to be coined out of the feelings of the people than out of their judgment. Now that the Revival passion is gone, and with the passion the profits that were in it, publishers take no further interest in the movement.[95]

Donald Gee remarks:

Perhaps the most formative result [of the Welsh revival] was the creation of a widespread spirit of expectation for still greater things. Men justly asked: Why Wales only? Why not other lands? Why not a world-wide Revival? Prayer to that end received a tremendous new impetus. And while so many were interceding for a wider outpouring of the Holy Spirit, others were pleading equally for a deeper work. Faith was rising to visualise a return to apostolic Christianity in all its pristine beauty and power.

Of special interest to British people is the little group that gathered around the godly vicar of All Saints' Parish Church, Sunderland. Alexander A. Boddy had been their spiritual leader since 1886. When the Revival broke out in Wales in 1904 he made a special journey to Wales, and stood beside Evan Roberts in the midst of some of the amazing scenes of Tonypandy.

When he recounted to his people at All Saints what he had personally seen in Wales, it stirred both pastor and people up to yet more earnest prayer and expectation of great things from God. Sunderland was being prepared in the purposes of God to become a centre of new and far-reaching blessing. The circumstances were humble enough. The meetings were held in a wooden barn-like structure now pulled down.

At around the same time as the Welsh revival, a similar revival broke out in Los Angeles. In many ways there are similarities here with what is happening today in Toronto, London and elsewhere. The revival was charismatic in theology, the leaders at first had little idea how to manage the phenomena responsibly, the media played a central role in advertising the meetings through their own reporting, people travelled thousands of miles to go there (a massive undertaking in those days), and the manifestations mainly attracted believers.

However, hundreds if not thousands were equipped and empowered and went out as evangelists and missionaries. The secondary effect was huge, as many think will be the case from what happened with such force in 1994. Frank Bartleman was at the heart of what happened in Los Angeles. This is what he wrote shortly after the 1905 revival began:

When we began to pray in the spring of 1905, no one seemed to have much faith for anything out of the ordinary. April 15, the

Lord called me to ten days of special prayer. I felt greatly burdened but had no idea of what He had particularly in mind.

Wednesday, April 18, the terrible San Francisco earthquake came, which also devastated the surrounding country. No less than ten thousand lost their lives in Francisco alone. I felt a deep conviction that the Lord was hearing our prayers for a revival in His own way. A tremendous burden of prayer came on me that the people might not be indifferent to His voice.

Thursday, April 19, while sitting in the noon meeting at Peniel, 227 South Main Street, the floor suddenly began to move beneath us. Many people ran into the middle of the street, looking up anxiously at the buildings, fearing they were about to fall.

I went home and after a season of prayer was pressed of the Lord to go to the meeting which had been moved from Bonnie Brae Street to 312 Azusa Street. Here they had rented an old frame building, formerly a Methodist church, in the center of the city, now a long time out of use for meetings. It was my first visit to 'Azusa Mission'.

I gave a message at my first meeting at 'Azusa'. Two of the saints spoke in 'tongues'. Much blessing seemed to attend the utterance. It was soon noised abroad that God was working at Azusa. All classes began to flock to the meetings. Many were curious and unbelieving, but others were hungry for God.

The newspapers began to ridicule and abuse the meetings, thus giving much free advertising. This brought the crowds. The devil overdid himself again. Outside persecution never hurt the work. I had the most to fear from the working of evil spirits within. Keen spiritualists and hypnotists came to investigate, and to try their influence. Then all the religious sore-heads and crooks and cranks came, seeking a place in the work. We had the most to fear from these. But this is always the danger to every new work. They have no place elsewhere.

This condition cast a fear over many which was hard to overcome. It hindered the Spirit much. Many were afraid to seek God, for fear the devil might get them. We found early in the 'Azusa' work that when we attempted to steady the Ark the

Lord stopped working. We dared not call the attention of the people too much to the working of the devil. Fear would follow. We could only pray. Then God gave victory. There was a presence of God with us, through prayer, we could depend on.

The leaders had a limited experience, and the wonder is the work survived at all against its powerful adversaries. But it was of God. That was the secret. I found the earthquake had opened many hearts.

The work was getting clearer and stronger at 'Azusa'. God was working mightily. It seemed that every one had to go to Azusa. Missionaries were gathered there from Africa, India, and the islands of the sea. Preachers and workers had crossed the continent, and come from distant islands, with an irresistible drawing to Los Angeles. 'Gather my saints together.' They had come up for 'Pentecost', though they little realized it. It was God's call.

Holiness meetings, tents and missions began to close up for lack of attendance. Their people were at 'Azusa'. Brother and Sister Garr closed the 'Burning Bush' hall, came to 'Azusa', received the 'baptism', and were soon on their way to India to spread the fire. Even Brother Smale had to come to 'Azusa', to look up his members. He invited them back home, promised them liberty in the Spirit, and for a time God wrought mightily at the New Testament Church also.

There was much persecution, especially from the press. They wrote us up shamefully, but this only drew the crowds. Some gave the work six months to live. Soon the meetings were running day and night. The place was packed out nightly. The whole building, upstairs and down, had now been cleared and put into use. There were far more white people than colored coming.

Some one might be speaking. Suddenly the Spirit would fall upon the congregation. God Himself would give the altar call, men would fall all over the house, like the slain in battle, or rush for the altar, en masse, to seek God. The scene often resembled a forest of fallen trees. Such a scene cannot be imitated. I never saw an altar call given in those early days. God

Himself would call them. And the preacher knew when to quit.

When He spoke we all obeyed. It seemed a fearful thing to hinder or grieve the Spirit. The whole place was steeped in prayer. God was in His holy temple. It was for man to keep silent. The shekinah glory rested there. In fact some claim to have seen the glory by night over the building. I do not doubt it. I have stopped more than once within two blocks of the place and prayed for strength before I dared go on. The presence of the Lord was so real.

Presumptuous men would sometimes come among us. Especially preachers who would try to spread themselves, in self-opinionation. But their effort was short lived. The breath would be taken from the throne.[96]

1906

June 22, 1906. In the 'Christian Harvester' I wrote, at the same date: At the New Testament Church a young lady of refinement was prostrate on the floor for hours, while at times the most heavenly singing would issue from her lips. It would swell away up to the throne, and then die away in an almost unearthly melody. She sang, 'Praise God! Praise God!'

All over the house men and women were weeping. A preacher was flat on his face on the floor, crying out. 'Pentecost' has fully come.

We had several all nights of prayer at the New Testament Church. But Pastor Smale never received the 'baptism with the speaking in tongues'. He was in a trying position.

I wrote further in 'Way of Faith', August 1, 1906: 'Pentecost' has come to Los Angeles, the American Jerusalem. Every sect, creed, and doctrine under Heaven is found in Los Angeles, as well as every nation represented. Many times I have been tempted to wonder if my strength would hold out to see it. The burden of prayer has been very great.

But since the spring of 1905, when I first received this vision and burden, I have never doubted the real outcome of it. Men are now in trouble of soul everywhere.

Persecution is strong. Already the police have been appealed to to break up the meetings. The work has been hindered much also by fanatical spirits, of which the city has far too many. The Holy Spirit Himself is taking the lead, setting aside all human leadership largely. And woe to the man who gets in His way, selfishly seeking to dictate or control. The Spirit brooks no interference of this kind.

The human instruments are largely lost sight of. Our hearts and minds are directed to the Lord. The meetings are crowded out. There is great excitement among the spiritual and unsaved.

Demons are being cast out, the sick healed, many blessedly saved, restored, and baptized with the Holy Ghost and power. Men's hearts are being searched as with a lighted candle. It is a tremendous sifting time, not only of actions, but of inner, secret motives. Nothing can escape the all-searching eye of God. Jesus is being lifted up, the 'blood' magnified, and the Holy Spirit honored once more.

The Lord wrought very deeply. Several were under the power all night on one occasion. There was no closing at 9 o'clock sharp, as the preachers must do today in order to keep the people. We wanted God in those days. We did not have a thousand other things we wanted before Him. And He did not disappoint us.

One sister sang and spoke in 'tongues' for five full hours. Souls were saved. The saints were wonderfully built up and strengthened by the presence of the Lord. A number received the 'baptism', and the mission became full fledged for 'Pentecost'.

One Sunday night the hall was packed out, to the middle of the street. I went to the hall one morning to look up at the folks who had not come home. Several had stayed all night. I found them lost to all but God. They could not get away. A very shekinah glory filled the place. It was awesome, but glorious.

The Spirit wrought very deeply in the meetings at Toronto, but the leader was very much tried with me because he did not understand the Spirit. He expected things done the old way, new wine in the old skins. The Lord had given me a premonition of conditions in Toronto before I reached there. Thus the Spirit often prepared me for my ministry. He put the quiet spirit on me for Toronto. There was too much 'flesh' there. The 'fleshly' ones largely dropped out – they could not live in such an atmosphere.

Donald Gee says of what happened in Los Angeles:

The news of what was happening in Los Angeles began to spread far and wide, and a little four-page paper, published free month by month, carried it even to distant lands. Sensational reports in the daily papers, though published from a very different motive, all helped to spread the news. Of course the main emphasis of the newspaper reporters was on the speaking with tongues, or anything spectacular that occurred. They had little interest in the times of tremendous heart-searching and emptying of self that were going on.

Visitors now began to come from many different parts of North America, and finally from overseas too. They were from various walks of life and church connections. The refined and educated mixed freely with the ignorant and lowly.

Christian workers, pastors, evangelists, missionaries and others came to investigate for themselves. Many were hungry for God and tarried to seek and receive a personal 'Pentecost'. Today (1963) they are leading large Pentecostal churches and organisations all over the world.

The first speaking with tongues that was made public in India really occurred as the result of a mission held by one of the Mukti bands in the Church Missionary Society schoolroom in Anrangabad in 1906.

late 1906

About the close of 1906 similar manifestations occurred in

Toronto, Canada, among those who had made no contact with any others. About the same time hungry Canadian ministers journeyed all the way to Azusa Street, while others received a personal 'Pentecost' in Chicago, and during 1907 hundreds received the Baptism of the Spirit in Winnipeg alone. Among these was Archdeacon Phair, an Episcopal minister among the Indians in North-west Canada.

The fire spread all over North America until it reached the great city of New York and eventually led to the establishment of Glad Tidings Tabernacle in 33rd Street.

When that eventful year 1906 drew to a close the Pentecostal Movement had not yet commenced in the British Isles, but there were, as we have already seen, prayer meetings being held all over the country for a yet deeper Revival than that which had so recently visited Wales.

The same kind of thing was happening in Sweden where, especially among the Baptists, there were many groups. The same spiritual conditions prevailed in Holland and Germany. By the end of 1906 it was evident that a powerful new revival movement had appeared, the main emphasis of which was upon a personal spiritual experience which was emphatically declared to be the 'Baptism of the Holy Ghost', and was invariably accompanied by speaking with tongues and other manifestations of a supernatural or deeply emotional character.

It immediately appealed to multitudes of those who had been prayerfully expecting just such a further world-wide outpouring of God's Spirit, and they naturally and legitimately saw in these things an answer to their prayers. There was, moreover, a scripturalness about 'tongues' recurring as an initial evidence of the Baptism of the Holy Spirit that was not only deeply satisfying in itself, but logically led on to an expectation of the restoration of other features of Primitive Christianity.

1907

Pastor Barratt was a church leader in Norway. Just before

he sailed for England at the end of August 1907, he received a letter from A. A. Boddy in Sunderland. Donald Gee continues:

...informing him that visitors were already gathering at Sunderland from many parts of England. They had been praying for months that God would send His servant over and that Pentecostal blessing would graciously crown his ministry.

Mr. Barratt records in his Journal a deep feeling of his own unworthiness, but a conviction that the call to the land of his fathers was of the Lord, and therefore he set forth in complete dependence upon God. He arrived on Saturday and that evening in Sunderland, they held the first prayer meeting in the vestry 'with great blessing'.

On the next day Pastor Barratt was asked to preach in All Saints' Parish Church immediately following the usual evening service conducted by the vicar. The service was followed by a prayer meeting in the vestry, where 'many received very marked blessings, and a few came through to a scriptural baptism in the Holy Ghost "for we heard them speak with tongues and magnify God"'. That meeting continued until 4 a.m. on Monday morning.

The Pentecostal Revival had commenced in the British Isles. The daily newspapers were used by Divine Providence almost more than any other agency to bring the news of what was happening in Sunderland before the notice of multitudes who otherwise might never have heard. Of course they fastened upon the more spectacular phenomena accompanying the services, particularly the speaking with tongues, but almost without exception the reporters were impartial, and not one paper contained a bitter word.

The extent of these reports probably justified Mr. Barratt's words on September 13th, that 'the eyes of the religious millions of Great Britain are now fixed upon Sunderland'. Yet the religious periodicals, as a whole, maintained a frigid silence.

A constant stream of seekers continued to come to Sunderland to see and hear for themselves these scenes of reported Pentecostal blessing and phenomena. Some were critical, and one local minister violently attacked the new Movement that had sprung up with such power in his vicinity. Those were busy days for an already busy parish minister, and the vicarage became a hallowed spot for many visitors.

Destined later to become an outstanding world-wide Pentecostal preacher was Smith Wigglesworth, then leader of Bowland Street Mission, Bradford, and a master-plumber who received the baptism of the Holy Spirit with the sign of tongues in All Saints' Vicarage on Tuesday, October 20th, 1907. In later years Mr. Wigglesworth was constrained to enter upon a remarkable ministry that took him to all the five continents.

Huge crowds, sometimes having to be controlled by special police, gathered in Scandinavia, Switzerland, Australia, New Zealand and America in response to his absolutely fearless preaching of faith and the willingness of Christ to perform miracles to-day. Much of this can be read in his book 'Ever Increasing Faith'.

In June, 1907, T. B. Barratt visited Copenhagen, Denmark, and a remarkable incident of his ministry was the conversion of the great Danish actress, Anna Larssen. These happenings only tended to increase the Revival in Scandinavia. Finland also felt the blessing and a great Pentecostal work started there too. Mention must also be made of Holland.

1914

One outstanding feature of the Sunderland Conventions right up to 1914 (outbreak of War) was the large group of German Pentecostal pastors who came every year, and whose ministry always formed a dominant side of the Bible teaching. There were reciprocal visits from the British Pentecostal leaders to the larger German Pentecostal Conventions.

1933

In 1933 the two-thousandth anniversary of Pentecost was celebrated. New pentecostal denominations had been formed over the previous twenty-five years as a result of the Welsh, Los Angeles and Sunderland revivals. It was, however, a time for soul-searching and questioning. The pentecostal movement, far from breaking out across the nation in a great awakening, was being marginalised and was in danger of losing momentum. In the foreword to *Pentecostal Rays*, a 1935 classic history of Pentecostalism, James McWhirter writes:

> The outbreak of revival was spontaneous and not organised, breaking forth in different parts, and among different groups of Christians at the same time.
>
> In consequence of the Church's official attitude, which was Pharisaical, numbers of Christians found themselves virtually excommunicated, and generally met together in back-street mission halls and in private houses. The result was that Pentecost went back to the upper room and stayed there, except for a few urgent souls who became foreign missionaries.
>
> Such was the condition that obtained in the British Isles when [George Jeffreys] was guided by the Holy Spirit to found the Elim Foursquare Gospel Alliance.
>
> Against fanatical opposition from sincere but mistaken people from within, and organised prejudice from without, Principal George Jeffreys led the movement to the public, and established its churches in main thoroughfares of each of the four countries of the British Isles, besides sending missionaries to different parts of the world.
>
> On the nineteenth centenary of Pentecost the largest hall in the provinces of England was packed for the conclusion of a campaign in that city through which ten thousand people were converted. For eight years the Royal Albert Hall, London, has

been crowded at the annual Easter Convention, and at Whitsuntide meetings in the same hall about three hundred received the Holy Spirit, with supernatural signs, in one day.

Every national newspaper has carried the news of the Principal's phenomenal success in his revival and healing campaigns.[97]

Donald Gee is clear about the problems the movement faced. The same problems threaten the 1994 movement today. His words ring out with sharp relevance. He lists the issues:

(a) Among the more conservative elements of the Christian Church all 'Revival' movements are looked at askance. Even the preceding 'Holiness' movements had been either rejected or treated with cool caution. The Welsh Revival had come in for much criticism in many quarters on account of its emotional scenes.

(b) Very few notable personalities were connected with the Movement in its beginning, and one looked in vain for any influential name that might have swayed multitudes among the masses of church members and pulpit admirers.

(c) Fear was inculcated through garbled reports of what actually transpired in Pentecostal meetings. The press naturally concentrated on anything spectacular or unusual. Among more select circles of spiritual Christians there began to be much talk of 'counterfeits', until there were those who bitterly condemned the whole Movement as satanic, in spite of so much 'good fruit' as evidence to the contrary.

Genuine and sincere warning as to the possibility of deception was justified and opportune, but in only a very few cases was it given in a loving and gracious spirit.

(d) Truth must honestly admit that there were scenes in the first rush of new spiritual enthusiasm and experience that no reputable Christian worker would now seek to defend or excuse. Emotions were deeply stirred, there was a reaction against the prevailing stiffness and formality of most of the churches, and some elements were bound to be attracted within the orbit of such a free Movement that possessed very questionable qualities.

There were, let it be quite frankly admitted, some scenes of indisputable fanaticism. At the beginning there were few leaders with sufficient experience of just this type of Movement who could lay their hand on extremists without fear of quenching the Spirit. That phase, however, has long since passed. Most of the early fanaticism in the Pentecostal Movement arose from the utmost sincerity, and in the midst of many mistakes hearts were right, and therefore God was able steadily to bring things into a healthier condition. This phase, also, is now passing away.

(e) Finally, there seems to be a law which students are compelled to observe, that the last wave of spiritual revival in the Church nearly always seems to offer the greatest opposition to the new wave of oncoming blessing and advance. It must be remembered, and that with deep sympathy, that where the teaching and testimony of the Pentecostal Movement came to the front there were great numbers of Christian leaders who already were claiming to have been baptised in the Holy Spirit in connection with preceding revival movements.

Only a most gracious spirit and an unusual humility of mind could accept the new and more scriptural standards which, certainly not always wisely nor winsomely, the Pentecostal preachers now set up. The Pentecostal testimony provided a personal challenge of a very searching nature.

Meanwhile, by 1933 a major revival had also broken out in mainland China. In that year, Dr Paul Abbot wrote an article called 'Revival Movements' in the *China Christian Year Book*, describing the revival and some concerns he had. There were several different moves of God among different missionary groups in his area, some quite extreme:

Stages along the road of 'spirituality' can be gauged by the number of the gifts received. The steps are confession, jerks, dancing, rolling, tongues, trances, visions, voices and direct revelation. What began as a free spontaneous revival has, in one large district, hardened into code which none dare violate or object to lest he be branded as unspiritual.

What started as simultaneous prayer has, in the same sections of country, degenerated into a ritual of chaos and a liturgy of disorder. Dancing, jumping and unrestrained actions in church are practised without check. The meetings are pandemonium. As if to break with the past and its quiet and dignified worship, the gatherings glorify noise; cacophonous praying splits the ear; wild wailing and tears, worked up in similar fashion to wailing at the graves, rob the services of all reverence.

Carried on often until the small hours of the morning, they degenerate into exhibitions of emotional debauchery as the devotees abandon themselves to the floods of emotion. The bodies strained with fasting and loss of sleep react with jerks and the vocal organs with gibbering. Hysterical laughter makes the gathering uncanny. Many go into religious swoons and remain in such for long periods, sometimes indeed for twenty-four hours. Not a few have lost their reason.

The description above was typical of one particular group of churches, while many others were also pentecostal or charismatic, but were less extreme in teaching and behaviour. As we have seen, the growth of the church in China since 1933 has been explosive, despite the severe oppression under the Cultural Revolution from 1949 until recently.

1935

The East Africa Revival began in 1935 in Rwanda, rapidly

spreading to Burundi, Uganda, Kenya and beyond, associated with people like Dr Joe Church. In 1975, when he was living near Cambridge, I talked to him about those remarkable days. There were many scenes of high emotion and manifestations of various kinds. The work and gifts of the Holy Spirit were clearly taught as being vital in the experience of believers, a normal expectation in a life of holiness and obedience.

That revival has continued in the region more or less without interruption for over sixty years, seeding large numbers of indigenous national churches, which do not have a colonial history of traditional denominations behind them.

1949

In 1949 a big revival broke out among a small group of people in the Outer Hebrides of north-west Scotland. This little group of islands was inhabited by a small number of crofters, often struggling against severe weather to eke out a living from sheep farming and subsistence cultivation on poor land. The people were strongly Christian, yet something changed.

Just before the revival started, a group of men met in a barn in the village of Sharda for three nights a week to pray. Duncan Campbell records:

For months they waited upon God in this manner. Nothing happened, until one night … one young man, a Bible in his hand, began reading from Psalm 24: 'Who shall ascend the hill of God and who shall stand in his holy presence?'… He shut his Bible and, looking down at his companions, said this: 'Brethren it seems to me so much humbug waiting as we are praying unless we are rightly related before God.' He then began to pray... At that moment something happened in the barn. A power was let loose that shook the parish from centre to circumference... God had visited them and neither they nor the Parish could ever be the same again.

Within hours the news had travelled up and down the crofts until all in the neighbourhood knew that there had been a visitation from God. People almost ran to be a part of it. The news quickly spread along the winding roads from village to village until even the most isolated crofters had heard what was happening. People travelled large distances to be together. Many remarkable conversions happened and there was a sense of awe which spread throughout the area.

1950

In the 1950s the pentecostal movement was still very much alive, despite the way it was looked down upon by many, and isolated from contact with the major denominations. It is probably true to say that in Britain, as in other nations, if you looked hard enough you would have found phenomena and manifestations of one kind or another in some churches throughout the 1940s, 1950s and certainly the 1960s.

Norman and Grace Barnes, well known for their international teaching ministry based in the UK, and for the work of Links International, clearly recall extraordinary events from 1950 onwards. Unusual things happened and they were confined to small groups, unlike today where phenomena have spread very rapidly across the denominations and networks, through lines of fellowship encouraged by years of bridge-building.

Grace recalls:

When I was 17 (in 1950) I was in a pentecostal church, part of Assemblies of God. About fifty of us went on a Youth Holiday at Sandy Bay in Exmouth at a place run by Mr and Mrs Cunningham. It was led by a Welshman called David Owen.

Every night we ate together in a big tent. Afterwards we would all turn round where we were sitting to hear him preach. He'd get one word out and then laugh! He laughed and laughed. He couldn't get another word out. And then we were all caught up in it, laughing and laughing for up to one and a half hours. Still laughing we then went to our tents to go to sleep.

It went on the whole week. It was the same with all the other groups over three months that went to the same camp. There was a great sense of the presence of God.

Norman Barnes was converted when he was sixteen years old. He recalls:

A month after I was converted it was Whitsun and I was at an Assemblies of God convention. Things began to happen. On the Youth Night, two days later, it all broke out. That night 15 to 20 of us were filled with the Holy Spirit. The meeting started at 8pm and was still going on at midnight. One of them was so incapacitated he had to be carried home. The guy spoke only in tongues for two days. He was totally drunk.

That Sunday we all piled into the church back home, and filled the front two rows, 20 of us. We stood up for the first song – and we were all on the floor. One of us had to be carried out into the vestry. Every week for months it happened, and most times all 20 of us had to be carried out one by one into the vestry to recover. But these were relatively isolated things that came and went. What is happening today is more widespread, more sustained, more intense.

Norman Barnes notes with sadness that all the rest of the group of twenty fell away from faith over the years, in contrast to the group Grace was with, many of whom were inspiring examples of faith in action.

1953

Many different revivals broke out in various parts of Africa at different times. One such 'surprise' was what happened in Central Africa in 1953. What follows here are fascinating extracts from a number of letters from missionaries, published in 1954 as *This Is That*, just a few months after they were received by the offices of the World Evangelisation Crusade. They describe a spontaneous, surprising arrival of very similar phenomena to what is happening in 1994. In different parts of Africa over the years such stories could be repeated from 1935 to today.

The violent manifestations they saw happened first to Christians and remained largely confined to believers or those who had lapsed. One of the writers remarked that the impact on 'the pagans' was relatively limited. However, many were set on fire with a new zeal and love for God which accelerated the process of mission throughout the area. The editor of the letters notes:

> The area in which there has been this recent mighty outpouring of the Spirit is the exact centre of the continent of Africa, in the North-east Belgian Congo. It was the field first entered in 1914 by C. T. Studd and A. B. Buxton, who founded there what later developed into the Worldwide Evangelization Crusade. From 1914 onwards an area of some 400 miles long and 250 broad at its widest part has been gradually occupied, a gospel witness being established among numerous tribes, with a staff averaging fifty missionaries in ten centres.

Here are extracts from the letters:

> In the evening, we Europeans were holding our usual prayer meeting in our house, while the Africans were meeting for theirs in the school. Suddenly we heard strange loud cryings coming from the building. Going along to see, we found people shaking all over the place. Many were quite overcome with a violent shaking, quite uncontrollable. After a time we sought to close the meeting, but it went on for hours. Many were standing with their hands raised, worshipping the Saviour. Some were bringing out hidden secrets, confessing them not to us, but to some unseen Person.
>
> My colleague was awakened about midnight by his boy, still shaking, coming to confess pilfering things in his house. And so it went on. We hardly knew what to say. We had been praying for a long time for revival, but were not expecting anything of this kind, and wondered if it were a spurious movement. Praise God, we found it to be a touch of revival.
>
> The next move was when Sena, the wife of a Lubutu elder, came up to Opienge on a visit. My co-worker and I were on trek at the time. She came to the Sunday service, and people noticed jerks and shakings of her body during the meetings. One or two approached her, thinking that she was ill. She told them she was not ill, but that the Holy Spirit was upon her. People were amazed, and not a few amused.
>
> Nothing else happened until the Tuesday night, when Peleza, the wife of the Opienge chief elder, woke up other folk with her loud singing and praises. They flocked to her house and saw her on the bed in an upright position shaking violently and saying, 'Thanks, thanks, thanks, Lord Jesus,' over and over again. They thought she had gone mad. As she got quieter, they went back to their houses, but at 4 a.m. she again woke them up singing 'There is light in my heart'. She told them she had seen a light come closer and closer to her, until it eventually burst upon her and filled her heart.

Folk were amazed, some laughed and said, 'She is gone off top,' but others rebuked them, saying it was better to wait and see if it was the Lord's doing. The following Sunday the Spirit again came upon Peleza in the service, and although she was asked to be still, the shakings were beyond her control.

As I said, we were out on trek when a letter reached us, telling us of these happenings. After I had read it, I got a vision from the Lord of what was going to happen. I saw the meetings with the people shouting, shaking, and making confession – all the manifestations which we have now seen. The vision shook me, and I got a fear of the whole thing. My own inability brought a fear, as I knew the people would crowd to me for help, and a great longing came to run away from it all; but I prayed to the Lord to help me, and came through willing to be used. It is one thing to pray for revival, quite another to be willing for it.

We had hardly started when we noticed a different note in the prayer of the evangelist who had struck his wife, a great pleading note, an earnestness which tended to be extreme. He seemed very agitated, and was soon crying, tears flowing freely. He ended by falling down on the seat. There was a silence for a few moments, then the chief elder, a very tall man, shot up to his full height, his hands stretched out, shaking and shouting at the top of his voice, 'Thanks, thanks, Lord Jesus.'

In no time the whole place was as if charged with an electric current. Men were falling, jumping, laughing, crying, singing, confessing, and some shaking terribly. It was a terrible sight. One man came upon his hands and knees from the back of the room right up to the front. A young man had a mighty filling. His shakings and jumpings were awful to behold, then he turned to praise and came out to a large place, praise ascending to the Throne such as I had never heard before from an African. He had nothing to confess, as he was already in a healthy place with the Lord.

During this time the women had come out of their meeting

and had gathered round the windows to see the wonderful spectacle of their men being so possessed, then instead of going back to their homes to prepare food, they turned and went back to their meeting place. Hardly had they got there, when the Spirit came down upon them, and the same manifestations were seen among them. Even when both meetings had finished, folks were falling down praising the Lord, or confessing their sins on the paths or in the village. The afternoon meeting was united, and what a meeting!

I had been reading *Rent Heavens*, by R. B. Jones, on the Welsh revival, and in it he mentioned that 'the evangelist could hardly make his voice heard above the din of the worshipping saints'. How true that has been of the meetings we have seen out here. This particular one can best be described as a spiritual tornado. People were literally flung to the floor or over the forms, yet no one was hurt.

It was here I was first led to challenge an excess of emotionalism, for one or two women who were flung to the floor did not take heed to their clothes, so I rebuked them, and later spoke of the Holy Spirit being a holy Spirit in the true sense of the word. The people responded well. Time after time they were willing to be taught, and accepted almost without question any exhortation backed by the Word. The girls from the school were present, and the Lord began a mighty work among them. The school boys, except for two or three, were not touched.

When the Spirit came upon him, he got up and made a full confession of all the things he had stolen from us, and brought back money to pay for them. He had also stolen kerosene from a trader, but was afraid to repay for fear of prison; but when challenged by the Spirit through a message on Zacchaeus he went and made it right. The same trader has been amazed at the number of people who have come to confess stealing. As for testimony and praise, there has not been time enough for all who wanted to testify, and there has never been such praise to the Lord in these parts.

The following Saturday the people from the villages began to arrive for the week of special meetings arranged long before, some walking nearly 100 miles to attend. 'What will happen in the coming week?' was the question on many lips. That evening there were about 400 people crowded into the building, and I gave a welcome message, urging them to be ready for the Lord and telling what had happened on the previous Thursday. Then, as I led in prayer, the Spirit came down in mighty power, sweeping through the congregation. My whole body trembled with the power.

We then saw a marvellous sight: people literally filled and drunk with the Spirit. Never have we seen anything like this. The power and presence of the Lord were awful indeed. Elders and evangelists were swept to their feet, reeling around like drunken men, shouting out, 'I am filled! I am filled!' Then some of them turned to me and asked for forgiveness for having criticized me. As soon as I said I had forgiven them, they praised the Lord in mighty and loud praises.

They went to one another, or called out a name at the other end of the building, asking for forgiveness for some wrong done. Another called out the name of his wife, telling her he was filled with the Spirit and urging her not to hold out against the Lord. One evangelist made public confession that he had made wrong entries in his report book.

There was unbounded joy in the meeting. One elder was clapping his hands and thighs in an ecstasy of joy, yet at the same time failing to stand upright and staggering like a man drunk, his knees refusing to function properly. Elder Leon became like a lion, marching up and down the aisle, praising the Lord with mighty shouts, then turning first to the men, then to the women, next to the schoolgirls and boys, urging them to turn to the Lord, saying that He was soon returning.

Others were dancing and jumping before the Lord through sheer joy, others shaking uncontrollably and shouting out, 'Praise the Lord!' over and over again. Others were singing away on their own, quite unconscious of what the rest were doing. I felt led to clap my hands and start the hymn 'Onward Christian Soldiers'. Immediately, like one man, the whole congregation was on its feet, and was there ever singing like it? No, not even in my native Wales, except perhaps during the revival.

On the singing went, every line, every verse with punctuated emphasis, people glancing at their neighbours with a smile, indicating their fullness of joy at the victory of Jesus. There was such a volume of praise that angels must have stopped their ministering to gaze down at the wonderful sight.

The people were amazed at the sensitiveness of the Holy Spirit to what they called small sins. The breaking of the sixth, seventh, and eighth commandments they understood, but heart sins like murmuring, evil thoughts, and criticism they had thought He would not be so particular about. But when they came under terrible conviction over such sins, then they saw them as God sees them.

Tunziako, for instance, had spoken a lot against a certain missionary. For days the Spirit strove with her. She would tremble terribly and get up to   confess a certain wrong, but still there would be no freedom or joy. Later she would tremble again and cry piteously, asking that a certain hymn be sung, but still no freedom, until one day I was asked to go and see her, as she couldn't walk.

My colleague and I went. She was sitting on a low stool and couldn't move her legs. I tried to help her rise, but it was impossible, her legs seemed fixed or stuck to the ground. We sat down near her, and all the time she was crying pitifully. Then she began to bring out with great sorrow of heart her sin of speaking against the missionary. As soon as she had finished, she was filled with joy, her knees straightened, and she stood and walked. There have been other cases of limbs fixed.

One who never comes to any meetings was on his way to his wine palm to drink, when he was arrested by a deep conviction of sin. Both his hands came together at the wrists with a sense of heat, and he could not part them. Then his legs came together in the same manner, and he fell into a sitting position on the road. He then confessed his sins. The Spirit then told him, 'I will release your legs so that you can walk back to your village and tell the folk, but your hands will remain fixed until you have obeyed.'

He did so, much to the astonishment of his wife and others, and as soon as he had obeyed his hands were released. An elder went out to visit him and teach him more fully the way of the Lord. He and his wife then accepted the Saviour.

A phenomenon, which we whites have not yet seen, but which some of our best evangelists and Christians vouch for, is that of seeing a holy light in some of their houses. Many people have seen it in the girls' dormitory on more than one occasion, here on the mission station (Acts 12:7).

From that day I found the messages to the girls charged with new power, power from on high. However short the message was, I felt God was working. He had answered prayer and given power. A week later, while we were having a short season of prayer, as the service closed, the same strange experience came over me and my body began trembling violently. Again afraid of the results, I brought the meeting to an abrupt close.

Three days later, while having a prayer meeting with the station women, the Spirit came upon one of the women in a similar way, and a few days previously this woman's husband had leaped from his seat in a prayer meeting, shouting and trembling as the Spirit of God came upon him. A few weeks later we began our week-end conference when close on a thousand people gathered with us from our district churches. We had as our guest speakers the two missionaries from Opienge, and the Africans who accompanied them.

God came down in our midst in a wonderful way, and the fire fell. My schoolgirls were leaving to go on holiday the day the conference was to close. I arranged to have a farewell meeting with them. Many confessed to sin of one form or another, such as little unrighteous acts, which had meant nothing to them until the Spirit of God had convicted them. We had a further time of prayer, but I felt a hardness come over the meeting.

As I was fervently and silently praying for my girls, this strange sensation I have mentioned came on me again, but now recognizing it for what it was, I did not resist: it seemed that Another Being had taken possession of me, as indeed was true; the Holy Ghost had come, surging through my whole body and reaching even to my finger-tips. In my hands and fingers were sensations like being in contact with live wires: the strangest sensation I have ever experienced, and such as I can never forget.

My heart and my whole being were praising God, and as I could keep silent no longer, I let out joyful bursts of hallelujah, which were echoed by my amazed schoolchildren. A few moments later an evangelist's wife came along saying she wanted to pray with the girls. She had heard our shouts and had come to see if she could help. I knew she was sent by God, for He had much more work to do in their hearts, and so I left them in her care. Soon the compound was ringing with their cries, as the Spirit came down in convicting power and confessions of deep sin were made. This went on until about midnight. Yes, revival has come!

It is impossible to record everything. We could fill pages with testimonies. The wild dancing and singing is more settled now, but the deep joy remains. Children and adults speak to themselves 'in psalms and hymns and spiritual songs, singing and making melody' in their hearts to the Lord.

Preaching is such a joy now. The simplest teaching is so new to the folk. They are all the time saying, 'This is new to us. We knew the doctrine before, but now we know the power.' That was all. Now they do not need reminding!

One elder from an out-church came under the power of the Spirit as he was returning to his village. He was actually on his cycle, and was so under conviction that he fell off. He got through to wonderful liberty. He has been much used since.

There have been a few cases of excess, or perhaps fanaticism would be a better word. Some have had visions and trances which were evidently not of God. We made an open challenge of this. Another began to meddle with engaged couples: 'A voice has told me that you are not to marry this person, but so and so.' But here again we have had no cases of obstinacy. We back up our rebukes and exhortations with Scripture, and hitherto our word has been accepted.

Words fail to describe it, but we know something now of what it must have been like on the day of Pentecost. As one prayed, another began to pray, and another, and then the whole congregation together. Such a noise as they poured out their souls in prayer and praise to God. Men, women, boys, and girls just drunk with the Spirit, many shaking beyond their control, others throwing themselves on the floor, some leaning, some standing.

One man danced about exhorting them to fear God and not hide sin, but his voice was soon drowned in the hubbub. We just stood there amazed, but were not afraid, as we knew the Spirit was working. We just walked about among them, seeking to help where we could, though it was impossible to make oneself heard. If this had not been of God, it would have been terrible, as they were beyond all human control.

Although many threw themselves about, or rather were thrown down, yet none was hurt. All this went on for about an hour, and then as it quietened a bit, a hymn was sung and the people dispersed. We got to bed late, but it was not to sleep much, as our hearts were so full of praise.

As the blessing continued through successive days, he wrote again, 'Praise His blessed name for all the wonderful things He is doing in our midst these days. As we have been trusting the Lord for years to pour out His Spirit upon us in revival, now we rejoice in the answer. We do not need to be afraid of any manifestations which are strange to us. Strange things have accompanied every true revival.'

1954

The 1950s were also the years of a new kind of high-profile evangelist: the 'healing evangelist'. People like Kathryn Kuhlman, William Branham and W. V. Grant drew great crowds in the US to meetings where the work of the Holy Spirit was 'demonstrated with power'. Detailed insights into the lives of strangers present in the large meetings (words of knowledge) would precede prayer for healing, with many remarkable stories of God's intervention in physical and emotional healing. It was common for people to collapse to the ground when prayed for or at other times.

In 1954, from a very different culture, without the emphasis on the supernatural, Billy Graham began a big mission in Haringey Stadium, North London, after an exploratory trip in 1946. There was a tremendous response, and he went on to preach in Scotland in 1955. Some estimate that over the next forty years a total of 9 million people in Britain attended meetings at which he preached, and perhaps some hundreds of thousands responded.

Michael Baughen, Bishop of Chester, recalls: 'There was a tremendous result from the first Billy Graham crusade. It produced a whole new encouragement and confidence, and there are considerable numbers of people in the ministry who came to faith or who were encouraged into a committed form of service through that original crusade.'[98]

However, there was a big problem. At the crusades many people saw a strength of life-changing faith that was truly inspiring. But when they went to church for the first time afterwards, they found something which in sharp contrast was very lifeless and dull. Pressure for change began to build.

From the 1960s onwards the most significant change in British church life was the spread of the charismatic movement, with the discovery of the dynamic power of the Holy Spirit by those outside of pentecostal circles. The big 'break out' was about to begin, with a transforming effect on thousands of churches. Meanwhile, revival accelerated in many of the world's poorer nations. The result was the series of events which in turn began to set the stage for what happened in Britain in 1994.

4
Making Sense of Enthusiasm

So how do we make sense of enthusiasm as often seen in revival or in national awakenings – of its disturbing aspects and its associated manifestations? What are the hallmarks of a revival? How do we know if we are on the edge of one?

Here are some answers, with one or two dissident voices, drawn from the last 150 years, from Charles Finney, George Jeffreys, Arthur Wallis, Martyn Lloyd-Jones, Jim Packer, Peter Nodding, Clifford Hill, Gerald Coates, Derek Munday, Alan Morrison and Seraphim Rose.

Charles Finney has been called 'the nineteenth century apostle of revival'.[99] He was a connecting link between the converts of the eighteenth-century revival and the associated American awakenings, and of the later revival of 1857-59. Wesley had left 50,000 Methodists in America alone, and died almost as Finney was born. Finney in turn lived to see Spurgeon become a major preaching force in Britain, and the beginning of Moody's work. Finney saw the centenary celebrations in the 1840s of the Great Awakening in 1740 with Jonathan Edwards.

Finney speaks with conviction from a time surrounded by the memories and experiences of recent revivals. Much of what he wrote seems laser sharp and relevant today, whether about being filled with the Spirit, or being involved in revival – both of which he saw as being closely related.

Of being filled with the Holy Spirit he warns:

1. You will be called eccentric; and probably you will deserve it. Probably you will really be eccentric. I never knew a person who was filled with the Spirit that was not called eccentric. And the reason is that such people are unlike other folk. ... you must and will act so as to appear strange and eccentric, to those who cannot understand the reasons of your conduct.

2. If you have much of the Spirit of God, it is not unlikely you will be thought deranged by many – we judge men to be deranged when they act differently from what we think to be according to prudence and common sense, and when they come to conclusions for which we can see no good reasons. Paul was accused of being deranged by those who did not understand the views of things under which he acted. No doubt Festus thought the man was crazy, that 'much learning had made him mad'. But Paul said: 'I am not mad, most noble Festus' (Acts 26:24, 25).

3. If you have the Spirit of God, you must expect to feel great distress in view of the condition of the Church and of the world. Some spiritual epicures ask for the Spirit because they think He will make them so perfectly happy. Some people think that spiritual Christians are always free from sorrow. There never was a greater mistake. Read your Bibles, and see how the prophets and apostles were always groaning and distressed, in view of the state of the Church and of the world....

If you have NOT the Spirit, you will be very apt to stumble at those who have. You will doubt the propriety of their conduct. If they seem to feel a good deal more than yourself, you will be likely to call it 'animal feeling'. You will perhaps doubt their sincerity when they say they have such feelings....

You will be had in reputation with the impenitent and with carnal professors. They will praise you, as a rational, orthodox, consistent Christian. You will be just in the frame of mind to walk with them, because you are agreed.

You will be much troubled with fears about fanaticism. Whenever there are revivals, you will see in them 'a strong tendency to fanaticism' and will be full of fears and anxiety. You will be much disturbed by the measures that are used in revivals. If any measures are adopted that are decided and direct, you will think they are all 'new', and will stumble at them just in proportion to your want of spirituality. You do not see their appropriateness. You will stand and cavil at the measures, because you are so blind that you cannot see their adaptedness, while all heaven is rejoicing in them as the means of saving souls.

Finney also has many warnings about ways in which revival grinds to a halt, and therefore ways in which God's sovereign work can be encouraged. One warning he has is that the excitement and business of revival can lead to total exhaustion and collapse. His list of reasons for the ceasing of a move of God seems so important for us today, perhaps on the brink of revival, that it is reproduced here, slightly edited.

1. The revival will stop when the Church gets exhausted by labour. Multitudes of Christians commit a great mistake here in time of revival. They are so thoughtless, and have so little judgment, that they will break up all their habits of living, neglect to eat and sleep at the proper hours, and let the excitement run away with them, so that they overdo their bodies, and are so imprudent that they soon become exhausted, and it is impossible for them to continue in the work.

2. A revival will stop whenever the Church believes it is going to cease. The Church is the instrument with which God carries on this work.

A revival will cease when Christians consent that it should cease. Sometimes Christians see that the revival is in danger of ceasing, and that if something is not done, it will come to a standstill. If this should distress them, and drive them to prayer, and to fresh efforts, the work will not cease.

3. A revival will cease whenever Christians become mechanical in their attempts to promote it. When their faith is strong, and their hearts are warm and mellow, and their prayers full of holy emotion, and their words with power, then the work goes on. But when their prayers begin to be cold and without emotion, and they begin to labour mechanically, and to use words without feeling, then the revival will cease.

4. The revival will cease whenever Christians get the idea that the work will go on without their aid. They are co-workers with God in promoting a revival, and the work can be carried on just as far as the Church will carry it on, and no farther.

5. The work will cease when the Church prefers to attend to selfish concerns rather than God's business... They begin to think they cannot afford sufficient time from their worldly employments to carry on a revival.

6. When Christians get proud of their 'great revival' it will cease. I mean those Christians who have been instrumental in promoting it.

7. A revival will cease when the Church begins to speculate about abstract doctrines, which have nothing to do with practice.

8. When Christians begin to proselytise. When the Baptists are so opposed to the Presbyterians, or the Presbyterians to the Baptists, or both against the Methodists, or Episcopalians against the rest, that they begin to make efforts to get the converts to join their Church, you soon see the last of the revival.

9. When Christians refuse to render to the Lord according to the benefits received. This is a fruitful source of religious declensions. God has opened the windows of heaven to a Church, and poured them out a blessing, and then He reasonably expects them to bring in the tithes into His storehouse.

I have known Churches which were evidently cursed with barrenness for such a course. They had a glorious revival, and afterwards perhaps their buildings needed repairing or something else was needed which would cost a little money, and they refused to do it, and so... God gave them up.

10. When the Church, in any way, grieves the Holy Spirit. When Christians do not feel their dependence on the Spirit. Whenever they get strong in their own strength God curses their blessings. In many instances they sin against their own mercies, because they get lifted up with their success and take the credit to themselves, and do not give all the glory to God... The Spirit may be grieved by a spirit of boasting of the revival. Sometimes, as soon as a revival commences, you will see it blasted out in the newspapers, and most commonly this will kill the revival.

There was a case in a neighbouring State, where a revival commenced, and instantly there came out a letter from the pastor, telling that he had a revival. I saw the letter, and said to myself, 'That is the last we shall hear of this revival.' And so it was. In a few days the work totally ceased. I could mention cases and places where persons have published such things as to puff up the Church, and make the people so proud that little more could be done for the revival. It is always fatal to the revival.

So too the Spirit is grieved by saying or pushing things that are calculated to undervalue the work of God. When a blessed work of God is spoken lightly it is not rendering to God the glory due to His Name, the Spirit is grieved.

11. A revival may be expected to cease when Christians lose the spirit of brotherly love. Jesus Christ will not continue with people in a revival any longer than they continue in the exercise of brotherly love.

12. A revival will decline and cease, unless Christians are frequently re-converted. By this I mean that Christians, in order to keep in the spirit of revival, commonly need to be frequently convicted and humbled and broken down before God, and 're-converted'.... In a revival, the Christian's heart is liable to get crusted over, and lose its exquisite relish for Divine things; his unction and prevalence in prayer abate, and then life must be converted over again. It is impossible to keep him in such a

state as not to do injury to the work, unless he passes through such a process every few days. I have never laboured in revivals in company with anyone who would keep in the work and be fit to manage a revival continually, who did not pass through this process of breaking down as often as once in two or three weeks.

Revivals decline, commonly, because it is found impossible to make Christians realise their guilt and dependence, so as to break down before God. It is important that ministers should understand this, and learn how to break down the Church, and break down themselves when they need it, or else Christians will soon become mechanical in their work, and lose their fervour and their power of prevailing with God.

13. A revival cannot continue when Christians will not practise self-denial. When the Church has enjoyed a revival, and begins to grow fat upon it, and to run into self-indulgence, the revival will soon cease. Unless they sympathise with the Son of God who gave up all to save sinners; unless they are willing to give up their luxuries, and their ease, and devote themselves to the work, the Christians need not expect that the Spirit of God will be poured out upon them.

14. A revival will be stopped by controversies about new measures. Nothing is more certain to overthrow a revival than this.

15. Revivals can be put down by the combined opposition of the Old School, and a bad spirit in the New School. If those who do nothing to promote revivals continue their opposition, and if those who are labouring to promote them allow themselves to get impatient, and get into a bad spirit, the revival will cease. When the Old School write letters in the newspapers, against revivals or revival men, and the New School write letters back again, in an angry, contentious spirit, revivals will cease.

Let them keep about their work, and neither talk about the opposition, nor preach upon it, nor rush into print about it. If others choose to publish 'slang', let the Lord's people keep to their work. None of the slander will stop the revival while those who are engaged in it mind their business, and keep to the work.

16. Any diversion of the public mind will hinder a revival. In the case I have specified, where the minister was put on trial before his Presbytery, the reason why it did not ruin the revival was that the praying members of the Church would not suffer themselves to be diverted.

17. Resistance to the Temperance reformation will put a stop to revivals in a Church.

18. Revivals are hindered when ministers and Churches take wrong ground in regard to any question involving human rights. Take the subject of *slavery*, for instance. The time was when this subject was not before the public mind. John Newton continued in the slave trade after his conversion ... the sinfulness of it never occurred to his thoughts until some time after he became a child of God.

19. Another thing that hinders revivals is neglecting the claims of Missions. If Christians confine their attention to their own Church, do not read even their missionary magazine or use any other means to inform themselves on the subject of the claims of the world, but reject the light, and will not do what God calls them to do in this cause, the Spirit of God will depart from them.

George Jeffreys, founder of the Elim movement, wrote a vigorous defence of Pentecostalism, manifestations and emotional experiences which I have already referred to (*Pentecostal Rays*, 1935). He describes common objections to manifestations and gives his own answers:

Critic: Speaking in tongues and other manifestations have much in common with the effects produced by hypnotism, mesmerism, spiritism and the like, and there can be little doubt that they may be attributable largely to such forces.

Answer: It were a sad state of affairs, were this true. Happily, we know better. We have often been told that to know a person one must live with him. In our ministry we have seen thousands baptised with the Holy Spirit, and we have heard them speak with tongues. Yet we have never known one real Christian who, having sought the baptism for service in the kingdom of God, receive an evil spirit. See Luke xi. 13.

Critic: The teaching with which the baptism of the Spirit and the speaking in tongues are connected would make the Holy Spirit the consciousness of the Church, whereas the Spirit has come to make the Lord Jesus Christ our consciousness. Speaking of these supposed miraculous signs as a whole, they are physical rather than spiritual in nature.

Answer: We have come into contact with hundreds of thousands during our ministry who have received the baptism of the Holy Spirit and the gift of tongues, and our testimony is that no people love and adore the Lord Jesus Christ more than they.

Even the thousands of young people, who characterise the great Pentecostal movement of to-day, have fallen in love with Christ to such a degree that their lives are laid upon the altar of service, many on the foreign mission field, in the extension of His glorious Kingdom. Love for Christ is best proved by obedience to His will, and there are no more obedient people to the will of God than those baptised with the Holy Spirit with signs following.

Critic: The present Pentecostal movement with its miracles and gifts encourages extravagances and abuses of all kinds. The leaders I know would disclaim any responsibility for these excrescences, but the movement is wider than its leaders.

Answer: History shews that every heaven-sent revival is 'wider than its leaders', and every revival, like the present one, has had its excrescences. They are unavoidable where the Spirit of God is mightily at work, for the enemy is ever near, and ready to hinder along counterfeit and other lines. Every real revival movement has had to contend with three relentless opposing forces – the world, the flesh, and the Devil – and the marvel is that revivals like the present one have experienced so little extravagance and excrescence.

In latter years the greatest and most continuous revival since the days of the apostles is in progress all over the world. Every tongue and nation seems to be coming under the copious showers of Latter Rain, and the miraculous signs and gifts are freely bestowed. In its soul-saving aspect, through which lives and homes are changed, there has been nothing to compare with it in history. Is it to be wondered at that this revival is like all others in history, and has to contend with some excrescences?

Critic: The Church needs revival, and it is encouraging to know that an ever-increasing number of saints are realising the great need. The prayers of God's people are everywhere ascending, and when the revival comes, it will be with the full and indisputable sanction of Holy Scripture, and will be confirmed by the fruit of the Spirit, and not by physical manifestations.

Answer: The revival which the Church needs has arrived, and there will be no other. It is useless praying and working if one is not prepared to receive. If the present heavenly visitation with its extensive soul-saving, its exhortation to holiness of life, its uncompromising stand for the whole Bible, its unshaken fundamentalism, its manifestation of the fruit of the Spirit, its exercise of supernatural gifts, its signs and wonders, and its implicit obedience to the commandments of Christ, is not accepted as the answer to prayer for revival, we should like to know what would be.

We see no other pattern for revival in the New Testament, and the church or leader who rejects this is rejecting the answer to their own prayers for revival.

Jeffreys also talks about the dangers of a completely 'hands-off' approach, when leaders take a back seat to 'let the Spirit flow' without taking responsibility for what is happening. The result, he says, can be disaster.

Controlling the power of God

So many a beautiful church is giving no indication of the power at her disposal. It is lying dormant within, all because proper adjustment has not been made in accordance with the clear declaration of God's Word. When this is done, revival breaks out and life manifests itself; spiritual dynamic forces are let loose, and the church is driven through even the raging seas of opposition, worldliness, and unbelief.

Controlled power. The great liner leaves her moorings, glides down the lough, and moves out into the boundless ocean beyond. She turns first in one direction, then another; she proceeds slowly or quickly, all at the direction of the controls on board. Every possible precaution is taken in case of emergency; the clear lines of the chart are carefully followed, for every movement is under control. She proves to be a blessing in every port where she makes harbour, and her gracefulness is admired by all.

What a splendid illustration she furnishes for the church which experiences revival. Adjustments to the requirements of God's Word have been made, and the dynamic of the gospel within has begun to manifest itself in unmistakable fashion. She gracefully leaves the cramped condition of the traditional quayside, passes through the trough of formal religion, and moves out into the great ocean of humanity. Her quest for lost sinners is rewarded, and perishing souls are safely quartered on board.

She brings life to the dying, healing to the oppressed, power to the faint, liberty to the captives, and blessing to mankind everywhere. What disaster there would be if those on board the big liner were to neglect the controls, and allow her to proceed anywhere and everywhere.

Uncontrolled power. But what if the boilers were filled, the fires kindled, and the dynamic powers released in action, without control of any kind? The great liner would soon pound herself to pieces right at the quayside. Who can possibly imagine the appalling disasters which would ensue if she were allowed to pass out into the great ocean uncontrolled? Alas! this is an illustration of what is allowed to happen occasionally in a church blessed with the dynamic of the gospel.

Having adjusted herself to the requirements of Holy Scripture, revival has broken out – the Spirit descends, the miraculous gifts are in evidence, and everything is on the move. Then, to the consternation of wiser heads, the hands are taken off the proper controls, and the power and gifts are allowed to run uncontrolled. The New Testament pattern of church equilibrium is upset, and it is not long before undue emotionalism, accompanied by excessive psychic forces, comes aboard, with the result that the church in due time is split into pieces.

The once powerful spiritual liner has become a wreck upon the rocks of excrescences and extravagance, and the end means disaster to all. If she had been controlled, and allowed to run according to the clear lines indicated by the inspired Chart, she would have been a blessing to a needy world.

In 1956 Arthur Wallis wrote his own reply to critics of manifestations associated with many new moves of God:

We must pause a moment and answer some of the objections that are always brought against revival. When God pours out the Spirit these arguments are sure to occur again, and there will be no time to deal with them then.

There is little that can be said to those who wilfully blind their eyes to the facts, and with wholesale antagonism to the work of the Spirit would seem to derive more from the enmity of the heart than the reasonings of the head. Some, however, speak against revival out of ignorance. They have never experienced it, do not know what it is, and are prejudiced against it from the outset. Influenced by enemies of the work, their opinions are based on hearsay. The effective cure for such, if they are willing, is to go and see for themselves.

Others object to revival because they consider that it is always accompanied by excesses and other undesirable features. That here is a tendency for such to occur where care is not exercised, and that at times excesses have occurred, cannot be denied. No one would pretend to claim that every revival burns with a smokeless flame. But let us test the depth of the argument.

Would these critics suggest that the early church ought never to have sold their possessions that distribution might be made to those in need, because this was abused by Ananias and Sapphira? Should the young churches have refrained from eating the Lord's supper, because in some places, e.g., Corinth, the ordinance had been abused? Ought there to have been no Reformation because occasionally Protestants gave way to excessive zeal and wrongs were perpetrated?

The picture must be seen in perspective, and the evils must be weighed against the overall good. 'After drought, the copious rains often deluge the land and sweep away bridges, and otherwise do very much harm. But no one is so alarmed by the evils of rain, as to desire a continuation of the drought' (Wm. Patton, D.D.).

There are always some who are desirous of revival until it comes, and then they bitterly oppose it, because it has not come in the way they anticipated. The instrument that God used, or the channel through which the blessing flowed, was not what their convictions had led them to expect. They looked to see an Elijah or an Abinadab chosen for this great work, but the Lord, who 'looketh on the heart', chose a David. They thought that their own local church, their own fellowship which was so scriptural and right, would see the beginning of the work, but God chose to work elsewhere, and this became to them a stumbling-block.[100]

Arthur Wallis also comments:

> True revivals have ever been marked by powerful and often widespread outpourings of the Spirit. Many many times the teaching had to cease because the hearers were prostrate, or because the voice of the preacher was drowned by cries for mercy. Who will deny that these were outpourings of the Spirit? Who could find a more appropriate description of such scenes as the words of Luke: 'The Holy Spirit fell on all them which heard the Word' (Acts 10:44)?
>
> Revival can never be explained in terms of activity, organization, meetings, personalities, preachings. These may or may not be involved in the work, but they do not and cannot account for the effects produced. Revival is essentially a manifestation of God; it has the stamp of Deity upon it, which even the unregenerate and uninitiated are quick to recognize.
>
> Revival must of necessity make an impact upon the community, and this is one means by which we may distinguish it from the more usual operations of the Holy Spirit.[101]

Martyn Lloyd-Jones was one of the most influential preachers and writers on Christian doctrine in Britain this century. On revival and manifestations he wrote this:

> It comes near to the rule that in revival phenomena begin to manifest themselves... Sometimes people feel the power of the Spirit to such an extent that they faint and fall to the ground. Sometimes there are even convulsions, physical convulsions. And sometimes people fall into a state of unconsciousness, into a kind of trance, and many remain in that kind of state for hours... These phenomena are not essential to revival... yet it is true to say that, on the whole, they do tend to be present where there is revival.
>
> We must never forget that the Spirit affects the whole person.

You see, man is body, soul and spirit and you cannot divide these. Man reacts as a whole. Something is happening which is so powerful that the very physical frame is involved.

Why should the Devil suddenly start doing this kind of thing? Here is a church in a period of dryness and drought, why should the Devil suddenly do something which calls attention to religion and Jesus Christ? The very results of revival, I would have thought, completely exclude the possibility of this being the action of the Devil... There is nothing so ridiculous as this suggestion that this is the work of the Devil.[102]

Jim Packer is widely respected for his scholarship and his biblical understanding. He has said of renewal and revival:

The phenomena of renewal movements merit much more study by church historians, theologians, and exponents of Christian spirituality than they have yet received. At surface level, they vary widely, as do the movements within which they appear, and we should not be surprised at that.

That would mean identifying past movements of renewal and revival, from the Old Testament records of Israel's return to Yahweh under Asa, Hezekiah, Josiah, Ezra, and others, and the New Testament story in Acts of revival in Palestine after Pentecost, through to the Cistercian and Dominican and Franciscan movements; the ministry of Savonarola; the Western Reformation; the early Jesuits; English Puritanism and Lutheran Pietism.

The Evangelical Awakenings in old England and New England in the eighteenth century, the repeated stirrings of the Spirit in Wales and Scotland between the seventeenth and nineteenth centuries; the first hundred years of the Protestant missionary movement; the frontier revivals in America; the worldwide quickenings among Protestants in the 1850s and again in the 1900s.

The East African revival, now fifty years old and still

continuing; the awakenings in Lewis, off the west coast of Scotland, in the 1950s, in Western Canada in the 1960s, and in Indonesia and the Californian 'Jesus movement' in the 1970s; the impact of the worldwide charismatic movement over the past twenty years; and so on.

But at the level of deeper analysis ... there are constant factors recognizable in all biblical and post-biblical revivals and renewals of faith and life, whatever their historical, racial, and cultural settings. They number five, as follows:

(1) Awareness of God's presence. The first and fundamental feature in renewal is the sense that God has drawn awesomely near in his holiness, mercy, and might.

(2) Responsiveness to God's word. The sense of God's presence imparts new authority to his truth. The message of Scripture which previously was making only a superficial impact, if that, now searches its hearers and readers to the depth of their being.

(3) Sensitiveness to sin. Deep awareness of what things are sinful and how sinful we ourselves are – conviction of sin, to use the old phrase – is the third phenomenon of renewal that calls for notice. No upsurge of religious interest or excitement merits the name of renewal if there is no deep sense of sin at its heart.

(4) Liveliness in community. Love and generosity, unity and joy, assurance and boldness, a spirit of praise and prayer, and a passion to reach out to win others are recurring marks of renewed communities. So is divine power in their preachers, a power which has nothing to do with natural eloquence.

(5) Fruitfulness in testimony. Revival of the church always has an evangelistic and ethical overspill into the world: Christians proclaim by word and deed the power of the new life, souls are won, and a community conscience informed by Christian values emerges.[103]

More recently, those caught up with these new events in

1993 and 1994 have also been struggling to make sense of their experience. Millmead Centre in Guildford was hit by the 'wave of the Spirit' in May 1994 after two leaders went to a conference at St Andrew's Chorleywood.

Peter Nodding, Pastoral Leader, later reflected on the tears, laughter, shaking ('nothing new. The Quakers were shakers, hence their name'), the 'weight of the Spirit' when people need to sit or lie down ('in most cases I believe people could stand up, but that would mean coming out of what the Spirit is doing'), and heavy breathing with other bodily movements.

He said to the congregation:

These experiences do not cause us to be afraid. Indeed on the contrary, they give us a sense of the love and acceptance of God. But what is actually happening? As the power of the Holy Spirit comes upon us, our spirits, souls and bodies are responding.

So what is the fruit of this so far? First, a greater passion for Jesus: I observe in myself and others that the person of Jesus has become even more precious to us.

We can be reassured that this is a move of the Spirit of God because he is highlighting the wonder and significance of his Son. There are several places in Scripture where we are told that the Holy Spirit will glorify Jesus.

Secondly, there is an accelerated growth in sanctification or holiness in the sense of our setting ourselves apart for the Lord. Some deeper changes may take longer to be evidenced.

Some who have been especially worried about laughter have asked where is the repentance in this move of the Spirit? Repentance is a change of attitude about God. It is to be consumed with the things of God rather than the things of earth or self. It is wanting to live the way that Jesus did, in humility and obedience. For many of us these attitudes are at the heart of this refreshing.

Thirdly, an accelerated growth in spiritual gifts. With the new anointing of the Holy Spirit comes the more natural flow of his gifts – prophecy, word of knowledge, healing, etc.

Allied with this I have heard wonderful stories that some members have been wonderfully set free in Christ. Personal difficulties that might usually take several counselling appointments to resolve are being healed in a much shorter time. Also the Lord is unearthing aspects of our lives with which he wishes to deal.

Then there is a greater capacity to carry on the work of God … a greater faith and boldness to see it through.

It will not happen for all of us at the same time. What is important is what the Lord is doing inside of us, not the outward. 'It is not the manifestation that is important, it is transformation.'

I believe that what we are seeing is a preparation for a move of God's Spirit in this country. Leaders have been saying for some time that we are near to a move that will affect the nation. So it is not Revival at this stage. There are dangers in any move of the Spirit, but the answer is not to quench him but to ask for more, because the more we have of him, the less we have of ourselves. Just as years ago when folk were getting up tight about spiritual gifts the answer was not 'no use' but 'right use'.[104]

Clifford Hill, editor of *Prophecy Today*, has distinct reservations. He wrote in July 1994:

There is nothing new about people falling to the ground. In numerous periods throughout church history when there has been a significant move of God, people have been struck down by the power of the Holy Spirit or fallen down under the conviction of sin. It has been a major mark of the charismatic renewal movement for the past 25 years. Indeed it is a healthy sign of the deep working of the word of God within the believer, leading to penitence and a longing for greater holiness, cleansing from sin and deeper commitment.

The new feature of this phenomenon is laughter. It is often described as joy but most of the reports also indicate that the laughter is often hysterical and even maniacal. Such manifestations are unlikely to be of the Holy Spirit and are more likely to be of the flesh or of an alien spirit.

That is not to deny that soft gentle laughter under certain conditions may not be an expression of joy in the Lord. But loud uncontrollable hysterical laughter has no precedent in Scripture as a manifestation of the Spirit of God.

Indeed, throughout the Bible, the great majority of references to laughter are associated with scorn, derision or evil. Psalm 126 is one of the few examples of laughter being an expression of joy. But this is one of the Songs of Ascent used by the pilgrims on their way up to Jerusalem.

It is not a description of formal worship in the Temple but a song sung by the pilgrims as they remembered, or even re-enacted, the scenes of uninhibited joy of those who had been slaves in Babylon and returned to the land of their fathers and to Jerusalem. 'Our mouths,' they sang, 'were filled with laughter, our tongues with songs of joy.'

Jeremiah associates roaring like a lion with the occult spirit of Babylon. He sees this growling turning to shouts of laughter which will be a prelude to their destruction. '"Babylon will be a heap of ruins, a haunt of jackals, an object of horror and scorn, a place where no-one lives. Her people all roar like young lions, they growl like lion cubs. But while they are aroused, I will set out a feast for them and make them drunk, so that they shout with laughter – then sleep for ever and not awake," declares the Lord. "I will bring them down like lambs to the slaughter like rams and goats"'(Jeremiah 51:37-40).

Another worrying feature of the Toronto phenomenon is the number of people who are travelling from one place to another in order to be ministered to by 'those who've got it' in order to take it back and to pass it on to others. Pastors are said to be travelling from all over the world to Toronto to catch it and take the blessing back with them.

On the other hand it needs to be borne in mind that there are few details given in Acts of the manifestations accompanying the outpouring of the Holy Spirit. It would be unwise, therefore, to rule out any manifestation unless it were blasphemous, destructive or sinful. There are good things happening as well as bizarre, the manifestations occurring alongside genuine revivals.

But are these accounts of strange manifestations indications of revival? In themselves they are not revival. It is noteworthy that the leadership at HTB has been careful to say that what is happening there is not revival. It is regrettable that some writers in the press, including the *Church of England Newspaper* have used sensational headlines about 'revival'.

There are very few reports of unbelievers being converted. Therefore this cannot be described as a revival. Most reports speak of God giving this as a time of 'spiritual refreshment' for the saints. If this is a genuine time of spiritual refreshment preparing the way for revival, as some believe, then we will be able to judge the truth of this by the fruit.

If it spills over into the secular unbelieving communities around our churches, and large numbers come under conviction of sin in repentance and turning to the Lord, then indeed it will be a mighty revival for which we will all rejoice and give thanks to God.

In the meantime, while we wait to see if the fruit of this new spiritual phenomenon is good, we should be reminded of some basic biblical teaching in regard to spiritual manifestations.

The first is that believers can be deceived, otherwise Jesus would not have warned his own disciples in Matthew 24:4, 'Watch out that no-one deceives you,' and again in v24 he warned, 'For false christs and false prophets will appear and perform great signs and miracles to deceive even the elect – if that were possible. See, I have told you ahead of time.' If these are indeed the last days, then we may expect 'the deceiver' to be active among us.

It is a common error to believe that Christians who are filled with the Holy Spirit cannot be deceived. In fact those who have been baptised in the Spirit are more likely to be deceived than conservative evangelicals or traditional orthodox believers who have had no such experience.

The reason for this is that the latter judge right or wrong by the use of their intellect or reason. They form a judgment based upon principle rather than experience or emotional reaction. The more the believer is soaked in the word of God the more likely they are to be able to make a sound judgment.

Those who are in greatest danger are believers who have been newly baptised in the Spirit and who lack maturity in the word of God. They have opened their lives to all things on an experiential rather than a rational basis. If they lack a depth of sound teaching in the word they are an easy target for the enemy.

The history of revivals shows that they often begin in a somewhat untidy and messy manner. When the Spirit of God comes down upon the people, demonic spirits are exposed, sometimes with frightening manifestations.

It is not unknown for people to laugh when experiencing the joy of the Lord. Laughter and joy are clearly associated, but uncontrollable hysterical laughter is an excess which believers ought to be able to control for the sake of courtesy to others. In a believer it is more likely to be giving way to the flesh than of the presence of a demonic spirit, but self-control is part of the fruit of the Spirit.

It would appear that the manifestations in some fellowships, although strange, are not out of control where the leadership is mature and those in charge of the meeting are well grounded in the word of God. On the other hand there are reports of fellowships where the leadership does not appear to be exercising wise control and where things are happening which are not in accordance with the word of God. Where there is a departure from Scripture there is a great danger of the enemy taking over.

The final test of this current phenomenon is its fruit. If it is genuinely of God and the church receives it joyfully and acts wisely, it will undoubtedly spill over into revival. In the current condition of Britain and many western nations, where there is great spiritual hunger alongside moral bankruptcy, the revival could be a mighty work of God and a great harvest for the kingdom.

It is possible, however, for this to be a true work of God but not lead to revival, thus not fulfilling God's intention. There is always a danger with the evangelical/charismatic sector of the church in the highly individualised western culture of the late twentieth century to internalise and personalise everything.

On the Day of Pentecost the disciples did not remain in the upper room praising God and enjoying the experience of exercising the gifts among themselves! They spilled out into the streets of the city with the power to fulfil the Great Commission and three thousand were saved on the first day! If this is a genuine move of God it will result in revival not simply in blessing the Lord's people.

We can, however, frustrate the purposes of God if we do not understand the times and recognise the very special significance of what is happening in our lifetime. We also need to know the unchanging word of God, his purposes and the way he works them out.

There will be no mighty revival, no great outpouring of the Spirit of God upon unbelievers in this nation, until there is a spirit of repentance among the believers.[105]

One of the commonest concerns among Evangelicals is whether such phenomena as have been seen recently can be justified from Scripture. Gerald Coates, director of Pioneer, believes that they can, despite some of Clifford Hill's reservations about laughter in particular. In August 1994 Gerald wrote:

One of the most frequently asked questions, particularly from conservative Evangelicals is 'Where is all this in the Bible?' They are of course referring to giggling and convulsive laughter, weeping and deep sobbing, shaking and trembling and people prostrate before the Lord or flat on their backs. The latter is sometimes accompanied by a feeling of a loss of control and an inability to get up. In the words of Jonathan Edwards 'bodily strength is withdrawn'. In other situations people are well able to get up, but feel it right to stay down.

There is plenty of biblical material covering all of these aspects, manifestations and reactions to the Spirit's presence. Some may regard biblical evidence for these manifestations as either slim or scarce. But it is well accepted, within biblical scholarship and evangelical circles, that the importance of an issue cannot be gauged by the number of times it is mentioned.

For example, 'born again' is only mentioned two or three times in the entire New Testament; the breaking of bread, again, is referred to on only a handful of occasions; dancing, while referred to by our Lord in terms of how people responded to his ministry (Lk 7:32) is nevertheless not mentioned in the Epistles.

But it is difficult to believe that in a culture where dancing on festive occasions was not only acceptable but promoted (see the Psalms!), that after the Messiah had come, forgiveness had been exercised, people groups had been reconciled and gifts of the Spirit had been poured out on people, they stopped dancing!

Before we look at some of the manifestations of the Spirit, or people responding to the Spirit, it should also be noted that the Bible is not given so that we can proof text everything. Most evangelical Christians are currently engaged in a wide range of activities for which there are no proof texts.

There are things God approves of in Scripture – we call them scriptural; there are things God disapproves of in Scripture – we call them unscriptural; but there are a lot of things that are plainly non-scriptural. The Bible is not a text book but a test book. We draw our experiences alongside Scripture to test them to see whether they are of God or not.

Things most Christians are involved in without much biblical data to support them include: church buildings, communion/Lord's supper (where people do not eat a meal or even talk with one another), the gospel preached to the converted at 6.30pm every Sunday evening, closing your eyes when you pray, sitting when you pray, saying 'grace' before meals, Sunday schools, youth clubs, women's meetings, and even a daily morning quiet time! That is not to say these things are wrong.

The point being made is that God wants us to grow up, and between those things he specifically approves of and others he specifically disapproves of, we are given liberty to develop a wide range of activities to broadly reflect things he approves of.

The same liberty applies to manifestations of the Holy Spirit, as well as reactions to the Holy Spirit (though it has been pointed out that even a manifestation is some kind of reaction to the presence and prompting of the Holy Spirit). Scripture gives more than sufficient evidence and endorsement for the following responses.

Trembling/shaking

'My flesh trembleth for fear of thee; and I am afraid of thy judgments' (Ps 119:120).

'Serve the Lord with fear and rejoice with trembling' (Ps 2:11).

The apostle Paul was deeply affected while with the mega-church in Corinth: 'I came to you in weakness and fear, and with much trembling' (1 Cor 2:3).

When Paul and Timothy wrote to the church in Philippi they told them: 'Work out your salvation with fear and trembling' (Phil 2:12).

Indeed (even in the Old Testament) the expected response from those who realised they were in the presence of God was clear. 'Should you not fear me?' declares the Lord. 'Should you not tremble in my presence?' (Jer 5:22).

Weeping

Interestingly, in our own church, Pioneer People (situated between Guildford and Kingston), we have had more weeping than laughing. In May 1990 it was prophesied that our church would be marked by weeping. This had not happened to any great extent prior to that time. The scripture around which this prophecy hung was: 'While Ezra was praying and confessing, weeping and throwing himself down before the house of God, a large crowd of Israelites – men, women and children – gathered round him. They too wept bitterly' (Ez 10:1).

Nehemiah, the Governor, and Ezra, the priest and scribe, along with the Levites actually discouraged the people: 'Do not mourn or weep,' they said (Neh 8:9). (There was no auto-suggestion here.)

Weeping is often a sign of maturity and sensitivity to our own personal sin or the needs around us. A compassionate heart is often marked by tears, even in the unconverted.

Tears of joy and gratitude were prophesied by Jeremiah when prophecy was to be fulfilled. 'They will come with weeping; they will pray as I bring them back. I will lead them beside streams of water on a level path where they will not stumble' (Jer 31:9).

Joel invites the people of God to return to God 'with fasting and weeping and mourning' (Joel 2:12).

John, Jesus' best friend, exiled on Patmos, gives future hope to the crushed and bereaved: 'He will wipe every tear from their eyes. There will be no more death or mourning or crying or pain, for the old order of things has passed away' (Rev 21:4).

Appearing drunk/trance-like

On the Day of Pentecost 120 people were filled with the Holy Spirit, spoke in tongues, made a noise, and as a result a crowd gathered. Some mocking observed, 'They have had too much wine' (Acts 2:13). Peter responded, 'These men are not drunk, as you suppose. It's only nine in the morning!' (Acts 2:15).

If you see a person speaking in a language other than their own, you don't assume they are drunk, rather that they are intelligent. So there was something about their behaviour that was so bizarre, out of the ordinary or unco-ordinated that led people to believe they were drunk.

Eli thought Hannah was drunk (1 Sam 1:13). Saul certainly appeared unusual (if not drunk) when he 'stripped off his robes … lay that way all that day and night' (1 Sam 19:24)

There are damaging effects on people who get drunk on alcohol (loss of self-control, violence). But other features include happiness, singing, laughter, generosity and warm affections. The Spirit of God would never lead us into a place where we are not responsible for our actions, or get physically violent. But we should note that many of the other features of drunkenness are positively encouraged in Scripture.

Convulsions

Most if not all references to do with convulsions have a demonic source. A man with an unclean spirit was silenced by our Lord, and the demon was commanded: 'Come out of him!' Mark records that this 'shook the man violently and came out of him with a shriek' (Mk 1:25-26).

Elsewhere Mark records that someone in the crowd spoke to Jesus about his son who was possessed with a spirit which made him mute. He added: 'Whenever it seizes him, it throws him to the ground. He foams at the mouth, gnashes his teeth and becomes rigid' (Mk 9:18).

That is why we need to be sure that we are operating in the name of Jesus, in the power of the Holy Spirit and of the word of God. We also need to ensure that wherever possible we are working in a team and we are not facing these issues on our own. The number of people who have been involved in the occult is considerable.

Laughter

Most Evangelicals are a little happier with tears than with

laughter, and I believe this is due to a completely wrong concept of reverence.

Laughter comes from heaven. 'The One enthroned in heaven laughs' (Ps 2:4). He laughs at the wicked as they come to judgement: 'The Lord laughs at the wicked, for he knows their day is coming' (Ps 37:13). Even the godly laugh at evil people: 'The righteous will see and fear; they will laugh at him' (Ps 52:6).

Jesus, giving prophetic kingdom teaching, declares: 'Blessed are you who weep now, for you will laugh' (Lk 6:21). It is possible our Lord was thinking of Psalm 126 written as a song of thanksgiving after the return from captivity: 'When the Lord brought back the captives to Zion, we were like men who dreamed. Our mouths were filled with laughter, our tongues with songs of joy. Then it was said among the nations, "The Lord has done great things for them." The Lord has done great things for us, and we are filled with joy' (Ps 126:1-3).

The *Oxford Dictionary* describes joy as 'vivid emotion of pleasure, gladness; a thing that causes delight'. The Bible has a great deal to say about joy in a wide range of situations.

The apostle Paul was not just joyful in tribulation – his joy knew no bounds (2 Cor 7:4). Being a Jew he was of course in good company. David wrote a prayer for rescue from his enemies: 'May those who delight in my vindication shout for joy and gladness; may they always say, "The Lord be exalted"' (Ps 35:27).

Perhaps most interestingly we have to ask: What is 'joy unspeakable' (1 Pet 1:8)? Indeed the mark of kingdom people is 'righteousness and peace and joy in the Holy Spirit'.

What is laughter? A joy that cannot be communicated with words.

Bodily strength diminished

This is in fact a phrase used by Jonathan Edwards, but the experience is found in Scripture.

Trembling (a partial withdrawing of strength as one might

find after an accident or traumatic experience) can also happen when there is a divine visitation (Ex 19:16) or angelic visitation (Mt 28:4), when people believe they have heard the voice of God (Mt 17:6), an individual has received a vision (Dan 8:27; 10:11); it could also have happened when Peter was having his noon-day prayers (Acts 10:10).

It certainly happened when Jesus made himself known to what could have been 600 men, a battalion of the Roman cohort (Jn 18:6).

Those travelling with Saul to arrest the followers of Christ having seen the light from heaven 'stood there speechless' while Saul 'could see nothing' (Acts 9:7-8).

All of this indicates a partial or full withdrawal of physical strength.

Given that Scripture is not there as a proof text for everything, the above is a mere selection of incidents and happenings which are worthy of closer study. I would like to suggest that readers do word studies on tears and crying, laughter and joy and the issues raised in these guidelines.

Nevertheless, we need to emphasise the fruit of these phenomena and make room in both public and private meetings for people to share what Christ has done for them.

A trained psychotherapist told a friend of mine that she was not yet a Christian, but that she and her colleagues would give their 'right arm' to see in their surgeries what was happening in his church building. She added, 'It takes us two or three years to get people to this place,' and she could see it was happening in twenty to thirty minutes and sometimes even two or three minutes! She concluded that it was very healthy.

While it is inevitable that there will be those who simply look for experiences (these are a lot less damaging than some things Christian adults have been involved in), we should focus on where Christ is at work, with or without manifestations.[106]

(For a fuller biblical basis see Appendix on page 297.)

Dr Derek Munday is an experienced general practitioner and the leader of a national British association of Christian charismatic doctors and nurses called CiCP (Christians in Caring Professions). In September 1994 he wrote:

It is a problem being a doctor because we always carry a burden of scepticism and questioning. Many in the professions are not used to accepting things at face value. Instead we dig to search for truth, recognising that things are not always what they seem.

Some of us have had to deal with Christians who have claimed healing when it has not occurred or have been living in unreality claiming some spiritual revelation, experience or call from God which does not seem to match up with reality. It is easy to become sceptical.

At a time like this, when things are happening in the churches (some of which are rather bizarre), it is easy to become cynical. We do well to remember that God has always broken out of traditions.

When one of the most significant events of the Christian Church occurred, ie the Day of Pentecost, it was marked by such bizarre behaviour that everyone around thought that the Christians were drunk. To our western minds that seems an extraordinary way to launch such an overwhelmingly important event as the founding of the Church. However, God's thinking is different. The Bible says that the foolishness of God is wiser than the wisdom of men.

We must also be careful about going to the opposite extreme of credulity. Satan has a very simple scheme for deceiving men and women. He tries with all his power to stop them coming to a knowledge of the truth.

If, however, he fails and they do come to know God, then he will try with all his might to distort truth or overemphasise one aspect and turn it into a parody of what it should be. Wherever there is a move of the Spirit, Satan will seek to move as well. There will be fleshly imitations. We need to seek the wisdom of God to know what is of God and what is not.

We must be those who have the word of God at the centre of our lives. We must understand it. We must live by its teaching. We must measure everything – every experience, every prophecy, every new movement – by what we see written here. God's truth is God's truth. It will not stretch or alter to fit in with the prevailing pattern and thoughts of society. Rather the opposite should happen. Society must take its foundation and basis from the word of God.[107]

However, some have even suggested that the recent phenomena are not only unbiblical, but may also be demonic. In London's Evangelical Library recently I found a tract by Alan Morrison of Crich, Derbyshire entitled *We all Fall Down*. Prompted by the recent headlines he wrote a severe criticism of the movement in August 1994 concerning the experience of so-called being 'slain in the Spirit', dismissing it as nothing less than evil, linked to possession in previous ages and hypnotism as discovered in the eighteenth century by the Austrian physician, Franz Anton Mesmer (1734-1815).

Some [of his] patients felt nothing at all, some felt as if insects were crawling over them, others were seized with hysterical laughter, convulsions or fits of hiccups. Some went into raging delirium, which was called 'The Crisis' ... There is an inescapable comparison here with the phenomena which have so bewitched numerous churches today.

...In contrast with the signs of a genuine Christian revival, we find that being 'Slain in the Spirit' results in a sensual yearning for psycho-religious experiences which then takes precedence over Christian spirituality and leads to a rejection of biblical revelation.

...To credit this occult experience to the work of the Holy Spirit is as close to blasphemy as one can get.[108]

Seraphim Rose wrote in 1979:

> It is only foolishness when some 'charismatic' apologists presume to compare these childish and hysterical experiences, which are open to absolutely everyone, with the Divine revelations accorded to the greatest Saints, such as St. Paul on the road to Damascus or to St. John the Evangelist on Patmos. Those Saints fell down before the true God (without contortions, and certainly without laughter), whereas these pseudo-Christians are merely reacting to the presence of an invading spirit, and are worshipping only themselves.
>
> If these 'charismatic' experiences are religious experiences at all, then they are pagan religious experiences; and in fact they seem to correspond exactly to the mediumistic initiation experience of spirit-possession, which is caused by an 'inner force welling up inside attempting to take control'.
>
> ...What is involved in these experiences – when they are genuine and not merely the product of suggestion – is not merely the development of mediumistic ability, but actual possession by a spirit. These people would seem to be correct in calling themselves 'spirit-filled' – but it is certainly not the Holy Spirit with which they are filled![109]

One angry dissident wrote in the *Church of England Newspaper*:

> It takes a form which is not found anywhere in Scripture; it is supported by verses taken out of context; it is offered in isolation, for its own sake, apart from any proclamation of the Cross of Christ and its purpose is to give those who receive it a feeling of peace.   Notwithstanding the affection and respect I have for many of the people who claim to have been blessed by this phenomenon, I still believe it bears all the hallmarks of a massive spiritual con.
>
> At best, it might be mass suggestion in which the emotional

is being mistaken for the spiritual; at worst, it could be the work of the deceiver, luring Christians away from reliance on God's word to seek signs and assurance in spectacular and bizarre experiences.[110]

Canon John Young, York Diocesan Evangelist and a member of General Synod, also wrote some reflections in the *Church of England Newspaper* following a visit to a Vineyard church in the UK.

The Bible describes some remarkable phenomena. We should not be surprised if the Spirit sometimes does a new thing among us. Nor should we be surprised if he repeats an old thing.

But the New Testament warns us that some new things can lead us down false tracks. We can easily be 'tossed back and forth like the waves, and blown here and there by every wind of teaching' (Ephesians 4:14).   There is more about crying than laughing in the New Testament.

I would distinguish rejoicing from laughing, while not doubting that the latter can express the former. And I continue to worry about hysteria. The New Testament letters while encouraging spiritual gifts, are very keen on orderly practice. The organisers of that Vineyard evening were in danger of ignoring Colossians 2:5: 'I delight to see how orderly you are.'

The invitation to receive ministry at the meeting was sensitively made. Those who wished to observe were asked to stand at the back; those who ministered were instructed to pray for 'more power' – nothing more. There was no conscious manipulation and there was no physical force. I have known 'slaying in the Spirit' to be accompanied by a hefty push! Not so here. Yet there was a psychological preparation which made ensuing phenomena likely.

Many people had come some long distances expecting such occurrences. Of course we can look back to the preaching of Jonathan Edwards – who was mentioned more than once – and others, which was accompanied by remarkable phenomena. But my understanding, perhaps wrong, is that this took place as he preached, not in a 'time of ministry' during which the chairs were cleared and the congregation stood, or lay on the ground. Much of the behaviour which I observed was bizarre and some was very noisy....

The speaker said, more than once, that the phenomena were unimportant. What really counts, he assured us, is whether we are drawn closer to Jesus. I'm very glad that he said this, but the medium was the message and any enquirers present, including Christians, were likely to focus on bizarre behaviour rather than on the death and resurrection of Jesus.

We are told to 'test the spirits'. One way of doing this is to develop and use one's Christian instinct and antennae – hopelessly subjective perhaps. Of course, the ultimate test is whether we say, 'Jesus is Lord.' But lips don't always express hearts.

I have arrived at a tentative conclusion following a lengthy conversation with a sympathetic and astute evangelical Anglican leader. Perhaps what we are observing is fundamentally a psychological phenomenon.

Get a group of people together, create a sense of expectancy, make suggestions about likely behaviour, clear a large space, move among them, and something like this is likely to happen. Some Hindus will walk on fire and levitate; some Muslims will speak in tongues and dance in ecstasy; some Christians will laugh and fall to the ground.

People are suggestible. We are not observing the work of the devil, though the leaders would be wise not to put too much stress on roaring like a lion (see 1 Peter 5:8)! Nor is this – as some leaders claim – a great outpouring of God's Spirit in revival. It is a movement which fits well into our secular and superstitious age which will believe pretty well anything, from energy pyramids to laughing in the Spirit.

Many humble souls, trusting the leaders and wishing to follow Christ more closely, will be renewed and inspired by the

Spirit. But others may be damaged; not only those who are suggestible or unstable, but some of those who 'feel nothing' and fear that they are being by-passed by God.

Tom Smail, whose charismatic credentials are pretty good (was he not Director of the Fountain Trust?), once said that spiritual gifts in most congregations are about 20 per cent of the Spirit and 80 per cent self-induced.

This is not to say that 80 per cent of those involved are wicked deceivers; it is to accept that we should not too readily discern the hand of God in the extraordinary. He is to be found in the ordinary too. I seem to remember something about a still, small voice as well as the wind and fire of Pentecost.

Meanwhile, let us honour one another – most motives are mixed and 'we all make many mistakes' (James 3:2, RSV). But I note a deep sincerity about all this. And at least it speaks of life. Perhaps the ultimate heresy is dead orthodoxy and that is one trap that the Toronto devotees certainly do not fall into! Above all, let us 'make every effort to keep the unity of the Spirit through the bond of peace' (Ephesians 4:3) and 'count others better than ourselves'.[111]

So then, over the last few hundred years many have struggled to make sense of their experience and that of others. There is clearly overwhelming evidence that emotional faith and physical manifestations are a normal, recurring part of historic Christian faith since the Day of Pentecost, and that many consider there is more than adequate justification for many of the phenomena in the Bible.

Despite this, even those most sympathetic to the current phenomena in 1994 and beyond, are deeply puzzled or concerned about some of the more bizarre manifestations – for example, animal noises in meetings. These have been attributed variously to emotional excess, demonic influence or the work of the Holy Spirit, either as a prophetic statement (eg, lions roaring) or just in order to humble sophisticated people obsessed about preserving their 'respectable' self-image.

I want to turn now to look at the link between spiritual experience and the way our bodies and minds function. It is clear that body, mind and spirit affect each other in many different ways. I also want to look particularly at laughter from the medical point of view, since many Christians have been puzzled as to why such a thing should be a gift from God.

5
Medical Perspectives on Manifestations

The big question in many people's minds is whether what we have been seeing is just emotion. We have seen how the accusation of hysteria has been brought against enthusiastic Christians for nearly twenty centuries. We have also seen how these manifestations seem to be infectious, suggesting that people influence each other. I now want to look at the way medical research over the last few years has given us a better understanding of some of the manifestations we are seeing today. These thoughts need to be read in the light of the previous chapter in particular.

Since so much attention has been focused on the 'new' phenomenon of laughter, I want to look first at the nature of laughter in more detail, and contrast it with crying. Then we need to look at the possibility of auto-suggestion, hysteria and crowd phenomena being responsible for some of the effects on people's minds and bodies. Finally, I want to look at how many things, including prayer, fasting and speaking in tongues, can affect our conscious state, allowing us to become more or less aware of a spiritual dimension to living, and how altered states of consciousness are produced in Christian experience, and are a normal part of charismatic faith.

Laughter

People often say that laughter is the best medicine. But why? Laughter is a God-given part of human design. Laughter or laughing is mentioned thirty-nine times in the Bible. As the writer of Ecclesiastes notes, there is 'a time to weep, and a time to laugh' (Ecc 3:4). So what do we conclude when people seem to be laughing far more than usual? Or when they cannot laugh but want to? Or when they start laughing and cannot stop?

In researching this book I employed computer technology to trawl through 5 million summaries of medical research papers published in every language since the mid-1960s. There are a couple of hundred on laughter. Mostly they are about pathological laughter, spontaneous inappropriate laughter triggered by epilepsy, brain tumours or other brain disease. These kinds of laughter are very rare, and are not to be confused with the current epidemic of laughter among normal men and women who have attended church meetings. So what do we know about laughter in general?

The first thing to note is that some people hardly seem to laugh at all. Everything is taken seriously. Such people are hard to live with and often have a tendency to be morose or depressed. The reason why so many people look for others who have 'a sense of humour' is that the ability to see the absurd, the ridiculous and the entertaining in the serious and the trivial is something that keeps us mentally stable and healthy.

For someone tensed up in an ultra-serious frame of mind, heavily burdened by cares and responsibilities, worn down by overwork, grief and suffering, laughter can come as a great flood of relief. Great gulping paroxysms of wonderful, releasing laughter are a marvellous tonic.

Someone who can never laugh is as emotionally

imprisoned as someone who can never cry. As the Bible says, there is a time for both. Each emotion is found towards the extremes of elation and sadness. It is true that some of us oscillate in mood more than others, while a number are very level headed. It is also true that pushed beyond the normal limits, elation becomes euphoria and finally mania, while sadness becomes melancholy and finally depression.

But excitement in the presence of God does not produce mania any more than awareness of sin produces clinical depression. Religion is often blamed for mental instability because those who are mentally ill frequently mix whatever they believe about life into their distorted thinking.

For example, a Christian who becomes depressed – perhaps through a hormone imbalance or another reason – may become pathologically convinced that he or she has committed some unpardonable sin. A Christian who has a chemical imbalance in the brain may become convinced he is seeing angels and demons – in fact he is hallucinating. This is not to be confused with demon possession (a very big subject) because once given special tablets to restore the normal neurotransmitter balance in the brain (special substances which transmit information between touching nerves), the person returns to normal. Demons do not respond to medication.

Enthusiastic faith does not send people mad, nor damage them psychologically, so long as it is balanced, biblical, Jesus-centred faith, rooted in a worshipping community. Time after time I have seen people who have been on the edge of serious mental illness completely recover through discovering the love of God for themselves.

So what about laughter? What role does it have in mental stability and health? Doctors and nurses are now realising that laughter is a powerful way to reduce tension and stress, creating a sense of well being, increasing contentment and alertness, helping us place the problems and difficulties of life in context. Many research papers have been published recently suggesting that doctors and nurses should learn how to make their patients laugh in order to help them get better.

The actual mechanism of laughing affects the whole body profoundly. For example, it alters the levels of various 'stress' hormones such as cortisol, dopamine, adrenaline and growth hormone – all hormones released when we are tense, working hard, worried or afraid. They are all part of the 'fight or flight reaction', released to prime the body for instant aggressive action. They enable us to overcome an attacker, or to sprint 300 yards from him! In typical office stress, all the hormones are released but no exercise follows and the body suffers. We develop stomach ulcers, our arteries clog up, we become irritable and develop a host of other problems – all because the body is pumping out hormones we don't need.

Laughter shuts down these hormone levels, keeping them low. Laughter helps prevent some of the damage that stress causes to us. Not surprisingly it also makes us feel more relaxed. Interestingly, endorphin levels seem to remain the same (natural morphine-like substances).[112]

Laughter is almost always a positive and beneficial thing.[113] We learn to laugh at four months of age, something which requires the action of fifteen facial muscles and changes in breathing. When we laugh, at first the heart rate rises as does the rate of breathing. After laughter subsides there is a period of relaxation, easing muscle tension, useful in breaking the muscle spasm in some neuralgias and rheumatism.

Laughter also aids lung ventilation, helping people with chest problems to clear mucus, although hearty laughter can make asthmatics wheeze. It can also (very rarely indeed), if severe enough, induce a heart attack or a stroke.[114] Extreme laughter gives the body exercise. Laughter also improves alertness and memory.[115]

If laughter does things to our brains, so does crying, and having a good cry can be very good for us too. Sometimes sad things happen to us, but we have no room to cry, either because our self-image prevents us, or because quite simply we were too preoccupied at the time. A doctor attending a serious traffic accident may cry later when the crisis is over. A mother nursing a dying child may have many tears, or she may find they only come fully after the end has come.

Sometimes we may be watching a film or singing in a church meeting, and for what seems like no reason at all we are deeply moved and our eyes fill with tears. Often what is happening is that the situation has triggered off deeply-rooted emotion, opening a floodgate, and out it comes. All the things we could have cried over before but did not are now welling up to the surface in a most healthy way.

This is normal. Indeed those who constantly stuff away sad feelings can find later that the pressure builds up so much that when another sad thing happens life seems to cave in altogether and they have a breakdown. So then, finding ourselves in tears should not surprise us.

Does this mean that we should regard someone who breaks down in a service, apparently overcome with a fresh realisation of sin, as just someone grieving over a past loss? Of course not. Such feelings are genuine and must be taken at face value, recognising however that if the same person is continually in a state over the same thing, then we may need to ask some questions. What are these tears really about?

This is a difficult area. After all, many people become Christians at a time of personal crisis and upheaval. Do we dismiss the feelings they have about God because of their situations? I hope not. Rather, we take the view that perhaps it has taken a series of unfortunate circumstances to cause them to stop and think about the future, the meaning and purpose of life, and what they are going to do about it all. The test is whether there is a lasting change.

If these things are true of tears, then they are true in a parallel way for laughter. Laughter is a releasing emotion. It affects the whole functioning of our brains. Feelings of elation in the presence of God may well be related to other factors, such as good news at home, falling in love, passing an exam, getting a new job, the birth of a child. That does not in any way lessen the validity of the joy in the presence of God. Indeed those circumstances become part of the celebration of life and of God's goodness.

Now a conflict can come if some in a congregation are out of cycle with others. For example, if two people walk into church whose husbands or wives have died recently, and all the others around seem to be joyfully singing, laughing and clapping, they may feel even more miserable and isolated. Some immature Christians can make things far worse with comments about the command to 'rejoice in all things', or 'He's with Jesus – isn't that wonderful?', failing entirely to understand that the nature of grief is the feeling of personal loss for those left behind. Jesus wept too – and we are told to weep with those who weep.

Then there is the other extreme, where we are so sensitive to the sadness of others – and there are always some in a large church who are grieving or going through tremendous suffering – that the whole church tiptoes around as if treading on egg shells, trying not to upset or offend, putting the lid on joy.

While being in God's presence can open the door for us to

express hidden sadness and joy, it is also the experience of many that God steps in sometimes to give us a joy beyond logic or rational understanding at a time of great pressure. After all, joy is part of the fruit of the Holy Spirit, closely linked to peace, the lifting of anxiety and worry (Gal 5:22).

If need be, God sometimes takes the opposite approach with us to knock us off a perch of self-satisfied contentment and mild euphoria until we reach the depths, where we understand our own depravity and sinfulness.

Some still say they have a big problem with 'holy laughter'. They can cope with joy as a gift from God, but not laughter. However, in that case we do need to ask what a massive gift of joy will feel like, particularly if it arrives at the same time as a big dose of peace, kindness, goodness and the rest. The result is surely a mental state beyond words; a sublime, inexpressible feeling of wonderful elation and lightness of burden, of release, of encouragement, of relief. And many laugh with relief. It is a natural response to lifting tension.

Laughter can be a final stage in the loss of awareness of immediate problems. It is hard to roar with convulsive laughter when you are consciously aware of an imminent disaster. Many people I have talked to who have recently found themselves laughing for long periods have told me that they felt an overwhelming sense of God's love and of relief, as if a massive weight of cares had been lifted away. People are laughing because they are happy. What is so wrong about that? And why shouldn't God want to see his children laugh? After all, a human father also enjoys seeing his children laughing away and having fun.

What about disturbance? It is also true that another fruit of the Spirit is self-control. Sometimes this can be confusing because if God seems to have given a wonderful gift of laughter to you, it is easy to feel that self-control to shut it all down again may not be the kind of self-control God wants, but just the old self-conscious adult brain wanting to take charge again before being made to look foolish.

The same is true of crying. Clearly someone deeply touched by God during preaching may begin to weep. What if the person is under deep conviction of sin, and crying out to God for salvation? Do we tell the person to shut up? That, of course, was Wesley's great dilemma.

Incidentally, Wesley would be hounded out of the country today. He would have no peace at all, inside or outside the churches, because of his message. Although he rarely preached directly about judgement and hell, the message people understood was seen in such vivid pictures that people were literally crying out in terrible distress and fright. When he talked of the forgiveness of God through the atoning death of Jesus, people were already dropping to their knees – no need to wait for an altar call at the end.

I have read accounts of children too afraid even to sleep – in great distress until they had found peace through faith in Jesus Christ. What would social workers and the media say about that sort of thing today? Yet Jesus talked often of judgement and Peter followed suit on the Day of Pentecost.

Getting the balance right between shutting all emotion down and total anarchy can be difficult and messy, but a way through *can* be found, as some of the guidelines at the back of this book reveal.

One thing is certain: human beings are emotional creatures, even if some cultures recognise it more than others (the British being notorious for suppression and inhibition). Living faith that leaves us emotionally untouched is a faith in the mind only, a mental assent process that has failed to touch the depths of our being. The church in Laodicea was harshly criticised for being lukewarm: neither enthusiastic nor apathetic, just plodding on from day to day. Enthusiastic faith is not an option, therefore; it is a command: we are to love God with all our hearts as well as our minds and our souls.

So then, we have seen that emotions are a normal part of the Christian life, and laughter is a part of that – so long as it is not mocking laughter at anything or anyone (except our spiritual enemy), and so long as it is not misused in a way that brings chaos and disorder. However, that is in some measure a responsibility of those who lead the meetings, in the way they direct proceedings, curbing excesses yet allowing people to respond to the promptings of the Holy Spirit.

Hysteria and other possibilities

But what about the serious charge that some of the meetings where emotional scenes are taking place are being manipulated by leaders, consciously or unconsciously, by their own actions? Is it possible that people are being reduced to a semi-hypnotic state; that mass hysteria is taking place or some other physical or psychological phenomenon?

Much of the medical literature on the subject is very negative for the simple reason that it is written by people without faith. Atheists have a fundamental problem when trying to make sense of religious experience. They cannot do so because it makes no sense to them, and they have no options by way of explanations but to rule out any possibility of divine influence or interference. For them the world is a neat closed system. The only explanations available are based on psychology or physiology. Their minds, by definition, are closed by the decision they have already made about the non-existence of God.

Christians, on the other hand, have a wide range of explanations they can draw from. They can attribute any situation to divine intervention, to psychological or physiologial factors, or even perhaps to the forces of darkness, demonic in origin. Christians may also reach a mixed conclusion, deciding that several factors may be at play to varying degrees, without an obsessive need to have to work it all out precisely. Indeed, the experiences of 1994 revealed how difficult it was to work out what was going on in an individual until after the manifestation was over.

It is important to recognise this bias of atheism. It is the reason why so many books on psychology and religion are so mechanistic and condescending about faith. After all, to concede even an inch of ground would mean acknowledging the possible existence of God.

Surprisingly few studies of psychology and religion have been made. It is one of the least researched areas of medicine. I ransacked the shelves of one of the largest medical school libraries in the country, pulling out every large book I could find on the workings of the mind and emotions. There was hardly a mention of belief in any of them. I also scanned 1.6 million research papers on a medical database and found a meagre handful on any aspect of religion and medicine or psychology or sociology – and many of those were on ethical debates, for example over homosexuality.

Perhaps that is partly why the book *Battle for the Mind* had such an impact when it was published in 1957. Written by William Sargant, Consultant Psychiatrist at St Thomas' Hospital, it claimed a common link between First World War shell-shock victims, converts to Christianity and brain-washing techniques.

Sargant noted that some soldiers returned from battle so

traumatised that they could hardly utter a word about their experiences. Trapped in an emotional prison they were profoundly handicapped in normal life. One controversial method of treatment was to drug them so they lost all inhibitions and felt relaxed enough to communicate what had happened. Often there was a massive flood of intense emotion released, after which the person recovered. He also found that if he could release massive emotion, the person could recover even though he had not fully talked about the past. The process was called not a reaction but an abreaction. Encouraging such a violent discharge of sudden emotion remains controversial today.

The changes in mental state were so great they were almost like a conversion experience. One day Sargant began to read about Wesley and felt that the descriptions of people crying out, falling down, and converting to faith had some similarities to his experience with the soldiers. Perhaps these things were having two effects: first, a release of suppressed feelings could in some circumstances be helpful in itself. Secondly, Sargant observed that after such an abreaction some people remained in a highly suggestible state, where thoughts could be suggested to them which seemed later to have become permanently part of their thinking.

The more he read, and the more he observed, the more he became convinced that severe emotional stress or sensory overload could completely alter brain function, brainwashing people from one view to another – permanently. This, he suggested, was the basis of torture (occasionally producing political conversions), religious cults, Christian conversions and a host of other things.

This suggestion was nothing new. In 1903, William James had written *The Varieties of Religious Experience*, a highly influential book in which he said:

Emotional occasions, especially violent ones, are extremely potent in precipitating mental rearrangements. The sudden and explosive ways in which love, jealousy, guilt, fear, remorse or anger can seize upon one are known to everybody. Hope, happiness, security, resolve, emotions characteristic of conversion, can be equally explosive. And emotions that come in this explosive way seldom leave things as they found them.[116]

Anyone who has been present at some of the meetings in 1994 will appreciate some striking similarities in a few who shout violently or cry out or otherwise express a sudden emotional outburst. So we need to follow this avenue through carefully before dismissing it prematurely as irrelevant.

Sargant researched a number of tribal religions still around in the 1940s and 1950s and discovered common features, such as rhythmic drum beats, ritual dances to the point of exhaustion, use of mind-altering substances, strong group identity and powerful suggestion from leaders and so on. He suggested that all conversions were influenced by their brainwashing techniques.

His book had a major influence. In a country like the UK where there is an innate mistrust of emotion in many people anyway, it fed people what they expected to hear. Even today you hear the ideas rumbling on, as a criticism of almost every aspect of modernising church culture.

For example, a band with a drum kit or a bass guitar might be affecting behaviour, repetitive chorus singing could be dangerous as well as mentally facile. And as for dancing during a time of worship – not only was it almost scandalous by being irreverent (despite the fact that King David danced before the Lord, and his psalms command us to dance), but also it might arouse dangerous suggestibility.

The problem with Sargant's work is that like most psychiatric theories it was based on little more than personal observation, a few anecdotes and a hunch, overlaid with a massive bias of his own personal beliefs or lack of them.

We had the same problem with Freud. No other individual in the last 150 years has so dominated thinking about the workings of our emotions for so long. Yet all his theories have come crashing to the ground because when challenged it is impossible to find any proper scientific basis for them. His writings are little more than a personal collection of observations and opinions.

Likewise, *Battle for the Mind* is a superficial and rather inadequate view of Christian experience, as we will see later. Sargant reveals a very limited understanding of the process of conversion. There is no crisis at all in the majority of cases, yet the transformation is huge and often permanent.

The other weakness in his argument is in the supposed power of music and beat to help alter the mind permanently. If only it were that simple – evangelists would be out of a job! Supermarkets play soft music to try and relax us, and dance venues play loud music with a hard beat to make us dance, but neither has any effect beyond the mood of the moment. Neither supermarket music nor a rock concert is likely to change your life or your choices at the time. Nor is a gospel choir or the best Christian band in the world likely to bend people's minds either.

Sargant said: 'Electrical recordings of the human brain show that it is particularly sensitive to rhythmic stimulation by percussion and bright lights among other things, and certain rates of rhythm can build up abnormalities of brain function and explosive states of tension sufficient even to produce epileptic fits in predisposed subjects.'

But what is the evidence? It is certainly true that a strobe at a disco flickering at a rate of around eight flashes per second will induce fits quite quickly in some people, and some computer games may have had the same effect on some subjects for the same reasons, but these are rare exceptions. Music alone does not produce fits in people who go to dance halls or raves, in the absence of other factors like drug abuse.

It is frankly absurd to suggest, as he has done, that the reason for changed attitudes among young people in the 1960s was because of brainwashing by rock music. If so, then all a communist state would have to do is play dance music to win national obedience.

It is true that at various times in history you can find people who work themselves up into a manic frenzy of dancing, with drums beating, usually using drugs or alcohol as well to heighten excitement, continued to the state of nervous exhaustion and collapse. However, that is not a common Christian experience! It is not recognisable as a description of charismatic worship. Induction of such a state requires a massive expenditure of energy for a long period, equivalent to running hundreds of yards at high speed.

However, I have seen one or two extreme manifestations, with particularly violent or vigorous physical activity over a long period (more than a minute or two), which could certainly have the potential to drive someone to a state of complete nervous exhaustion or help to induce an altered state of consciousness (an ASC – see below).

It is true, for example, that patterns of drumming such as those practised in voodoo can alter a mental state, but here you are talking of an extreme situation with extreme fear of 'the power' and, many Christians would say, a spiritual (occult) dimension as well.

The problem for Sargant is that his theory just does not fit with general experience. While his understanding of traditional torture and brainwashing techniques is helpful for some extreme situations of war or religious cults, it does not help us with the current manifestations.

The 1994 manifestations are happening often in a room which starts off silent, after minimal low-key worship and a bland, non-emotional talk. People fall over – not out of manic exhaustion, but with a sense of weakness. Brainwashing theories will not do. Nor will theories that people are converted through a mass hysteria or hypnosis effect.

I can accept, however, that the style of worship in some Vineyard meetings could slightly predispose some to a very mild hypnotic effect. The music is often gentle, almost soporific. But then so is Gregorian chanting in an ancient cathedral, or the chanting of a long metricated psalm.

We cannot easily attribute manifestations to a particular style of meeting or to the effects of music – for one simple reason. I have seen identical manifestations develop in a near identical way in meetings large, small and tiny, hyped up or low key, silent or noisy, strongly led or with an absence of clear direction, after worship or with no music at all.

Simplistic explanations just will not do. What we are seeing are highly complex phenomena of varying kinds, caused by a variety of different factors, often mixed together, in people of different backgrounds, different expectations, different histories and different personalities. Therefore the results can be confusing.

One of the biggest problems with Sargant's work is that his thesis stands or falls to a large extent on his stereotyped view of conversion. But despite the impression given by Sargant, the fact is that more than two-thirds of conversions are gradual, not as a result of a crisis, and certainly not ones that can possibly be attributable to 'brainwashing' in highly emotionally charged meetings.

A report published on 29th October 1992 ('Finding Faith Today', Bible Society) showed that most adults find God through the help of a friend, relative or minister. Only 4% are converted at rallies or special meetings. The most effective method of all is from one partner to the other, especially women to men. Hardly brainwashing.

Canon John Finney, author of the report and the Church of England officer for the Decade of Evangelism, said: 'All those surveyed felt more integrated as human beings because they had become Christians.'[117]

The reason why over a million new people every month become Christians is because they become convinced, step by step, that the claims of Jesus make sense as they check them out in the Bible, in the light of the life-changing faith they see in their friends, and the love they see in the church.

So friendship with someone who believes is more effective than a powerful meeting. Indeed, in the churches I am a part of, new believers and enquirers are often encouraged more to attend Bible studies in people's own homes rather than come to big noisy meetings, which many find hard to cope with at first.

People complain about emotional church meetings, saying that emotion is infectious and manipulative of others. It is true that all emotions can be temporarily affecting and we will return to that. But faith spread one to one is permanently catching.

So Sargant may be right when looking at the extremes of religious cults, with mind-bending rituals and total submersion in a strange culture at a time of emotional crisis, but that is simply not the explanation for the rapid growth of the tens of thousands of charismatic evangelical churches worldwide.

However, Sargant may help us to understand one or two of the more extreme and sudden emotional outbursts in meetings, and the beneficial cathartic effect when some people 'roar their heads off', weep, groan, shout or otherwise discharge pent-up emotion.

If we leave the issue of conversion, what about these short-lived strange behaviours, such as laughter and falling over, that start up in meetings and usually finish before the person leaves or shortly after, beginning in waves as they spread across a church or an area?

We have already seen beyond the shadow of any doubt that all these phenomena are such a common feature of 'lively Christianity', revival, renewal, awakenings, call it what you will, that it is hard to see how the current explosion of church growth worldwide could possibly take place without them. But why do they happen?

Many believers are happy with God-centred explanations such as, 'It is the move of God's Holy Spirit,' or, 'Just a repeat of Pentecost,' or, 'God is sovereign – he can do what he likes,' or, 'God has chosen what the world counts folly rather than what the world counts as wise.' However, for many others that could just be ducking the issue. Even if all those things are true, is it not possible or inevitable that imperfect human beings will get in the way?

The first thing to acknowledge is that all behaviour patterns are infectious. Take a look next time you sit in a circle around a room. Look at what people are doing with their legs or arms. If one person crosses their legs, there is an increased statistical probability that another will do so very soon. It is part of our social conditioning.

We are all sensitive to group identity. Although we retain individuality we pick up cues from each other which help us to behave in a way appropriate to the group we are with. So, for example, we are naturally inhibited from telling a loud joke at a funeral, and tend to feel happy when surrounded by reasonably cheerful people. We all give off 'atmosphere', which is why people often complain of the bad atmosphere at work. It is the collective mood, if you like, which builds us up or grinds us down.

The same factors operate in any church meeting. In a quiet traditional communion service a mother is likely to be on edge with a fractious toddler who wants to shout and laugh or run up and down the aisle. She may want to sing her heart out, full of joy at what God has done, yet has to keep her voice down and her body still in case others are distracted and think she is a little odd. She might want to have 'a good cry', but feels that she has to bottle it all up until she goes home.

Likewise, in a large charismatic celebration when everyone is clapping and swaying to the music, a believer who would in all sincerity prefer to be quietly kneeling in contemplative prayer may feel under tremendous pressure to clap along to the beat instead, and may do so.

Thus every church service has its own culture, and almost all cultures are very dominating and powerful, providing clear signals about the limits of what is acceptable and proper. Almost every person will try hard to conform, even those with no faith at all, blending into whatever kind of church they happen to be sitting or standing in.

Indeed, one of the stressful things about being in some meetings where manifestations have taken place has been confusing signals about how to behave. The boundary posts about what is acceptable or unacceptable have changed in some churches within a week! Last week someone yelling and thrashing about might have been asked to be quiet or quickly escorted out. This week someone has just explained from the front that many strange things may break out shortly throughout the congregation, but we are to be relaxed about it all because God is at work.

Last week someone giggling or laughing raucously might have been asked not to interrupt the speaker, particularly if it had happened the previous week as well. This week, as soon as ten people start laughing, the speaker, instead of frowning, starts to find the situation amusing also.

This raises another issue. When these manifestations are about to break out – you know a number of individuals in the church have already been affected and Sunday is drawing near – do you say nothing to warn the church and then have to cope with a shell-shocked congregation who have no idea what has hit them? Or do you risk accusations of auto-suggestion and explain to people something of what has already been happening and give some clear biblical teaching so that human experience becomes subject to a scriptural yardstick?

The fact is that in many cases the manifestations have only broken out after someone has got up to speak, explaining in some detail about what has happened to them, what is happening elsewhere and what might happen to people present if they are open to God. And even then in many situations the manifestations have only begun after a specific time has been set aside expressly for the purpose of praying for people to be touched by God with the expectation that a number will experience them.

Clearly both suggestion and pressure can be operating in such a situation. The degree to which that is significant as an explanation of some of what happens to some people will depend of course entirely upon the atmosphere, the way in which things are communicated, the words and attitude of the ministry team as they pray for individuals, and a host of other variables.

However, if a leader says that in the last three churches he or she has spoken at, there have been some mooing like cows, others crying 'cock-a-doodle-doo', and barking like dogs, without any comment about the merits or otherwise of such behaviour or whether it is of God, the flesh or the devil, is it any surprise if another begins to miaow like a cat or neigh like a horse?

How much we worry about the possibility of 'suggestion' will depend largely on whether we rate any of these manifestations and related experiences as positive or not. If they are regarded on the whole as helpful and healthy, and we want to encourage them without being manipulative, then it will matter far less. If we regard some manifestations as very unhelpful, distracting and destructive, then we will want to be very careful indeed not to act in any way which might appear to promote them.

I must stress that it is clear to me that we are dealing with a very mixed picture. You can arrive in a church one week and suggest what you like and probably nothing will happen at all unless God is present and affecting people by the Holy Spirit. However, you could be in another situation where God is clearly touching people and by a turn of phrase or a word of encouragement or direction make a particular manifestation many times more likely. This imposes a grave responsibility on those leading such a meeting and on those who speak about such things. We need to choose our words with care, bringing the central attention onto the person of Jesus in all things.

If we say that there may be some scriptural parallels with intoxication or drunkenness, and some present are euphoric, disinhibited and in a suggestible state, then more or less any kind of behaviour could be sparked off, either by a word from the front or by the various behaviours of others in the same meeting. I am not saying that these things are happening often, or in all cases. I am simply saying that these are all things we need to be aware of.

Some people react to pressure and make a deliberate point of not conforming, perhaps concerned about integrity, wanting to be the same wherever they are. I can remember a time in a meeting almost twenty years ago in a barn near Cambridge where I was called up (against my better judgement) with a group of friends I had gone with. The speaker prayed for us all in a line, having explained that we would fall over. I did not, despite firm pressure on my forehead which meant I had to work hard to resist. The speaker became angry with one woman because she was 'resisting the Holy Spirit'. What nonsense!

This was a total abuse of power and it backfired badly. It was a charade and very foolish, for years putting me off any kind of meeting where such things were taking place, as well as causing cynicism in others. Some of those who fell over just let themselves fall because they were too embarrassed to do anything else. I say this to show that even where pressure and suggestion are at their most extreme, we are still free spirits. A small minority may yield control in some way to whoever is attempting to abuse power, but the majority will not. Incidentally, I have not seen anything remotely near such abuse in any of the 1994 meetings I have attended, nor have I heard any such reports from others.

If pressure or suggestion is an element of what has been happening recently, it is only that: an element. It does not appear to be a major element in most people, although it may be in some. One of the main explanations appears to lie elsewhere – in a profound religious experience which is hard to explain in words.

Incidentally, just as all meetings create pressures and

boundaries, so some people are natural conformers and others are natural protesters. Protesters are unusual, because the conformist instinct in us is so strong as part of our social conditioning. For example, a person who is a non-conformer may be waving both hands in the air or bashing a tambourine in a traditional service (what a nerve!), or someone from a quieter background may be standing with mouth closed and arms folded during a time of lively celebration and praise.

It is very unfair to point the finger only at energetic meetings and say that is where you will particularly find emotional pressure. The pressure is everywhere you look, and felt whenever you are out of sync personally with what is going on.

So it is inevitable that in any meeting where many people begin to feel a particular emotion, others are likely to feel it to some degree as well. Moreover, others may feel confused and disturbed if they do not feel the same thing, because the group effect on most of us is so strong.

Mature and wise leadership will always try hard to make room, as far as possible, for a wide variety of people from different backgrounds and situations, who may be experiencing a whole range of different emotions or none at all, needing room to find God in their own way. After all, we are all part of the body of Christ.

In fact one surprising feature of the latest sweep of new enthusiasm through different churches is the unusually wide range of responses being accommodated – often at the end of the meeting when the proceedings are formally closed to allow some to leave and others to be prayed for. The extremes of joy and weeping are being expressed together at the same time in the same place, as well as the opportunity to observe quietly or withdraw altogether for coffee and a chat.

In most of the meetings I have attended where these phenomena have appeared, they have been regulated in time (towards the end of the meeting), in space (by clearing an area for ministry) and in people (most people affected actively choose to open themselves up to that possibility). Those being prayed for are usually told not to try and work something up or to judge what God is doing by how they are feeling, or by an outward sign, or by what is happening to others nearby. In this way the inevitable pressures that can build up in people's minds are being minimised.

What about accusations of hysteria? This is a specific medical diagnosis which in its classical form, as described in the nineteenth century, is now very rare in industrialised countries. Indeed the term itself is not really used any more by doctors.

The basis of the diagnosis is when there is a 'conversion reaction' (not to be confused with a change of belief), where severe anxiety is converted to some kind of physical symptom, such as paralysis of both legs or loss of speech. It can happen after a major trauma such as sexual abuse, or another powerful guilt-inducing event.

It happens more commonly in those who are relatively unsophisticated and of lower intelligence. There may be loss of sensation in areas of the skin, loss of hearing, complete paralysis, tremors, convulsions, loss of speech, coughing, nausea, vomiting or loss of memory where a person can't even remember his or her own name or where he or she is. Sometimes hysterical symptoms are connected to other neurotic or psychotic illness – part of some kind of mental breakdown.

So how do you make the diagnosis of such a 'conversion reaction'? First, there is often a history of similar things in the past. Secondly, in most cases you will find that there was a serious emotional crisis immediately prior to the event, and thirdly, the conversion itself has an obvious benefit to the person, almost 'solving the problem'. For example, someone is caught shoplifting and arrested. Within minutes the person loses the power of speech and is paralysed from the waist down. This is not consciously put on. The person genuinely is unable to speak or move. No amount of threatening or other behaviour will solve the situation. The result is that the person lands up in hospital on a psychiatric ward instead of in a cell.

Clearly it is conceivable that one or two cases of strange losses of power, sensation or other things may be linked to 'conversion reaction', but this is not a common explanation for the manifestations seen in 1994. Hysteria is a non-starter as a general description of what is going on.

We also need to be careful in throwing around these emotive words, or, as we have seen, we may be drawn to conclude that the apostle Paul was merely hysterical after Jesus spoke to him on the Damascus Road and he lost his sight (Acts 9), as was Zechariah when he could not speak for almost a year (Lk 1). We are told that both cases were caused by the direct action of God.

Anyway, appearances can deceive. For example, when is paralysis really paralysis? Take 'faintings' or 'being slain in the Spirit'. In many cases I have observed, and in perhaps the majority of people I have talked to afterwards, complete loss of consciousness is unusual, as is an instantaneous loss of power in the legs. Unsteadiness is very common – a gradual loss of co-ordination and a feeling of utter weakness so that standing becomes harder and harder work. Few are 'struck down' who would have preferred to have remained standing, and few fall who are not able to control in some small way the manner or timing of their falling.

As Nicky Gumbel of Holy Trinity Brompton expressed it recently, for him it was not so much falling down, but just that he was so aware of God's presence that he felt weak, and 'quite simply, lying down was the most comfortable and sensible place to be'.

It is true that once lying down – whether laughing, crying or just resting quietly – many report a feeling of separation from everything around them, and simultaneously an extraordinary sense of God's presence.

Some complain that people ought to be lying face down, not face up – following the biblical pattern. How absurd! Who has not prayed while lying on their back in bed? I cannot think of a better place to be at the end or start of the day, in the moments of falling asleep or waking, or in the stillness of the night, to be quietly aware of God's presence and intimacy.

We pray standing, walking along the road, driving a car. What is so terrible about praying while lying on our back? Position is very important: kneeling, standing, lying on front or back – all are expressions of our relationship with God. Lying on our back is a place of resting, of being quiet, still and aware; a place where every part of the body can relax and be washed of tension by God as he brings a gift of peace and an awareness of his accepting love and forgiveness.

Lying on our front is a place of adoration, prostration, awareness of God's splendour, might, majesty and holiness. Perhaps we are sometimes better at kneeling at God's feet than at enjoying his love. Many have called this a time of refreshing, a time of resting rather than interceding; of laughter rather than struggling; of melting through tears rather than fighting.

That brings me onto another criticism of what is happening. Some feel that we are in danger of creating spiritual junkies or tourists, who are for ever searching for the latest experience in a kind of restless nomadic wanderlust or spiritual consumerism. I see little danger of this while the emphasis continues to be on equipping or refreshing for service. Obviously one might have very serious questions if someone proposed to spend their life savings on a trip to Toronto, and no doubt some *have* spent time, energy and money unwisely as part of their own immature response to what is happening.

In the vast majority of cases, however, people are receiving what they feel is a special and helpful touch from God in their own churches, in the context of church meetings. Where churches have been in the early stages of seeing these things, it is true that many have gone to other places locally to 'receive', and that process has continued where leadership has been opposed to these things. Many have felt the need to spend a considerable time 'resting' in God's presence. However, profound changes seem to be taking place in their lives, and such things are very rarely instant.

I now want to turn to what appears to be the most obvious and complete explanation I can find in all the medical literature for what is happening – an explanation which combines our experience of God's presence and power with what we know about how our body and mind work: altered states of consciousness.

Altered states of consciousness

My own view is that we are not witnessing brainwashing on a grand scale, as Sargant would try to convince us, nor mass hysteria. We are, however, witnessing what happens when a large number of people experience an altered state of consciousness at the same time, as part of a profound spiritual experience.

Clearly, as we have seen, other factors may be operating in some people, including copy-cat behaviour, exhibitionism and spiritual conflicts of various kinds. However, my own observations lead me to conclude that a great many manifestations are due to this other effect, related to prayer, the work of the Holy Spirit and other factors all working together in a group setting.

Dr Simon Wessely, senior lecturer at King's College School of Medicine, commented in *The Observer* on 4th September 1994: This religious experience appears to be cathartic. The people feel rather good about it and appear to go for the purpose of group ecstatic experience. It is not mass hysteria or any form of mental disorder – it may be rather un-English, but there is nothing sinister about it at all.'

So what is a group ecstatic experience? Is his description correct? The problem is that we are lacking the language we need. Ecstasy implies something that is uplifting in mood, while for some the experience may be a sad one.

What is an altered state of consciousness (ASC)? Our normal state is considered to be our waking state. Then there is the sleeping state. However, the brain can also function in other states too – altered states of consciousness. In our day-to-day vocabulary we may refer to ASCs as trance, hypnosis, dream or ecstasy, depending on the situation and our worldview. Yet there are no satisfactory definitions of any of these terms in psychiatry.

Many things affect our conscious state. Most Christians would say that prayer does this. Depending on their background, some would say it happens as a result of contemplative meditation in stillness, while others would say it happens when they speak in tongues, or when fasting and praying.

For those without faith, taking hallucinogenic drugs like

LSD instantly creates an altered conscious state where the person feels they are having a profound and deeply meaningful spiritual experience, which later is so 'deep' that they cannot put it into words. Aldous Huxley did much of his writing, it seems, in an ASC.

ASCs are generally regarded negatively in Western culture and little research has been carried out in this field. Yet I believe it is the key to making sense of Christian experience, particularly what is happening in many churches today.

When Peter was caught up in a trance on the roof one day, and had a dream which showed him that non-Jews could also become Christians and be accepted by God, he experienced an altered conscious state. So did Isaiah when he had the vision of God's glory (Isaiah 6). Daniel, Ezekiel, John when writing Revelation, the apostle Paul 'caught up into the third heaven' – all are describing ASCs. They are almost universal in the writing of Christians over the centuries.

One could argue that ASCs, in the context of faith in Christ and prayerful obedience, are the basis of dynamic, personal, relevant, living faith. William James describes primary and secondary religious experience. Primary experience is when someone has a personal experience of their own, which is a part of their own faith. Secondary experience is when someone believes, but hardly feels God at all, yet is carried along by the primary experience of others. An ASC is the place where we usually find that primary experience.

So let us take a closer look at ASCs, what triggers them, the role of prayer and why ASCs are so vital to dynamic Christian faith and so common in meetings where there are manifestations.

Some manifestations are an obvious indicator that the person is in an ASC. Other manifestations may be a sign that the person is about to enter one, and may help induce it or cause an ASC to exist. (By the way, I am not in any way ruling out the direct work of the Holy Spirit in any person at any time. I am merely suggesting that one of the first things that happens when the Holy Spirit touches us is that our state of consciousness is altered so the temporal drops away and we become more spiritually aware. Nor am I describing here the way in which Scripture teaches that demonic forces can disturb people in their bodies or minds.)

So what then are the characteristics of an ASC?

Characteristics of ASCs

I am particularly grateful to the work of Arnold Ludwig, who in 1966 described how ASCs can be classified. Not all these characteristics apply, of course, to those who are having a profound experience of God, but as we will see, some aspects do describe quite well what is happening to many people, and perhaps shed some light on some aspects of these complex experiences.[118] Also there are degrees of alteration from normal waking state. Many people may experience an ASC only to a slight degree.

1. Alterations in thinking

Disturbances in concentration, attention, memory and judgement, and changes in perception of reality. We are seeing these all the time in meetings where there are manifestations. Don't bother trying to get a sound engineer to sort out a fault in the PA system after he has been on the floor for half an hour laughing. Let him sober up first.

2. Altered sense of time

Feeling that time is standing still, timelessness, of infinite or infinitessimal duration. This is one of the commonest experiences of those who lie on the floor 'resting in the Spirit'.

3. Loss of control

As an ASC begins, a person often experiences fear of losing self-control, or their grip on reality. Some may resist, while others give in readily to the experience. There may be feelings of impotency or helplessness, or greater power through gained knowledge of divine truths. So what about these things? I would say they are common in those experiencing manifestations. For example, someone becoming dizzy and beginning to feel weak, but afraid to 'let go' and enter further into the experience. Others may be overwhelmed by feelings of physical inadequacy, and still others struck by remarkable insights into God's truth.

4. Changes in emotional expression

Sudden and unexpected displays of emotion occur, ranging from extremes of ecstasy to profound fear and depression. Sudden indeed. So sudden in fact that sometimes the person praying may be thrown off balance by an irrational, violent unleashing of frustration, heartache, anguish, fear, anxiety, sadness, euphoria, elation, delight, enthusiasm, or 'hyper' energy.

Disinhibition is a key part of this, so that what is in the depths of the heart comes bubbling out. This suspension of some of the normal 'censoring' of what we say and how we move is quite typical of some people 'under the influence' of the Holy Spirit at some of these meetings. People afterwards may be quite embarrassed at what they said and did.

Jesus himself said that out of the mouth comes the overflowing of the heart (Mt 12:34), but usually in our normal conscious state we spend a lot of mental energy 'censoring' and filtering our thoughts and inner impulses, so what is communicated is socially acceptable, appropriate and fits with how we want others to see us. Despite this the words of Jesus hold true.

What is inside us comes out in one way or another in subtle or not-so-subtle ways. When someone is in an ASC, a great flood may be unexpectedly released. It might be a flood of adoration to God, tears of repentance, a struggle of inner conflict outwardly expressed, or joy and laughter. Part of the disinhibition may be responsible for some of the behaviour which seems almost like a reversion to early childhood.

5. Body image changes

The body image often becomes distorted, with a gap between mind and body, a feeling of distancing from what is going on around and feelings of 'oneness' with God being very common. The body may feel heavy, weightless, strange, with dizziness, blurred vision, weakness, numbness, tingling and insensitivity to pain. These changes are very commonly described by those receiving ministry or on the floor. 'Dissociation' can occur to one degree or another so that the person on the floor is hardly aware of wild laughter or crying around them, or if they are it seems far removed from their reality. It is also common for limbs to feel impossibly heavy, or as if their shape has altered in some way.

6. Perceptual changes

Hallucinations, increased visual imagery, heightened sensory awareness... A Christian would prefer to call the changes in visual perception visions. A friend of mine was dying and saw angels and a glimpse of heaven as he lay on his bed. His brain function was half shut down because of the toxins in his body – a similar effect to if he had been fasting, which indeed he was since he could not eat. He was in an altered conscious state at that moment, a place where he became sublimely aware of the reality of the spiritual world all around us. For him it was a wonderful, comforting experience of communion with God. He could see the angels protecting him and ready to carry him away.

7. Change of meaning or significance

Feelings of profound insight, illumination and truth; increased significance. Many prayed for have felt afterwards that they have understood God in a new way, as if God had turned a light on in their minds.

8. Sense of the ineffable

Vivid memories may persist afterwards, but they cannot be communicated in words. This is a classic diagnostic feature of an ASC. Because it is an experience taking place at another level altogether, 'in another world', it is impossible to communicate properly afterwards. Language cannot convey what is beyond human expression. This is a profound spiritual experience. To some degree it may be felt by believers during a traditional service of worship – as the choir sings a beautiful anthem or as the sun streams through a stained-glass window while familiar words are being read from the liturgy.

9. Feelings of rejuvenation

New sense of hope, renaissance, rebirth. People have frequently reported that it seemed like God was cleaning them out completely, or that he was closing a chapter on the past, or that he was giving them a new start, as a result of the Holy Spirit touching them deeply.

10. Hypersuggestibility

People may uncritically accept the ideas and commands of others while in an ASC. This is something to be aware of. In entering an ASC the mind is often in a relaxed state. We seek to open our minds to all God has for us, but we need to recognise that such a state could be hazardous under certain circumstances. This is not a hypnotic state, and control is not passing to another human being. However, the degree of influence by one person on another may be greater than usual. This is a variable effect, but may explain in part why laughter becomes so infectious in people with ASCs. In an extreme case, the degree of dissociation may be so great that the person is less likely to be influenced rather than more – 'completely drunk'. In such a situation you may not get much sense out of the person until they have sobered up a little, which will probably happen quite quickly if they open their eyes, sit up and are removed to another room and left quietly without other intoxicated people around them.

ASCs can have profound effects on body functioning, as well as on the mind. Some research has been done on people using transcendental meditation techniques to alter their conscious state – a mixture of concentration and relaxation. The only reason they were chosen by researchers is that they have all been taught a standard mental technique to attempt to produce an ASC.

Researchers wired them up to complex measuring equipment. They found oxygen consumption tumbled rapidly, and brain-wave patterns changed, as did the electrical conductance of the skin. These effects are not the product of some occult power but a simple physiological response to being deeply relaxed. Of course, spiritual assessment can also be made of someone in this state, but not based on purely physiological monitoring.

The oxygen consumption falls more rapidly and far lower than that of sleep, with a slowing of the heart and reduced rate of breathing within fifteen minutes. Hypnosis does not do this. A similar study of people 'resting in the Spirit' or just speaking in tongues would be fascinating. I am certain that profound changes would also be found in some people.

Remember that an ASC only allows temporal awareness to drop away so that one is more aware of the spiritual dimension. An ASC cannot bring you a personal relationship with God. Only faith in Jesus can do that, because of the barrier of sin to friendship with him. However, someone who has experienced an ASC who is not a Christian may then be far more open than, say, a militant atheist who denies there is anything more to life than what can be seen and felt.

What triggers ASCs?

How are ASCs induced? What is the role of prayer in increasing our awareness of God's presence?

Altered states of consciousness can be triggered or encouraged by many things, and some of these have been known and used by people of faith for centuries. An obvious example is fasting, which is not only an exercise in self-denial, but also affects the body and mind profoundly, making ASCs far more likely.

1. Lack of food

Someone in a fasting state is more likely when praying to

feel a powerful sense of the presence of God, to be able to shut out all the distractions of the world around, to be hyper-receptive to spiritual things, to feel they have an extraordinary insight into God's truth and purposes. No wonder Jesus told his disciples to fast and pray. If it were just an exercise in denial, then giving up a luxury or time would be as effective. No. This is food denial. Jesus therefore was teaching his disciples a means by which they could more easily and effectively pray, without temporal distractions. We will look at the usefulness of the gift of tongues later.

When the gut is empty of food, the levels of blood sugar soon begin to fall. To start with these are maintained by limited energy stores in the liver. However, these soon run down. As this happens the body changes over to burn up another fuel: fat. That is like converting a car from petrol to diesel. When you are running on fat reserves the whole of your body has to adjust, hormone levels change, and so does the functioning of the brain. Some people are more sensitive to these effects than others, and some have greater fuel reserves than others before they have to convert to fat use.

The effect of low blood sugar is seen most obviously in small children, whose behaviour alters as they become tired and hungry. They become fractious, irritable and spaced out, as if their batteries have run down. Within a couple of minutes of a sugary drink or a chocolate bar, or within ten minutes of beginning a meal, they have lit up again with a new dynamism. Adults also slow down without food, becoming more thoughtful, less energetic, quiet, introspective – and clumsy as the brain struggles to run all its electrical circuits at normal speed.

2. Reduction of sensory stimulation

Sensory deprivation is a well-known method of altering conscious states in people: prolonged solitary confinement with no indicator of day or night in a cell (whether a prison or as a recluse or hermit), extreme social isolation, loneliness in the desert, the Arctic or on a solo round-the-world cruise, or solo high-altitude flying: all these may cause rapid disorientation so that the person thinks they are going mad – losing their grip on reality. They may hear voices, hallucinate and have other strange experiences, particularly if deprived of food, sleep and material comfort, and living with great fear of physical assault.

Constant, repetitive or monotonous noise or light, extreme boredom, complete immobilisation of the body in a cast or in traction or in people paralysed –   these things act in the same way.

So then, closing the eyes and sitting or lying completely still in a perfectly relaxed state will make an ASC more likely, while opening one's eyes and talking will make it less likely. This is simple and obvious, and something all those with an effective prayer life are aware of. Going to stay in a flat on one's own for a week, during which there is no human contact; walking for extended periods in hill country alone; sitting motionless watching the waves of the sea or the shaping clouds in the sky – all are examples of this category, and have been found helpful by Christians in every age, no doubt, as a setting in which to pray.

However, the opposite is also a potential ASC trigger.

3. Increased sensory stimulation

When the nervous system is bombarded with sound, light, touch and other stimulation, or by extreme emotion, the brain can 'blow a fuse', unable to process all the data, partly shutting down to produce an ASC almost as a protective reflex. Examples might include a strange feeling of unreality experienced by someone lined up in front of a firing squad, or a Christian about to be tortured for his or her faith, emotional groups or mobs of people, someone unable to remember a traumatic experience such as rape, shell-shock in battle, panic reactions, fugues, or hysterical conversion reactions where a person about to be faced with unpleasant reality shuts off into a private world where things may be forgotten.

If someone feels terribly guilty in the presence of God or just overwhelmed by his love, 'overload' of normal brain function can be quickly reached. A noisy worship meeting where the person is dancing, clapping, has eyes open and is speaking in tongues and feels very emotional may help lead to an overload-induced ASC. This is not a harmful overload any more than the first example of sensory deprivation is necessarily harmful. Both, in mild degrees, are a normal part of the range of Christian experience. They explain why people go to 'find God' in church meetings and in solitude.

4. Increased alertness or concentration

Here attention is intensely focused on one thing, a thought or a task, literally blocking out almost everything else. Intense mental absorption in any task can do this: reading, writing, problem-solving, watching a radar screen, listening to a dynamic speaker, concentrating on the sounds of one's own breathing in a quiet room or fervent praying. As we pray we may be concentrating on one aspect of God's character, purpose, identity or creation. For hundreds of years Christians have found focusing on a symbol or picture that reminds them of some aspects of God's nature can also be helpful. Others may prefer to allow their eyes to rest on the outline of distant mountains, the beauty of the sky, light reflected by the leaves of trees or the detail of a rose in bloom.

5. Decreased alertness or relaxation of critical faculties

Day-dreaming, semi-awake or almost asleep, inspiring music, experiences which are soothing and relaxing, nostalgia, sunbathing. Some Christians say that their most profound experiences of God have been in that twilight zone between waking and sleeping. Perhaps they have woken in the night and had a vision. Perhaps kneeling at the side of the bed in the drifting from one conscious state to another they have felt a profound sense of God's touch on them.

Those 'resting in the Spirit', lying on the floor having been prayed for, may find that in a state of complete relaxation and in an atmosphere of love, acceptance and worship all around them, it is almost as if they are lifted into another world.

Those who have received the gift of tongues often find it is a vital God-given tool which helps them in prayer. I know many people who will pray in tongues for the express purpose of bringing themselves 'into the presence of God', especially if they wish to bring their rational, logical minds under God's authority in order to 'move in things of the Spirit' more freely, for example, exercising other gifts such as prophecy or prayer for healing.

When we speak in tongues, we are not just praying – something is quite definitely happening to our minds. We are speaking, yet we are in a 'language-free zone', where comprehension is turned off, as are grammar, punctuation and vocabulary. The brain is forced to stop processing language – a very rare event in our waking state because most of us (some would say all of us) think in language.

It may be that the repetition of very familiar words as part of a liturgical ritual may be deeply relaxing to the mind too, because it requires very little mental effort. The mental machinery is so well oiled. Without necessarily concentrating on the meaning of every word, but rather on the context (say the death and resurrection of Jesus remembered in a communion service), the mind is being lulled into a less active state. Temporal awareness may be diminished and a profound spiritual experience may follow. All repetitive tasks are helped by the cerebellum, the hind brain, not just the cortex. 'I could say or do it in my sleep' becomes almost literally true.

This could be the reason why changes in liturgy can be so traumatic for many who have worshipped in a certain way for years. Perhaps it is not merely that they like the beauty of the words, but quite literally something happens to their conscious state as the words are heard or spoken. If the words are changed, more mental effort is required to participate and an ASC becomes less likely – for a start they may have to read the words from a book. Also the language itself may be less poetic in rhythm and so less likely to be helpful to them. Perhaps unfamiliar surroundings too may be a distraction – rearranged seating, sitting in a different part of the building, changes in music, a new church building.

Thus abandoning, say, the old 1662 prayer book text could mean that some are robbed of a weekly experience of a mild ASC. They may come out of the church deeply dissatisfied and frustrated for reasons which are almost impossible to explain. No amount of logic or rational argument can convince them that the new order of service will do, because their own experience is beyond logic, or language, and is transcendental in nature.

The good news is that with the passage of time the brain will become as programmed by increased familiarity with new liturgy so long as it is kept to fairly rigidly. People may then find they still have aesthetic objections to exact phraseology but that it is easier to 'find God' spiritually.

I am not arguing for conservatism any more than for change for its own sake. We need to be open to the Holy Spirit in us. I am just pointing out that liturgy may have a potent ASC effect in some people by the nature of its context and familiarity.

Many charismatics look down on formal liturgy of any kind, preferring spontaneous, informal prayer. Yet so-called 'Spirit-filled' churches have some form of worship of their own which is usually highly predictable. Charismatics are not in a strong position to criticise 'mindless repetition', say of the Lord's prayer, when the gift of tongues seems to use even less of the mind, and may produce a not dissimilar effect. Some anti-liturgy campaigners point to Jesus' criticising of people 'babbling like the pagans' but that is perhaps a rather different thing (Mt 6:7)!

6. Body chemistry alterations

We have already looked at the powerful effects of fasting. The opposite can also help induce an ASC: the lethargy seen in many people after a large meal, especially in the middle of the day. There is also dehydration, adrenal or thyroid gland dysfunction, sleep deprivation, auras happening in some people prior to an epileptic fit or an attack of migraine, delirious states caused by infections and high fever, poisons, withdrawal from addictive drugs such as alcohol or barbiturates, anaesthetics, psychedelic drugs and other substances.

Hyperventilation or overbreathing can also affect the

mind. This is an important area to consider since it is so common and some have suggested it could be responsible for some manifestations in church meetings. So why does overbreathing make us dizzy, with tingling in the hands and other strange ASC experiences?

When the body burns up sugar or fat, which every cell does all the time, it uses up oxygen and releases carbon dioxide. Small amounts of these gases dissolve in water, which is just as well or we would have bubbles of fizzy gas in our blood, just like in bottles of opened soft drink. When carbon dioxide is dissolved in the water which makes up most of the blood, a chemical change takes place. It turns the water acid.

The acidic effect of carbon dioxide is why coke and other drinks taste so sweet when they go flat. The carbon dioxide actually affects the taste, giving the drink a 'tang' or 'bite'. Now the amount of this gas in the blood is far less. The blood also has special 'buffers' in it to help prevent the blood becoming more acid as it picks up waste gas, and then more alkaline after it dumps the gas and takes up fresh oxygen in the lungs.

So the blood is kept in a balanced state all the time. If you run upstairs, more carbon dioxide is released, the blood becomes acid, your brain reacts by telling your lungs to breathe more, and the blood returns to normal.

However, it can all go the other way. If you try to blow up twenty balloons quickly, or a large air-mattress, the oxygen level in your blood rises and the carbon dioxide level falls. As too much carbon dioxide is washed out of the blood, the effect is as great as a fizzy drink going flat. The blood balance is upset and the whole body begins to dysfunction.

It is easy to hyperventilate without realising, even when sitting quietly in a chair, or in church meetings. So what are the effects? The blood pressure falls as small arteries dilate and the heart begins to race. Tingling can appear in the hands, feet and face, with numbness of limbs and face as well. The person may feel light-headed, dizzy and faint. In more severe cases spasm begins to occur (tetany) in some muscles, especially common in the hands, with sweating of the palms.

You cannot easily tell if someone is hyperventilating just by looking. It can happen with a normal breathing rate but just with larger breaths than normal. Treatment simply consists of asking the person to breathe into a paper bag for a couple of minutes, so that the carbon dioxide level begins to rise back to normal.

The commonest cause of hyperventilation is anxiety. However, the question is: Are some hyperventilating during or before manifestations? While this may be possible in extreme cases, this is not an adequate explanation for what is happening, as most doctors attending these meetings will agree. Slight changes in breathing will not have this effect. It needs to be quite prolonged for some of the more marked effects to occur – and we all know what the early signs feel like, from blowing up balloons or air-beds.

However, we should be aware that someone standing still in a meeting who begins to pant quickly, or to take great violent, gasping lungfuls of air, one after the other over several minutes, is more likely to experience an ASC as a result. The combined effects are hard to calculate in, for example, someone who has been fasting for three days and lost a lot of sleep, who is emotionally drained, and then begins to hyperventilate in a meeting where there is gentle soothing music.

Even if we were to conclude that a certain proportion of those experiencing manifestations are doing so because of one or other of the mechanisms above, rather than just being purely 'overcome by the Spirit', it does not in any way invalidate the experience. ASCs seem to be a normal, common part of Christian prayer and worship, even if we never recognise them as such, and even if most people have only felt them to a slight degree until they have a powerful experience of the Holy Spirit. In previous ages it was quite common for people to withdraw from social contact for long periods to be with God in prayer. Fasting was often a part of that, as well as contemplation – either concentrating on one aspect of God's nature or perhaps seeking to empty the mind of all worldly influences.

In contrast, the charismatic may use the gift of tongues as a tool to bring the mind under God's authority, to a place of openness to the supernatural, as part of an experience of worship and adoration. In the classification above, tongues could be emptying the mind of logical, language-related thought, and helping to induce a trance-like state.

Some may find such thoughts threatening if they have been using their own subjective experience as a direct proof of the existence of God. It is hard to be certain God exists on the basis of feelings which are transient, and whose origins can be questioned. Strong faith will rest on an understanding of who God is from the Scriptures, rather than on emotion.

Feelings confirm our faith, but we are in danger if they are the basis for that faith. If faith is no more than the product of feelings, then we will believe in anything that makes us feel good – or bad.

If someone says that the reason they believe in God is because they fell over in a meeting, what happens to their faith when they see that people can also fall over in public gatherings for emotional reasons, or for occult reasons?

Feelings may be the start of a growing understanding of

who God is, and for some they may be part of a crisis experience of conversion, but future stability as a Christian will come through mature understanding, albeit an understanding in which feelings may well play a significant part.

Many believers have experienced what has been called 'a dark night of the soul', a time when they know in their minds that God exists, but do not feel his presence. It is as if God has left them alone, as a trial of faith. Do we love him only for the feelings he gives us? Do we follow only in the quest for experience? Or do we love God sacrificially, obeying and serving because he is God, rather than because we feel the warmth of his love in us?

So, in summary, human beings are emotional creatures and were designed by our Creator to be that way. We are social creatures and God designed us to worship and experience him together, hence the church as a worshipping community was God's idea. We enjoy group emotion. That is why we go to see films in the cinema with others, not merely for a big screen. There is a corporate atmosphere which enriches and stimulates us.

God intended church meetings to affect us profoundly, otherwise we would just worship him on our own. Emotion is part of every relationship we have. Therefore there can be no deeply meaningful relationship with God unless emotion is touched in some way.

The Bible teaches us to meet together, to sing, to pray, to fast, to meditate, to reflect – all things likely to alter our conscious state, causing us to rise above the temporal and immediate until we sense the eternal.

Most important of all, however, is that unlike other religions which stress some kind of technique to bring us to a transcendental spiritual realm, the Bible teaches us that no efforts of our own will produce a close relationship with God without repentance of sin and forgiveness through the sacrificial death of Jesus.

All an altered state of consciousness does is to confront us with the reality that there is more to life than we ordinarily see, feel and touch. There is a spiritual dimension to existence. An ASC does not bring us into God's presence, but it can make us aware of a presence to be brought into. The nature of a spiritual experience during an ASC will depend on the beliefs of the person and those around him or her.

Many Christians would agree that all ASCs are likely to open doors, but the question is – open them to what? An ASC in the middle of a seance or during a voodoo ceremony could be highly dangerous. However, an ASC during an act of Christian worship could be a helpful and healing experience which is life-changing and long-lasting in its beneficial effect on body, mind and spirit.

Some may find this whole discussion uncomfortable, denying that they have ever had an ASC. But who has not knelt at the communion rail and felt something outside themselves? Who has not sat in a place like King's College Cambridge and been transported to a sublime height with the soaring ethereal notes of the choir? Who has not for a moment imagined they have caught a glimpse of heavenly glory itself in a fading sunset, or been aware of the presence of God in the instant between sleep and wakefulness?

The charismatic and pentecostal movements have been driven perhaps by a celebration of altered consciousness and the recognition that our normal conscious state is a very shallow place from which to cultivate an awareness of all God is. There has been a widespread discovery that the experiences of prophets like Isaiah and the apostle Paul, while unique, are an indicator of what the prophet Joel promised when he said that old men would see visions and young men would dream dreams when the Holy Spirit was poured out.

In Jesus' day there were indeed a number who followed him around because they liked seeing miracles, rather than because they wanted to obey what he said. Spiritual consumerism is idolatry, where experiences in themselves replace sacrificial devotion to Jesus. The key is keeping central in our lives that the purpose of refreshing, the purpose of filling, the purpose of empowering or anointing, is for service.

Jesus calls us daily to take up our cross and follow him, reminding us that it is only as we lay down our lives, allowing ourselves to be lost for his sake, that we will find our true selves. Once we lose sight of what the blessing is for, we will quickly become walled up in the Christian ghetto, with only one aim in our minds: to spend time with other believers, or go to another remarkable meeting.

Every renewal needs to become a revival of the church, and the test of true revival is when a generation of believers becomes so filled by the Holy Spirit that it feels compelled by God's love to make huge sacrifices to tell others about its faith, giving up jobs, money, time and other commitments as God directs, in the supreme challenge of reaching every man, woman and child with the good news of Jesus. Then revival becomes an awakening of a nation.

Looking at the world situation, there is a certain inevitability about it all. The scene is set, with pre-millennial tension in the air; the collapse of the communist and socialist ideals, the apparent moral bankruptcy of materialism and capitalism, disenchantment with politics and apathy about democracy; with increasing terrorism, civil wars, ethnic genocide and unrest; with the collapse of family life and spiralling crime in the cities; with urban decay, mega-slums in mega-cities, shortages of resources and lack of direction. Is it any surprise that people are wanting to find faith?

There is a spiritual hunger greater than for over a generation. While the wave of revival and great spiritual awakening continues gradually to engulf nation after nation in much of the developing world, it is surely now inevitable that the very nation in which the greatest missionary movements began two centuries ago, will once again find itself touched, this time through missionaries from the same countries we sent others to so many years ago.

We may debate about the hour or the day. We may argue over predictions that may or may not have been made, but one thing is certain: the wind of revival is in the air. God's Spirit is moving and future generations of believers will judge us severely for how we responded.

History will record one of several things: either that we criticised and analysed the latest move of God until the rise of faith was all but crushed; or that the flame continued to burn, bringing limited revival to some groups, some churches, some areas, before fading away under apathy and neglect; or that the church reached to God in fervent prayer, willing to pay the cost of change, repenting of personal sin, corporate sectarianism and lack of mutual love, embracing the mighty power of God, and bringing the whole nation a challenge of repentance and new life, with a national awakening, the like of which numerically we have never seen.

6

Where Do We Go From Here?

Personal observations

When I first heard of the manifestations described in the first chapter of this book I was greatly disturbed – even more so when I found out people were spending vast amounts of money on what I called 'spiritual tourism', almost as if they were addicted to the next experience. I was unhappy about the noise, the lack of control of meetings which sounded chaotic, and I felt the whole thing was due to emotionalism which was likely to be damaging.

I gradually changed my mind after measuring what was happening against Scripture, particularly noting that 'drunken behaviour' is a consequence of the Holy Spirit. I also noted that 1 John 4:6 tells us that the (only sure) way to tell the work of the Holy Spirit from the demonic is that what is of God produces the recognition that Jesus is Lord. In other words, confusion was a feature of the early church too. They sometimes couldn't tell by mere appearances which was which either. On this test, though, the answer about the 'new' phenomena was very clear. Jesus was being directly acknowledged as Lord and Saviour.

I also read about the past and was shocked to find how

many accounts of revival had been 'sanitised', with manifestations played down or ignored. Thirdly, I listened to those affected, who invariably described the positive fruit in their lives. Fourthly, with a little reluctance, I went along to observe. I found myself reacting to noisy excesses, but I lingered long enough to recognise and experience the working of God too.

I was prayed for first at the Pioneer leaders' day on 4th July 1994 at Fairmile Court. I became aware of strange sensations in my body. In twenty-five years of being a Christian I have never experienced anything like it, and have tended to dismiss such feelings in others as largely emotionalism. Indeed, I have been puzzled by them, as they did not fit with my own experience at all.

I was not singing, not dancing, and certainly not over-breathing. There was little build-up and no hype. Two people had told us what had been going on and we had all stood to pray in silence.

In fact I was so curious to know whether hyperventilation could possibly be an explanation for what I was feeling that I consciously restricted my breathing until it became impossible to do so any more – and still the sensations continued. I am certain hyperventilation had nothing whatever to do with it.

While standing quietly with hands outstretched I became unsteady, as if my sense of balance was being disturbed. I became alarmed that if it got any worse I would fall over. As this happened I began to sway. As I swayed forwards I was more balanced than when I swayed back and saw immediately that if I was to fall over it would be more likely to be backwards than forwards. This is a simple feature of human anatomy – the direction of our feet being somewhat a decisive factor.

I have had mild vertigo attacks in the past, but not for a long time and this felt just like one. I was also aware of weakness in my knees. It was a real effort to stand. All the time I was tremendously aware of the nearness of God, of his love, of his blessing. I was also simultaneously aware of my own inadequacy, my own failings, my own weakness and sinfulness. As I inwardly confessed that to God I was filled with joy, until I was grinning from ear to ear. The whole experience was intensely pleasurable.

As the person praying for me continued to stand by I became so unsteady that I realised I would either have to sit down or be helped to the ground. I let myself be supported as I flopped to the ground, and was immediately relieved to be in touch with the safety and solidity of the floor. The world stopped moving.

I felt very odd. My body was tingling all over and my limbs felt very heavy. I could have moved, but it was a real effort, and it was almost as if to have moved would have made the world around me (chaos and noise) intrude into the quietness and intimacy of the world I was in with God. I felt strangely distanced and aloof from what was happening, yet in control and able to hear or see – although I did not want to open my eyes.

Lying on the floor was like being transported to a different plane of awareness of God's presence, a sublime experience.

And then the laughter started in people near me. And the floor space began to fill with people heaving with belly-laughter. Others were still standing praying for each other in huddles, but becoming more and more intoxicated themselves, until with a mighty crash and loud giggles several of them careered through chairs and all over the floor, landing up in a confused heap of laughter.

By now the whole room was alive with a sense of the

ridiculous. People were talking and laughing in the excited way you get at a party which is going well, with people really enjoying being together. The whole situation was utterly absurd. Here we all were, grown adults as helpless as babies, roaring with laughter, unable to get up, trying to get up and staggering around or falling down again!

It was as if the whole room was filled with laughing gas or some other powerful intoxicant. I laughed until my body was more than half off the floor, and then some more until it hurt and I started to wheeze. Yet I carried on because although I suppose with some effort I could have forced myself to stop, it was such a wonderful sensation, to feel free in the presence of God, in a place of worship, touched by his power, made to feel ridiculous, with pride, self-image and false sophistication melting away.

When the meeting gradually calmed down and the room became quieter, lying there felt like sunbathing or perhaps that should be 'Son bathing', being washed in the presence of God. A joyful, peaceful, refreshing, wonderful thing.

After the room was almost empty for ten minutes or so, and after I had been lying motionless for some fifteen minutes, I decided to try and get up. I was weak and unco-ordinated and had to grasp onto a chair as I rose. I stood, looking round blinking as if in some stupor and negotiated the hallway to the dining room with some difficulty.

At the meal table I was in trouble, almost knocking over glasses or the salt container. My pouring was clumsy and my attempts to load food onto a fork with a knife were awkward. Conversation was a little odd and stilted, and I continued to feel dazed and distant until halfway through the meal. I had no real desire for conversation. After all, what was there worth saying after an experience of the presence of God that could never be conveyed in words? Nothing else was worth the air to make the words.

I considered at the time that if I had tried to drive instead of stop for lunch I could easily have had a serious accident. I was as if drugged or drunk – definitely 'under the influence'.

The effect on my ongoing Christian life has been significant, but not dramatic. Perhaps it is most dramatic in those who have felt the most distanced from God, or the 'driest'. I have been through such times, as we all have perhaps, but in the summer of 1994 I felt close to God and the warmth of his encouragement. I also felt his power in my life, whether in medicine, in the AIDS work, in the church, in writing, in public speaking or with the family. When I first heard about these new happenings I therefore felt no great desire or need to go rushing off anywhere in search of something that was missing. It would have been very different just eighteen months earlier when times were really tough.

The most significant thing has been conviction of sin, realising that attitudes and feelings had crept into my life that were not right. Also, I have felt far more confident and assertive about explaining faith to others, and more aggressive regarding plans for evangelism in the church. I have been more willing to step out and take risks, which has helped as we have sought to plant another church.

I have also been more aware of God's power and more confident that he is willing to release his power into the lives of others through me. So then, a time of repentance, recharging and refreshing, empowering for service.

I have no doubt that profound physiological changes are taking place linked with these manifestations. I am convinced too that there is a group dynamic with an infectiousness about some of the emotions experienced. That does not invalidate them in any way – after all, God gave us emotions and he made us social creatures and the church as a close community was his own idea.

I am also convinced that there is a powerful spiritual dimension operating in many people, the result of repentance, faith and obedience. God's Holy Spirit blows where he will, causing renewal, revival and awakenings.

While we can point to 'signs of the times' (Mt 16:3) in culture, expectations, events, social conditions, spiritual hunger or repentance, ultimately the time and place of any great move of God is a mystery. God is sovereign. There is no recipe for revival. We are all called to prayer and obedience at all times. God does the rest as he wills.

We cannot earn revival. It is like God's grace: a gift to us, not a reward for work done. There is nothing for anyone to be proud of. This is God's work (Eph 2:8-10).

We will be surprised and humbled – disturbed even – as we seek to test in the fire of the future the fruit of recent manifestations and emotional faith. For that is the greatest test and the one we cannot carry out today. It will be for a future generation to assess.

In the meantime, I pray that hundreds of thousands in the UK alone will find faith in Christ, with an impact felt for ten generations to come, unless our Lord has returned by then.

But for today, how should we respond practically? Here are some suggestions from Gerald Coates which many have found helpful.

Guidelines for church leaders
by Gerald Coates

1. Make a swift response to the work of the Spirit

We must be willing to embrace the work of God's Spirit, even if it means changes to our structures, programmes and agendas. The main key is the entire leadership submitting themselves to the Holy Spirit and being willing to receive prayer.

2. Respond with humility and faith

Faith will overcome our fears, uncertainty and doubt. Humility will keep us from superiority and elitism. We have been praying for renewal and revival so we should not be surprised if God responds. 'Which of you, if his son asks for bread, will give him a stone? Or if he asks for a fish, will give him a snake?' (Mt 7:9-10).

3. Take responsibility for what is happening

The elders in Corinth had a hands-off approach. It was a mixture of manifestations of the Spirit, the work of the flesh and even the devil. As leaders, we have to give an account for what we allow and encourage in our churches. God puts no premium on ignorance. While it is a time of refreshing, it is also a time when we as leaders must help the church understand what is happening.

4. Ensure that we are directing and administrating what is going on

We do not want things simply to become introspective. We want to see people ultimately look to those outside the Christian community. Otherwise self-indulgence will take root, and either we will be responding to people's needs and manifestations or, eventually, we will dry up.

Practical help

1. Ensure that you do not seek personal gain, prominence or benefit from what is clearly a divine visitation.

2. Do not develop a ministry of manifestations, when God is wanting to do something deeper.

3. Do not hype meetings. Be relaxed, but full of expectancy.

4. Maintain a focus on the source of the blessing – Christ himself – and do not transfer people's faith either to a person, a place or a method.

5. Endeavour to read Scripture into what is going on, without becoming preachy or sermonising. We must not be awash in a sea of subjectivity.

6. Create a worshipping environment and give room for testimonies that speak of the fruit rather than the manifestations.

7. Encourage people to 'drink', as Jesus promises to quench our thirst. Also encourage people to allow the rivers of living water to touch those outside the Christian community.

8. Wait on God. Things cannot be rushed. Jesus told the early disciples to wait with expectancy in the Upper Room. It took days, not moments.

9. Encourage a continual response. C. H. Spurgeon, when asked why he needed to be continually filled with the Spirit, responded, 'I leak.' We should not be surprised when people keep responding. They are thirsty and needy. It is better than not responding at all.

10. Encourage people to release their emotions. We are still a very controlled people. We are suspicious of anything emotional. Laughter, tears, shouting or physical jerks must be allowed to happen.

11. Ensure that those leading meetings or praying with others share the vision of the church, support the leadership and are open to the activity of the Holy Spirit.

12. Do not become so taken up with the meeting that you fail to oversee the event. Ensure you have a group of trusted, senior people who can minister to those responding.

When you pray for people

1. When people's strength fails them, keep praying for them. Encourage them to stay down where they are and receive from the Lord. It is not unusual for people to stay down on the floor for significant periods.

2. Do not be afraid of having people catching those falling down. It removes the unnecessary fear of falling, bumps or collision, and while it is not vital, it is helpful.

3. Create floor space, even if it means moving chairs. We are responsible for facilitating the work of the Holy Spirit. Do not in any way manipulate the activity of the Holy Spirit. People must not be allowed to believe this is the work of human beings, but the work of God.

4. Encourage people to remain open to God – not looking for manifestations, but a work of the Spirit seen or unseen.

5. Do not be afraid of praying with children as well as adults. Most children believe this to be a little like heaven and are much more responsive than some adults. When praying with children it is helpful to have parents or a parent present. If parents have been touched by God, we should be responsible for their children.

6. Explain any unusual activities. They may be of God or the devil, but you will be responsible for determining which. Do not leave the church confused.

7. Endeavour to understand that events like these place great demands on you as leader, both emotionally and physically. Ensure that you rest. Do not stagger in from meeting to meeting.

8. Enjoy what is going on. Do not become over-heavy, serious and certainly not religious.

9. Be prepared for criticism. Some will not understand what is going on, and others will be fearful. This is the time for sensitive action, not emotional reactions.

10. While not discouraging people from visiting other churches to see what is happening, be wary of competitiveness and comparisons. Also beware of people simply running around to 'get blessed' without that blessing being allowed to bring about a radical change of life.

11. Be careful about prolonged times of men praying for women, or vice versa. It is preferable that prayer should be single sex or in groups.

12. If there is a fleshly or demonic manifestation which you are unable to deal with, make sure someone is drawn alongside you immediately. Such manifestations can be a distraction to the rest of the meeting.

13. Encourage people when they feel that nothing has happened. Some have sat under this sort of ministry for up to twelve hours with nothing happening, but now they are prominent channels of this blessing.

Opposition

There has never been a move of God which hasn't faced serious opposition. We see this in Jesus' ministry and in the Acts of the Apostles, from the religious as well as the godless. So we need to minister to the Lord and his people with 'clean hands and a pure heart'.

Therefore let us ensure that our behaviour is in line with the biblical mandate, with as little physical contact as possible, never pushing people over, or saying things which amount to triumphalism or pure fantasy. Don't invite criticism and opposition.

When we are attacked by people in the church, or other churches, or in the Christian press, it is easy to be reactionary, cynical, dismissive or superior. This could be more a matter of attitude than word, and it comes across with a sort of what-do-they-know? attitude. Remain calm, rational and reasonable. Learn to disagree without being disagreeable.

We must be prepared for opposition. We should expect it and count it a joy when we go through it, and simply be willing to pray for people, bless them and treat them with courtesy.

A caution

Continually giving out, without receiving, can lead to exhaustion and burnout. Take time to receive, rest, read Scripture and do 'normal' things. God wants us around for the long haul, not a short sprint!

(Gerald Coates acknowledges several sources including Bryn Jones [Covenant Ministries]; Sandy Millar [Holy Trinity Brompton]; David Pytches [St Andrew's Chorleywood] and Vineyard USA in helping him to prepare the notes above. For further advice from Vineyard, see pages 324-330.)

I leave the final word to Clive Calver, General Director of the Evangelical Alliance and a national figurehead for 1.2 million Evangelicals in Britain. Speaking at the Focus '94 Bible week in Morecombe Bay he said this:

> After 400 years of silence between the books of Malachi and Matthew, John the Baptist arrived with a word from God. It was not expected or anticipated and didn't rest well with the religious establishment.
> Normally when God moves it does not rest well with the religious establishment. Today, if we are seeing a move of God, it will not rest easily with the religious establishment. God always rocks the boat. He rarely does what I want him to. And

he very rarely does what I say he is going to do. That's why he is so uncomfortable.

When you look around everywhere today, something is happening. Just after this move of God started I was in a group of churches and they said, 'Is this an awakening?' And I said, 'No. An awakening is what God does in the world when he turns society round as he did in the eighteenth century.'

They said, 'Is this a revival?' I said, 'I don't think so. Revival is what God does when he brings the world into the church.' They said, 'Is it a renewal?' I said, 'Yes, definitely. It's as important as this: you have never had an awakening in history that hasn't started in renewal and revival.'

Now I want to see an awakening. I want to see God touch our nation and to see God turn our society upside down and inside out. But he won't start in society. He'll start with the people of God.

If this is an end in itself, I've got to confess to being slightly disappointed because I've spent the last twenty years waiting for God to turn society round. This is the beginning – God is after a people broken before him.

God forgive those who've condemned this as a work of the enemy. I believe that God starts with us. But we don't want it to finish here, do we? I like laughing, but I'd like our world to laugh too.

I believe we are waiting for God in the church in this country. Some of us have been waiting for a long time. But I also believe that God is waiting for us. God wants a people who will offer themselves so totally and completely that he can blow by his Spirit in a way that we have never seen.

This is just a beginning – and as God gets surrendered lives, he wants to take us out to make a difference.

It's a call to repentance. It's a call to follow Jesus. It's a call to surrender ourselves. When we do that we'll stop waiting for God and find that God's waiting for us.

And when he's found us, I believe he's going to use us to change this nation in a way we haven't seen since Wesley and Whitefield.

Appendix

I am very grateful to Bill Jackson, associate pastor of Champaign Vineyard, Illinois, and to other members of the leadership team, including Happy Leman, for permission to reproduce this important and helpful document in full. Written in the early part of 1994, it represents well the current understanding of manifestations with many Vineyard churches and the guidelines on pages 325-330 have been widely adopted.

Attention is drawn to the special copyright notice on page 331, allowing reproduction of pages 295,330 under certain conditions.

What in the World Is Happening to Us?
A biblical perspective by Bill Jackson

Introduction

Historical review

1. Randy Clark is the founding pastor of the Vineyard Christian Fellowship in St. Louis, MO. After years of seeing little fruit and power in his ministry he became desperately hungry for God. Hearing of unusual manifestations of God's presence through the ministry of South African evangelist, Rodney Howard-Browne, Randy attended one of Rodney's meetings in Tulsa, OK. Randy was powerfully touched and, in going home, began to see a similar outbreak of the Spirit among his people.

2. At the Regional meeting of Midwestern Vineyard churches at Lake Geneva, WI, in October, 1993, the Regional overseer, Happy Leman, asked Randy to share what was happening in his church. Again, a powerful demonstration of God's power broke out at the meeting. There was a limited outbreak at the Champaign Vineyard the following Sunday.

3. At the Vineyard National Board meeting in November, Happy shared the results of the regional meeting with John Arnott, pastor of the Airport Vineyard in Toronto, Canada,

and Area Pastoral Coordinator of the Vineyards in Ontario. John immediately went home and invited Randy to come to Toronto to speak and minister in January. Two days of meetings in Toronto turned into what, to date, have been 90 days of almost continuous meetings in numerous locations in Ontario and in the United States.

4. The meetings have been dubbed a 'renewal' rather than a 'revival' by psychiatrist and author John White and by John Wimber, international leader of the Association of Vineyard Churches. Randy and those who have been associated with him say that this move of God is more associated with refreshing the church and calling home the prodigals than salvation for the lost. People are coming to Christ, but not in the numbers one typically sees in times of revival.

5. On March 4-5, Randy spoke in Marion, Illinois, and several people from the Champaign Vineyard, including Bill and Betsy Jackson, went to hear him. Bill and others from the church were deeply impacted and came back to share with the church on Sunday what had happened. Again, there was an outbreak during the Sunday ministry time, this one larger than the one in the fall.

6. Happy and his wife Dianne went to Toronto on Bill's recommendation. Happy wound up staying for almost a week, and in coming home saw an even larger outbreak than the previous two. Manifestations of God's presence have continued every week since. Happy Leman has reported that he has seen more changed lives in one month than in all his years of ministry. Our purpose in putting this paper together is to develop a biblical apologetic for what we see happening among us. Much of what we are seeing is strange to the

natural mind. The following are some of the phenomena that we have seen in our meetings.

Falling
Shaking
'Drunkenness'
Crying
Laughter
Prophetic revelation

Any thinking believer is going to ask some basic questions.

1. Is what we are seeing biblical?
2. What are these phenomena for?
3. How can you be sure it's God?

Even if satisfying answers can be given to these questions, still more objections can be raised. How could it be God if:

1. It's hard to understand?
2. It makes me afraid?
3. It causes division?
4. He overrides my faculties?
5. It's so emotional?
6. It causes me to be the center of attraction?
7. It's so disorderly?
8. It doesn't happen to me?

We will now take up these questions and objections in order and try to give some biblical answers.

Are these manifestations biblical?

First, it needs to be said that it is perfectly normal and even necessary to inquire into the biblical nature of Christian experience. It is also OK to admit that much of this looks 'weird' as long as we don't prematurely judge it. When Paul first went to the Greek city of Berea, the book of Acts says that the Bereans were more noble than the other Jews Paul had encountered in Greece because they 'searched the Scriptures daily to see if what Paul was saying was true' (17.11). When we ask, 'Is it biblical?', we're probably asking for what is commonly called a 'proof' text. A proof text is a portion of Scripture that, when taken in context, validates a particular position we are taking. In order to ascertain whether these phenomena are biblical, we need to lay down some ground rules for solid interpretation.

There are three basic doctrinal headings in the Bible

1. Christian theology (what Christians are to believe)
2. Christian ethics (how Christians ought to behave)
3. Christian experience or practice (what Christians do)

You can call a verse/passage a proof text when the writer clearly states what God wants us to believe, do or practise. These texts can be labeled 'primary.'

There are many beliefs, behaviors and practices, however, that are not clearly taught but rather are implied. These texts can be labeled 'secondary.' This doesn't mean unimportant, only that a clear statement cannot be found. Let's take baptism for instance. The Bible clearly states that Christians are to be baptized. There is a primary text that says so (Mt. 28.19).

How we are to be baptized, on the other hand, is never explicitly stated. This is why different groups baptize different ways. There are, however, clear biblical passages that show that it was normal in the early church to immerse people in water. Even the word 'baptize' means to immerse. This doesn't prove that this is the way the church should baptize for all time. It does, however, imply it. At the very least it illustrates that this is what was done. The mode of baptism, therefore, is a secondary, not a primary issue.

When dealing with supernatural phenomena, we are dealing with the area of Christian practice. While there is a primary text dealing with prophetic revelation, there are no primary texts that clearly state that Christians are to fall down, shake or look drunk during seasons of divine visitation. There are, however, a number of secondary (remember, secondary does not mean invalid or unimportant) texts that illustrate that these were some of the responses people had during moments of divine visitation. We will examine some of these passages where they relate to a particular phenomenon.

There are also numerous examples of similar phenomena in church history, especially in seasons of revival. We will also briefly examine them. All historical quotes are taken from two sources. Material concerning Jonathan Edwards comes from his original writings as gleaned from a paper by church historian, Guy Chevreau. Guy is currently researching these phenomena in church history. The other quotes are taken from a priceless out of print volume by James Gilchrist Lawson called *Deeper Experiences of Famous Christians* (copyright 1911).

Falling

The most common phenomenon we have seen in our meetings is people falling down, commonly called 'resting in the Spirit.' Often they remain conscious but engaged with the Lord. They feel weak and find it difficult to do anything but rest with God. We have seen that as they lie with the Lord, they have had significant changes in their lives. What, if any, biblical precedent is there for this?

Gen. 15.12: 'Abram fell into a deep sleep and a thick,

dreadful darkness came over him.' This literally reads, 'a deep sleep fell on Abram.' The Hebrew word *radam* means to be in or fall into a deep sleep. This is the same word that is used when God put Adam to sleep when he made Eve (Gen. 2:21; cf. 17.17: 'Abraham fell face down').

1 Sam. 19: 'Saul walked along prophesying...he stripped off his robes and also prophesied in Samuel's presence. He lay that way all that day and night. This is why people say, "Is Saul also among the prophets?"' This text shows that for something close to a 24 hour period Saul lay in a prone position with God speaking through him.

2 Chron. 5.13-14: In the context of the temple priests worshiping and praising God, all of a sudden 'the temple of the Lord was filled with a cloud, and the priests could not perform their service because of the cloud, for the glory of the Lord filled the temple of God.' This is a fascinating text. It never says that the priests fell but it does indicate that under God's glory they were essentially immobilized, physically unable to perform their duties. What happened seems to be connected to the Hebrew word for 'glory' (*kabod*) which means 'a weight.' The phenomenon of falling in God's presence might be understood as being overcome by the weight of God forcing them to the floor. Ezek. 1.28: 'This was the appearance of the likeness of the glory of the Lord. When I saw it I fell face down...'

Ezek. 3.23: '...And the glory of the Lord was standing there, like the glory I had seen by the Kebar river, and I fell face down.' Dan. 8.17: 'As he (Gabriel) came near...I was terrified and fell on my face.' Dan. 10:9: In another divine encounter with an angelic being, Daniel says, 'When I heard the sound of his words I then was lying stunned (*radam*) on the ground and my face was toward the ground.'

Mt. 17.6: 'When the disciples heard this, they fell face

down to the ground, terrified. But Jesus came and touched them. "Get up," he said. "Don't be afraid."' Mt. 28.4: 'The guards were so afraid of him (the angel) that they shook and became like dead men.'

Jn. 18.6: As Judas and the soldiers came to arrest Jesus, they had an interesting encounter. 'When Jesus said, "I am he," they jumped back and fell to the ground.' Here we see an immediate falling back in response to the presence of Jesus. They were apparently able to get up shortly thereafter because they went on to arrest Jesus.

Acts 9.22-26: When Paul was apprehended on the road to Damascus by a light from heaven, he says, 'I fell to the ground and heard a voice.' Again we see that falling was a normal response to a divine visitation. Acts 10.10: While Peter was on the roof of Simon the tanner, it says that 'he fell into a trance.'

In 2 Corinthians 12.1-4, Paul describes an amazing experience where he didn't know if he was in his body or not. He was 'caught up in paradise' where he heard inexpressible things that he was not permitted to tell. Again, while the text does not say that he had fallen, this experience was not described as a dream which happened to him when he was asleep, but rather as a vision/revelation (12.1). This implies that he was awake when the revelation came and that for whatever time the experience lasted, he was in some sort of trance-like state, most likely in a prone position.

Rev. 1.17: In the visionary experience that resulted in the book of Revelation, John, speaking of his angelic encounter, says, 'When I saw him I fell at his feet as though dead.' Here we see an experience similar to Adam's and Abram's where the person not only falls but is also unconscious for an extended period of time.

Jonathan Edwards, the main instrument and theologian of

the Great Awakening in America (1725-1760), says in his *Account of the Revival of Religion in Northampton 1740-1742*: 'Many have had their religious affections raised far beyond what they had ever been before; and there were some instances of persons lying in a sort of trance, remaining perhaps for a whole twenty-four hours motionless, and with their senses locked up; but in the mean time under strong imaginations, as though they went to heaven and had there a vision of glorious and delightful objects. It was a very frequent thing to see outcries, faintings, convulsions, and such like, both with distress, and also admiration and joy. It was not the manner here to hold meetings all night, nor was it common to continue them till very late in the night; but it was pretty often so, that there were some so affected, and their bodies so overcome, that they could not go home, but were obligated to stay all night where they were.'

Charles Finney (1792-1875) was one of the most powerful revivalists since the reformation. At a country place named Sodom, in the state of New York, Finney gave one address in which he described the condition of Sodom before God destroyed it. 'I had not spoken in this strain more than a quarter of an hour,' says he, 'when an awful solemnity seemed to settle upon them; the congregation began to fall from their seats in every direction, and cried for mercy. If I had had a sword in each hand, I could not have cut them down as fast as they fell. Nearly the whole congregation were either on their knees or prostrate, I should think, in less than two minutes from the shock that fell upon them. Every one prayed who was able to speak at all.' Similar scenes were witnessed in many other places.

Conclusion: In light of the biblical data, the things that we are seeing now are both similar and dissimilar. It is clear from the text that there is a precedent for sometimes falling during a manifestation of God's presence. The cause of the biblical falls seemed to vary from God putting man to sleep for a specific purpose, to falling out of holy fear, to falling as almost a forced prostration in the face of human arrogance and rebellion. Interestingly, the majority of biblical men fell face down. The examples from Edwards and Finney seem to support this varied pattern. In Edwards' account, the people were overcome by the presence of God while in Finney's, it was clearly a falling from holy fear. The kinds of falling we are seeing now seem to parallel more the action of God to put to sleep for the purpose of divine intervention, rest and healing rather than contrition. While some fall face down, the great majority fall backwards. John Wimber believes that falling face down is some kind of indication of a man's stature in the Lord. Francis McNutt (*Overcome by the Spirit.* Grand Rapids, Baker, p. 85) thinks that the more common falling backwards comes from the heaviness of the glory (*kabod*: weight) of God.

Shaking

Shaking is also common in our meetings and is one of the hardest phenomena to understand. The kinds of shaking vary greatly. Sometimes the shaking is accompanied by all sorts of bodily contortions; sometimes mild, sometimes almost violent. What, if any, biblical precedent is there?

Dan. 10.7: 'I, Daniel, alone saw the vision. For the men who were with me did not see the vision. But a great quaking/trembling fell on them so that they fled to hide themselves.' Ps. 99.1: 'The Lord reigns, let the nations tremble; he sits enthroned between the cherubim, let the earth shake.' Ps. 114.7: 'Tremble O earth at the presence of the Lord.' Jer. 5.22: 'Should you not fear me?' declares the Lord. 'Should you not tremble in my presence?'

Jer. 23.9: In speaking of his prophetic experience, Jeremiah says, 'My heart is broken within me; all my bones tremble. I am like a drunken man overcome by wine because of the Lord and his holy words.' This is a significant verse because Jeremiah is relating that what happened to him on at least one occasion involved a trembling/shaking of his bones. His wording seems to imply that he shook from the inside out. It would take a powerful force to cause his bones to quiver inside his body. The analogy to being overcome could also be a reference to being entranced by the coming of a prophetic word. This text is an answer to God's plea in Jer. 5.22.

Hab. 3.16: 'I heard and my heart pounded; my lips quivered at the sound; decay crept into my bones and my legs trembled.' Mt. 28.4: See above. Acts 4.31: 'The place where they were meeting was shaken.' Js. 2.19: 'The devils also believe and tremble.'

George Fox (1624-1691, founder of the Quakers), after a life-changing experience with the Holy Spirit, had some remarkable experiences. After passing through the experience described above, Fox was mightily used of God, and great conviction of sin fell upon the people to whom he preached. 'The Lord's power began to shake them,' says he, 'and great meetings we began to have, and a mighty power and work of God there was amongst people, to the astonishment of both people and priests.' Later, he says, 'After this I went to Mansfield, where there was a great meeting of professors and people; here I was moved to pray; and the Lord's power was so great, that the house seemed to be shaken.'

A remarkable power seemed to accompany the preaching of Fox wherever he went, whether in Britain or America, Germany, Holland or the West Indies. He usually went about the country on foot, dressed in his famous suit of leather clothes, said to have been made by himself, and often sleeping out of doors or in some haystack. He was ridiculed and persecuted, beaten and stoned, arrested and imprisoned, more frequently perhaps than any other man, and yet the Lord seemed to greatly bless and own his labors. Describing his meetings at Ticknell, England, he says: 'The priest scoffed at us and called us "Quakers." But the Lord's power was so over them, and the word of life was declared in such authority and dread to them, that the priest began trembling himself; and one of the people said, "Look how the priest trembles and shakes, he is turned Quaker also."'

Conclusion: There is a biblical precedent for shaking in God's presence. In the verses where the cause of shaking is mentioned, it has to do with holy fear. The shaking we are experiencing seems to be related more to prophetic ministry and impartation of spiritual gifts of which parallels can be seen in Fox's ministry.

'Drunkenness'

See Jer 23.9 above. Acts 2.13ff: 'Some, however, made fun of them and said, "They have had too much wine." Then Peter stood up with the Eleven, raised his voice and addressed the crowd... "These men are not drunk as you suppose. It is only nine in the morning! No, this is what was spoken by the prophet Joel: 'In the last days I will pour out my Spirit.'"' Compare Acts 10.44-46 where apparently the same kinds of phenomena occurred with the Gentiles. That the 120 newly filled believers were acting in a 'drunken' manner is what is known as an argument from silence. The text never says that they were but it is obviously inferred. They would not be accused of being drunk because they were speaking in different languages. They would have been accused of such because they were acting like drunks, i.e., laughing, falling, slurred speech by some, boldness through lack of restraint, etc. The analogy of the gift of the Spirit being 'new wine' would lend itself to the connection.

Eph. 5.8ff: In a passage dealing with the Ephesians putting off their old carousing lifestyle, Paul exhorts them, 'Do not get drunk on wine which leads to debauchery. Instead, be filled (Greek present tense: "keep on being filled") with the Holy Spirit.' Paul is contrasting carnal drunkenness with spiritual filling. Given the tense of the Greek verb, he appears to also be making an analogy as well as a contrast. Being filled with God's Spirit is similar to being drunk on wine. The difference is that the former is holy while the other is sinful.

Conclusion: While there is not much to go on here, the two NT passages are important texts. The possibility of being 'drunk' in the Spirit is consonant with the overall flow of biblical precedent.

Crying

Neh. 8.9: 'All the people had been weeping as they listened to the words of the law.' 2 Chron. 34.27: 'Because your heart was responsive and you humbled yourself...and you tore your robes and wept in my presence, I have heard you.' Acts 2.37: 'When the people heard this, they were cut to the heart...' This text doesn't say they wept but it's hard to imagine being 'cut to the heart' as not evoking that emotional response.

John Wesley (1703-1791, Founder of the Methodists): On April 17, 1739, there was another remarkable case of conviction of sin, in Bristol. Wesley had just expounded Acts 4, on the power of the Holy Spirit, 'We then called upon God to confirm His Word,' says he. 'Immediately one that stood by (to our no small surprise) cried out aloud, with the utmost vehemence, even as the agonies of death. But we continued in prayer, till "a new song was put in her mouth, a thanksgiving unto our God." Soon after, two other persons (well known in this place, as laboring to live in all good conscience towards all men) were seized with strong pain, and constrained to roar for the disquietness of their heart. These also found peace.' Many other wonderful cases of conviction of sin attended Wesley's preaching. It was a frequent occurrence for people to cry aloud or fall down as if dead in the meetings, so great was their anguish of heart, caused, no doubt, by the Holy Spirit convicting them of sin.

Conclusion: Crying is a natural and normal response to the movement of the Holy Spirit. It comes as a result of the Spirit's ministry to release grief, bring repentance or as a sign of joy.

Laughter

While there are not a lot of texts that describe laughter as a response to divine visitation, the key passage of Scripture on this subject comes at a very important moment in redemptive history. Both Abraham and Sarah had laughed in unbelief when God told them respectively that they would have a child in their old age. When God performed a miracle in giving them the child of promise, Abraham named him 'he laughs' (Isaac). John Wimber believes that laughter accompanies revivals because it represents God's sovereign activity to heal the barrenness of his people.

Ps. 126: A Psalm of joy and laughter. 'Our mouths were filled with laughter...those who sow in tears will reap in joy.' Ecc. 3.4: 'A time to weep and a time to laugh.' (See Js. 4:9 for the opposite progression.) Jn. 17.13: 'I am coming to you now but I say these things while I am still in the world so that they may have the full measure of my joy within them.' If there is any prayer in the Bible that will be answered, it is the high priestly prayer in John 17. Certainly the full measure of joy within the Trinity is full of laughter.

Jonathan Edwards: 'It was very wonderful to see how a person's affections were sometimes moved, when God did as it were suddenly open their eyes, and let into their minds a sense of the greatness of His grace, the fullness of Christ, and His readiness to save … Their joyful surprise has caused their hearts as it were to leap, so that they have been ready to break forth into laughter, tears often at the same time issuing like a flood, and intermingling a loud weeping. Sometimes they have not been able to forbear crying out with a loud voice, expressing their great admiration. The manner of God's work on the soul, sometimes especially, is very mysterious.'

Conclusion: Again, laughter fits within the general flow of Scripture. Christians can be so filled with the joy of the Lord that they are given over to fits of laughter.

Prophetic revelation

One of the things we are seeing is that people are having visions, dreams and prophetic words while under the power of the Spirit. All throughout the Bible, prophetic revelation occurs during periods of divine visitation. There is no way we can cover this subject in this context so a few key passages will have to suffice.

Num 11.29: In response to Joshua's complaint that some of the elders were prophesying outside of the tent of meeting when the Spirit rested on them, Moses says, 'Are you jealous for my sake? I wish that all the Lord's people were prophets and that the Lord would put his Spirit on them!' This is a very significant passage. It shows that prophecy can be a response to the Spirit's coming. The phrase 'when the Spirit rested on them' (v25) is also reminiscent of the Spirit alighting on Jesus like a dove at his baptism. Num 11.6: When Miriam and Aaron opposed Moses, God revealed how he speaks to the prophets, in contrast to speaking face to face with Moses: 'When a prophet is among you, I reveal myself to him in visions, I speak to him in dreams.' 1 Sam. 10.10: In fulfillment of Samuel's prophetic word to him, Saul met a procession of prophets. The text says, '... the Spirit of the Lord came on him in power, and he joined in their prophesying.'

Acts 2.17-18: On the day of Pentecost, Peter quoted the prophetic word of Joel saying, 'In the last days, God says, I will pour out my Spirit on all people. Your sons and your daughters will prophesy, your young men will see visions, your old men will dream dreams. Even on my servants, both men and women, I will pour out my Spirit in those days, and they will prophesy.' This is the only primary text concerning the phenomenon that we have been able to find. Peter conveys quite plainly: 'God says' that when the Spirit comes upon his people, they will prophesy and receive dreams and visions. 1 Cor. 14: An entire chapter of 1 Corinthians is devoted to the exhortation to be eager for spiritual gifts, especially the gift of prophecy. When an unbeliever comes into a meeting and hears someone prophesying, Paul says that, 'he will fall down and worship God, exclaiming, "God is really among you!"'

George Fox: 'And a report went abroad of me, that I was a young man that had a discerning spirit; whereupon many came to me, from far and near, professors, priests, and people; and the Lord's power brake forth; and I had great openings and prophecies; and spake unto them of the things of God, and they heard with attention and silence, and went away, and spread the fame thereof.'

Conclusion: When the Spirit comes in power, God's people will prophesy.

What are the phenomena for?

Signs of the Lord's presence

In Ex. 33.14-16, in response to Moses it says, 'The Lord replied, "My Presence will go with you."' The promise of God's presence is the distinguishing mark of God's people. Moses says to God, 'What else will distinguish me and your people from all the other people on the face of the earth?' (v.16). The abiding presence of the Holy Spirit is in each Christian and, since Acts 2, has been continually active in the Church. Jesus, speaking of the Spirit, says to the disciples, 'he is with you and will be in you' (Jn. 14. 17). There are times, however, when God allows us to see his presence to build our faith and show us where he is working.

2 Ki. 6.17: When Elisha saw that his servant was afraid of the surrounding armies, it says, 'And Elisha prayed, "Oh Lord, open his eyes so he may see." Then the Lord opened the servant's eyes and he looked and saw the hills full of horses and chariots of fire all around Elisha.' Here God allows his presence to be manifest. The phenomena we have been describing are biblical manifestations of God's presence.

The phenomena can best be described as prophetic signs, even as Ezekiel and Jeremiah were signs that pointed to God. Those that have moved in these signs have noticed over time that certain phenomena mean specific things, especially shaking.

Certain shaking motions preceding prophetic utterance
Certain shaking meaning empowerment

Certain body movements indicative of demonic presence
Etc.

God is shaking us to wake us up! In Eph. 5.14 Paul says, 'Wake up O sleeper, rise from the dead and Christ will shine on you.' This command precedes the exhortation to be filled continually with the Holy Spirit. We are to wake up and seek to be continually filled with the wine of God's Spirit.

If we haven't heeded God's previous wake up calls, perhaps he is now shaking us to arouse us and get our attention. To humble us.

When Randy Clark asked God why he was bringing all the phenomena to Toronto, God replied that he was looking for people who were willing to look publicly foolish for the honor of his name. Paul Cain said, 'God offends the mind to reveal the heart.' The bottom line issue is one of control. God wants to know who among his people will be willing to play the fool for his glory.

Anointing

The filling of the Holy Spirit is a repeatable experience and one we are commanded to continually experience (Eph. 5.18). God will sovereignly move on us to impart supernatural ability to do certain things. See 2 Tim. 1.6: 'I remind you to fan into flame the gift of God which is in you through the laying on of my hands.'

Charles Finney: '...the Holy Ghost descended on me in a manner that seemed to go through me, body and soul. I could feel the impression, like a wave of electricity, going through and through me. Indeed it seemed to come in waves and waves of liquid love; for I could not express it in any other way. It seemed like the very breath of God. I can recollect distinctly that it seemed to fan me, like immense wings. No words can express the wonderful love that was shed abroad

in my heart. I wept aloud with joy and love; and I do not
know but I should say, I literally bellowed out the
unutterable gushings of my heart. The waves came over me,
and over me, one after the other, until I recollect I cried out,
"I shall die if these waves continue to pass over me." I said,
"Lord, I cannot bear any more;" yet I had no fear of death.'
Finney continued for some time under this remarkable
manifestation of the Holy Spirit's power. Wave after wave of
spiritual power rolled over him, and through him, thrilling
every fibre of his being.

Note: Signs are pointers to a destination, not the
destination itself. Our destiny is to become conformed into
the image of Christ (Rom. 8.29). We have also been called,
as the Church, to bring the gospel to every nation and then
the end will come (Mt. 24.14). When the Holy Spirit comes
in power, he comes to make us like Jesus, to heal us and
empower us for our particular roles in the mission. The
results are what he's after, not the phenomena. If, under
God's sovereignty, he chooses, during seasons of divine
visitation, to do his work without phenomena, that is his
choice. So also, it is of no benefit to shake or fall, and have
no long lasting fruit. Ultimately, what God is after is a
willing, humble heart. He decides how to sanctify, heal and
empower.

Jonathan Edwards: 'Neither a negative nor a positive
judgment should be based on the manifestation alone
because the Scripture nowhere gives us any such rule.' John
White (*When the Spirit Comes With Power*, InterVarsity
Press, 1987, p. 81-82): '...manifestations, while they may be
a blessing, are no guarantee of anything. Their outcome
depends on the mysterious traffic between God and our
spirits. Your fall and your shaking may be a genuine express
of the power of the Spirit resting on you. But the Spirit may

not benefit you in the least if God does not have his way with you, while someone who neither trembles nor falls may profit greatly.'

Just remember Lk. 10.20: '...do not rejoice that the spirits submit to you, but rejoice that your names are written in heaven.'

How can you be sure it's God?

Options

People do it themselves (psychological)
Preachers do it (mass hypnosis)
Devil does it
God does it
Mixture

Biblical warnings

Mt. 24.24: 'For false Christians and false prophets will appear and perform great signs and miracles to deceive even the elect – if that were possible.' 2 Cor. 11.14: '...Satan himself masquerades as an angel of light.' 1 Jn. 4.1: 'Dear friends, do not believe every spirit but test the spirits to see whether they are from God because many false prophets have gone out into the world.'

Key texts for proper discernment

Lk. 11.9-12: 'So I say to you, ask and it will be given to you... Which of you fathers, if your son asks for a fish will give him a snake instead? Or if he asks for an egg will give him a scorpion? If you then, though you are evil, know how to give good gifts to your children, how much more will your father in heaven give the Holy Spirit to those who ask him!' Simply put: If we ask for God, we aren't going to get the devil. Remember Mk. 3.24, 'A kingdom divided against itself cannot stand.' 1 Jn. 4.2-3: 'This is how you can recognize the Spirit of God: Every spirit that acknowledges that Jesus Christ has come in the flesh is from God, but every spirit that does not acknowledge Jesus is not from God.'

Simply put: If the person praying exalts Jesus, the Holy Spirit will be the one who will come to answer his/her prayer.

The devil wants to slander Jesus' name, not exalt it. 1 Cor. 12.10: Discerning of spirits is a spiritual gift. We have demonstrated that when we pray and ask for God, the Holy Spirit will come in answer to our prayers. The next question is whether the manifestation we are seeing is God blessing, empowering, etc., or whether it is what missionaries have called a 'power encounter,' i.e., the light of God exposing an area of darkness. In the case of sin, this would call for repentance. In the case of demonization, this would call for deliverance along with repentance.

Another possibility is that the person is performing acts of manifestations himself. In this case, proper pastoral judgment must be used. 1 Cor. 14:40: 'Everything should be done in a fitting and orderly way.' This criterion concerns the way the meeting is being conducted. The 'everything' Paul is referring to is the coming of the gifts of the Spirit into the meeting. By nature, this looks a bit messy at times. Look for the way the meeting is being conducted. Are the leaders humble? Exalting Jesus? Maintaining order in the way the gifts are moving? If they are, and the atmosphere is peaceful and not carnal and hyped, then it will be the Holy Spirit who will come to build Jesus' Church, not the devil.

Mt. 12.33: 'Make a tree good and its fruit will be good or make a tree bad and its fruit will be bad, for a tree is recognized by its fruit.' Gal. 5.22: 'But the fruit of the Spirit is love, joy, peace, patience, kindness, goodness, faithfulness, gentleness, and self-control.' Simply put, if the long term fruit is Gal. 5.22, it's God. The character of Jesus is the destiny of the Church (Rom. 8.29).

Summary of judging criteria

Are the people being prayed for asking for God? They will get God. Are the people praying asking for God and exalting Jesus? The Holy Spirit will come in answer to their prayers. Are you asking for the gift of discernment? Are the leaders humble and exalting Jesus? Is the atmosphere peaceful, even though perhaps noisy? If yes, then these are signs of the Holy Spirit's presence. Is the fruit good? Then it's God.

God, I still don't get it!

Further objections – 'It's hard to understand.'

Our presupposition: 'If it were God, I would understand it.' All throughout the Bible, God revealed himself in ways that were hard to understand. God's chosen people for the most part missed Jesus. The Pharisees called him 'Beelzebub' which was a term for the devil. The disciples didn't understand the mission of Jesus until the Holy Spirit came in Acts 2. The Jews as a whole never understood that God's heart was for all the nations. Even the disciples were shocked that God would offer the gospel to the Gentiles, law free. They muse in amazement in Acts 11.18, 'So then God has granted even the Gentiles repentance unto life!'

Historically, God has moved in ways that are hard to understand. The classic example of this is martyrdom. Martyrdom has always been an explosive key to church growth. One of the early church fathers, Tertullian, said, 'The blood of the martyrs is the seed of the church.'

'It makes me afraid.'

Our presupposition: 'If it were God, I wouldn't be afraid.' Visitations produce fear throughout the Bible. Lightning, thunder, and smoke on Mt. Sinai (Ex.19). Daniel in Chapter 10 had a great vision: 'I had no strength left, my face turned deathly pale, and I was helpless.' The angel, Gabriel, had to say, 'Don't be afraid,' because he was terrifying. Great fear seized the whole church in Acts 5 when Ananias and Sapphira dropped dead through a prophetic word when they lied to the Holy Spirit. Note: This fear is not the same fear as that which comes from Satan. 2 Tim. 1.7 says that God has not given us a spirit of fear. The devil's fear robs us of faith and hope and renders us incapable of love. There is, however, a godly fear that the Bible says is the beginning of wisdom (Prov. 9.10). It is this kind of fear that is produced by divine visitations. It results in a more godly life. How could a visitation of a holy God on sinful men not produce fear? How could our finite minds expect to understand the infinite ways of God? He is completely beyond us, and holy. Fear is caused by: The holiness of God coming in contact with our sinfulness. Our anti-supernatural world view: since we have no category in our western world view, when we encounter the supernatural, we encounter the fear of the unknown. It causes the psychological state known as 'cognitive dissonance.' We receive data that does not fit and it causes feelings of insecurity.

'It causes division.'

Our presupposition: 'If it were God, there would be no division.' There are two kinds of division. When the kingdom of light clashes with the kingdom of darkness, it causes godly division. Jesus said that he had not come to bring peace but a sword. 'A man's enemies will be the members of his own household' (Mt. 10.36). Backbiting, slander, and rebellion are ungodly because they cause the kingdom to be divided against itself. Godly division is thoroughly biblical: Korah was judged for his rebellion against Moses in Numbers 11. Jesus caused division wherever he went. The inclusion of Gentiles caused division (Acts 15). Godly division is thoroughly historical.

The Great Awakening broke out in New Jersey in 1725 and was violently opposed by more traditional churches. G. Campbell Morgan called the Pentecostal Movement 'the last vomit of Satan.' The last move of God usually persecutes the present one.

'He overrides my faculties.'

Our presupposition: 'God is always a gentleman and would never force anything upon us.' The Bible seems to say something else. God is God and he does what he wants. In Isaiah, God says, 'I say my purpose will stand and I will do all that I please' (46.11). God overrode Balaam in Numbers 23 and caused Balaam to prophesy against his will. God overrode Saul and his men in 1 Samuel 19 and caused them to prophesy instead of killing David. Jesus blinded Paul on the road to Damascus against his will. God's killing of Ananias and Sapphira is the ultimate override. Far from treating us gently, God has promised his people persecution.

'It's so emotional.'

Our presupposition: 'If it were God, there would be very little or no emotion in it.' Again, the Bible says something else: Pr. 4.3: 'Above all, guard your heart for it is the wellspring of life.' There is a full range of emotion seen in the scripture: David danced, wept, fought. Jesus wept, was joyful, angry. Peter wept, rejoiced, felt convicted. God is emotional because we are. We have been created in his image. Historically, emotions have been seen in the movements of God. Jonathan Edwards saw no distinction between the head and the heart: 'Nothing of religious significance ever took place in the human heart if it wasn't deeply effected by such Godly emotions.' John White says, 'The lack of emotion is just as sick as being controlled by emotion.' Emotion comes from seeing reality (truth) clearly. When the Spirit of truth comes, we see things as they really are which opens up our emotional being.

'It causes me to be the center of attention.'

Our presupposition: 'If it were God, he would not do it publicly.' Quite to the contrary, God often uses the person to be the message. In Ezekiel 4-5, Ezekiel is told by God to lie on his side, naked, to shave his head and beard, etc. God made him the center of attention because he, himself, was the message. Jeremiah was told to smash a jar in Jer. 18-19 to draw attention to his message. Hosea was told to marry a prostitute as a message to the nation of Israel. Ananias and Sapphira can be used as yet another example because their dead bodies were the message. Stephen was 'glowing' when he was killed.

'It's so disorderly.'

Our presupposition: 'If it's God, it would be always spiritual, tidy, and orderly.' Both the Bible and history show just the opposite. Until Christ returns, there will always be a mixture of the Spirit and flesh. This is why we are told to pray that the kingdom would come. We are at war, and war is always ugly. The disciples were rebuked for their mixed motives. They wanted great position while genuinely trying to serve Jesus. Paul rebuked Peter to his face in Galatians 2 for being in the flesh but this didn't discredit Peter's ministry. Paul and Barnabas split up over the issue of taking John Mark with them on the second missionary journey. Luke never tells us whether either Paul or Barnabas was in sin. The point is that the kingdom continued to advance despite division in the ranks. John Wesley himself had bitter disputes with other godly men over issues of doctrine. Remember Satan's trick is to try to discredit what's true by infiltrating it with what's false. He wants to tempt the flesh that is at war with our redeemed spirit in its attempt to serve God. He wants to expose the sinful character within us. This fact does not negate the genuineness of our ministries any more than it did Peter's or Paul's.

It always smells in a nursery. The very nature of discipleship is trial and error. We have grace for our children as they learn to walk. Praising the good and reprimanding in love the bad is part of parenting. To debunk a new movement for not getting it all right is not fair. Godly correctives, on the other hand, are necessary to keep that movement on course. We need a 'free to fail' environment in order to learn. 1 Cor. 14.40 says, 'Let everything be done in order.' Let's put the emphasis on 'everything' and later focus on the 'order.' The biblical order is that you build the fireplace around the fire, and not vice versa. Function always precedes form.

'It doesn't happen to me.'

Our presupposition: 'When God moves, the same things happen to everyone.' It's simply not true that some people seem to be 'favored' while others are not. God's love is for the whole world. Under his sovereignty he treats everyone in a way that is beneficial for them. God ultimately determines what is best for us. Jesus healed only one man by the pool of Bethesda despite the fact that there were many more sick present (Jn. 5). This in no way meant that God loved the man who was healed more than the ones who weren't. Jesus said that he only did what he saw the Father doing and the Father was somehow loving all those at the pool that day.

A final caution

It's OK to have questions about what is happening but we must try to be honest about the motive behind our questions. If it's because of your personality, that's OK. But let's not let our personalities keep us from being touched by God during this season of divine visitation. If it's because you are a 'noble Berean,' that's to be commended. Search for the truth diligently. When you find it, press in. If it's because you are afraid: Ask God why. Don't run – if this is God, then you would be turning your back on him. After the crucifixion, the disciples had questions too. The Jesus who walked with two of them on the road to Emmaus and opened their minds so they could understand the Scriptures is the same Jesus who walks in our midst by the person of the Holy Spirit (Lk. 24. 13-35). He will open our minds as well.

A final word

When we ask the question, 'What in the world is happening to us?', it is clear from what we are seeing and hearing from all over the United States and Canada, that we are in a sovereign move of the Holy Spirit. Peter told early onlookers to the Spirit's activity to repent so that times of refreshment would come from the Lord's presence (Acts 3.19). What should be our response to such a season of divine visitation? The clearest passage in the NT on the subject of a local church's response to the coming of the Holy Spirit is 1 Corinthians 12-14. Paul's purpose in writing 1 Corinthians was to answer a set of questions delivered to him in the form of a letter from the church (see 7.1; 16.17). He had also received some oral information from 'Chloe's people' (1.11).

When Paul proceeds to answer their questions about spiritual gifts, he does so in a section where he is dealing with questions related to when they gather together for church (11.17). In chapter 12, Paul encourages the activity of spiritual gifts when they gather together. He also said that the church was Christ's body which was to be built up as spiritual gifts are exercised. His admonition in chapter 13 is that they exercise gifts in love. Herein lies the most important point of all as we press into the season that is upon us: without love it profits us nothing.

In chapter 3, Paul had already established that whoever co-labors to build on Paul's apostolic foundation will have his/her works weighed on the day of the Lord. Some works will be labeled 'gold, silver and precious stones.' Others will be labeled 'wood, hay and stubble.' It is the quality of each man's work that will make the difference. How do we know that our work is the kind of quality that will pass the fire test on that day? I believe the answer is in the motive. In chapter 13, Paul says that the motive must be love.

In Matthew 7.15-23, in a passage dealing with false prophets who would be known for their fruit, Jesus said, 'Many will say to me on that day, "Lord, Lord, did we not prophesy in your name, and in your name drive out demons and perform many miracles?" Then I will tell them plainly,

"I never knew you. Away from me you evil doers.'" This passage allows for a category of person in the church that amazingly are able to move in spiritual gifts but at judgment day will be counted among those that do not know Jesus. The difference is that they are not doing the will of the Father. Their motive is not one of love for God or men, but is self serving.

Jesus is clear: self serving activity, no matter how powerful, doesn't count. Paul finishes his response to the Corinthian question of spiritual gifts in chapter 14 where he says that the sign of a loving exercise of gifts is the building up of Christ's body. If the exercising of gifts does not, in the end, build up the church, it has been counter productive. Whether because of ill motive or because the leaders have not been facilitating the operation of the gifts in the meeting 'decently and in order' (14.40), the fact of the matter is that the gifts have not been allowed to work to build up the church for the common good.

Conclusion: The final word, then, about the season that is upon us, belongs to the apostle Paul. He calls us to embrace the Holy Spirit's ministry in our midst. He exhorts us to exercise the gifts with a loving heart posture in such a manner that the church is edified. The leaders need to see that this is done in an orderly way. What counts in the end is not whether someone fell or shook or even was healed. No, what counts ultimately is whether they are loved and built up. What happens as a result of the Spirit's sovereign intervention is up to God. This is his work, not ours. Our job is to love and pray in faith for the kingdom to come, watching, as we do, for what the Father is doing so we can bless it.

Postscript

So what has Father been doing during this season that has been upon us? As we conclude, we need to ask whether we are seeing any long term fruit. This is the ultimate test in determining if it is God. In Acts 3.19, Peter called his onlookers to repentance so their sins could be wiped out. The result in their lives was that times of refreshing would come to them from the presence of the Lord. One of those seasons of refreshment is upon us now. In talking to John Arnott, the pastor of the Airport Vineyard in Toronto where this visitation has continued non-stop for over three months, the overriding theme has been joy. This is thoroughly consonant with the New Testament which sees joy as a sign of the presence of the Spirit in the believer's life (there are over 60 references to joy in the NT). God's people are simply having fun in him.

In the early days of the apostles, as they were searching for a word that would communicate to the Gentiles the ecstasy in having their sins forgiven and being in right relationship with God through the atoning blood of Christ Jesus, they choose the word *euanggelion* which we now translate 'gospel' or 'good news.' It was a completely secular word that was used in reference to the emperor's birthday. It was a holiday, a day of good news. The apostles traveled throughout the ancient world preaching that the day of God's party had come.

We are learning to party in God again because the Spirit of the Lord has come among us to teach us grace, mediate forgiveness and reveal the Father's love in Christ. The second characteristic of this renewal, then, is a return to our first love, Jesus. Reports are coming from every corner about people falling in love with Jesus in a whole new way, about a new love for the Bible, about being taken up into heaven in the form of visions and dreams. In the arms of Jesus is fullness of joy.

The third characteristic of the renewal is healing. Reports too numerous to count tell of physical healings, deliverance from demonic influence and deep emotional wounds being touched. It seems that as people spend 'floor time' with God, he meets them where they are, at their point of need. He is removing barriers that have kept us from moving forward with God.

Much of the shaking has to do with empowerment for service. Spiritual gifts are being imparted through the laying on of hands. We have seen impartations for intercession, evangelism, healing, prophecy and pastoral care. Finally there has been a significant return of prodigals to the church. God is healing old wounds and drawing lost ones back into fellowship with himself and with the church.

There have been numerous salvations but not enough to characterize this as a genuine revival. Revival is characterized by masses coming to Christ. Those that have been on the vanguard of this move of the Spirit believe that its purpose is to refresh the church and to prepare it for the mighty and genuine revival that is on the horizon.

The Vineyard Archives

VINEYARD CHAMPAIGN SUGGESTED MINISTRY TIPS

Written to help teach the Champaign Vineyard church body wholesome techniques for enhancing times of ministry, this paper contains some helpful hints about four specific areas:

Tips for facilitating ministry as a leader
Tips for praying for people
Tips for catching people
Tips for receiving ministry

Written by the church staff, it is not intended to be considered an official 'position paper' about how the Champaign Vineyard, or any other church – Vineyard or otherwise – should handle times of ministry. These tips have been compiled based on the experience of the Champaign staff and the suggestions of others.

Tips for facilitating ministry as a leader

1. It is usually helpful to begin every time with worship followed by testimonies of people who have been touched. Immediately after the testimonies, invite the Holy Spirit to come upon these individuals again and do a further work. There seems to be a special grace for these people to receive another 'drink' of the new wine when they are up front giving testimonies. They often begin to experience the same outward manifestations again.

2. When ministry begins, look for those who are most obviously anointed. This can be done by looking for manifestations such as crying, shaking, laughing etc.

3. If you don't notice any outward manifestations of the Holy Spirit, ask those who sense a strong anointing within

them to come for ministry. This might manifest as a burning, tingling, 'knowing,' etc.

4. Encourage people to freely receive ministry. It's OK to receive several times of prayer in the same meeting. It's also OK to receive prayer every time we gather. In fact, people seem to receive better and more fully each successive time. The more the 'soaking,' the deeper the impact.

5. Keep reassuring people that it's OK if they do not manifest anything unusual when they receive prayer. God works differently in different people. Remember to encourage people that it's not manifestations we are after but changed hearts. The manifestations are simply a by-product.

6. Encourage people not to be fearful of what God is doing. This requires reassuring words from the leaders.

7. Be willing to be prayed for yourself. People always respond best when the leaders are also responding. It seems that the leaders are the gatekeepers and what they will allow, the people feel confident to allow.

8. Sometimes children are afraid to receive until they see their parents or other known adults receive. Some children have even been reported as being fearful of some of the manifestations they have experienced, such as being pinned to the floor.

9. Keep the 'environment' light and easy. This is not a season for heavy ministry, great deliverance, or deep inner healing. It seems the Holy Spirit is emphasizing joy and release from heaviness.

10. Please refer to these manifestations as 'times of refreshing' (Acts 3:19) or renewal rather than revival. Revival has the connotation of touching the larger

community. Use the phrase 'resting in the Spirit' rather than 'slain in the Spirit.'

11. When the number of people wanting prayer is large, it seems that the quality of prayer goes down and vice versa. We've found that the people who linger around the longest and get multiple times of prayer generally get the most. Meeting and prayer times seem to move from low anointing to higher as time goes on.

12. Current prayer methods do not contradict the Vineyard prayer model. Both are important and should be used as led by the Spirit.

13. The 'event flavor' of this season does not nullify the idea that some things happen as a process.

14. Let's be careful about pride and presumption.

Tips for praying for people

1. When praying for individuals, watch closely what the Spirit is doing (John 5:19). If no manifestation of the Holy Spirit comes within a few minutes, it is often wise to simply allow that person to 'soak' and come back later. We've found it is even advisable to say something like this, 'I want you to soak a little while, and I will be back to you later.' Meanwhile, others will pray for them, or you can come back when you are done with the next individual.

2. When people fall in the Spirit (called 'resting in the Spirit'), keep praying for them. It seems that everyone wants to get up way too quickly. God continues to do work even when we are down on the floor. Sometimes it will be noticeable and other times it might be quiet and inward.

Allowing people to get up too quickly seems to work against what the Lord wants to do.

3. Generally, it is helpful to have people stand to receive ministry. This seems to allow the Holy Spirit more freedom to move. Be sure to put someone behind the person receiving ministry to catch them.

4. Be careful not to push people over. This is offensive and will backfire by causing people to grow resistant to the real thing.

5. Don't force ministry. If the Spirit is not doing something, relax and remember that there will always be another opportunity.

6. There is at times a 'backwash phenomenon.' This means that the anointing is not received by the individual you are praying for and can actually come back to you.

7. If the person is one of the 'hard ones,' you might help them do the following. Help them to deal with a tendency to rationalize, with their fears, or with a loss of control. Calm their fear of loss of control by helping them know what to expect. For example, let them know that they will have a clear mind, that they can usually stop the process at any point if they want to, and that the Spirit comes in waves.

8. Pray biblical prayers such as some of the following. Come Holy Spirit. Let the Kingdom of God come on earth as it is in Heaven. Outpouring of the Father's love for them and for others. A deeper revelation of the Father's love in Christ. Anointing for service. Release of the gifts and callings. Bring the light and expel the darkness. Note: 'More Lord' is just a shortened form of blessing what the Father is doing, from John 5:19.

9. If you are getting 'words of knowledge,' pray biblical prayers related to those words.

10. Some people have 'fear of falling' issues. Help them to sit down or to fall carefully, especially if they have back problems, pregnancy, or fear of falling.

11. It's OK to talk to the person during the engagement process.

12. If your hand/body is shaking, pray with hands slightly away from the person so as not to distract them.

13. Don't project what God has been doing with you on to the person you are praying for. For example, if you've been laughing, don't pressure them to laugh. Find out what God is doing for them and bless it.

14. Encourage the people you pray for to put testimonies in written form immediately. Please use the forms 'New Wine at the Vineyard' for adults and children.

Tips for catching people

1. Please do not push or pull anyone over. This will ultimately backfire.

2. Do not hold anyone up by grabbing their shoulders or upper back.

3. When laying hands on people, do just that. Do not rub or do other things that might be annoying.

4. When catching someone, put your hands lightly in the small of their back. This gives people confidence that you are behind them and does not interfere with the prayer process.

Tips for receiving ministry

1. Come humble and hungry. Forget preconceived ideas and what has happened to others.

2. Experience it before trying to analyze it. It is something like worshipping God which has no rational explanation. Others have likened it to kissing which is more emotional than analytical.

3. Face your fears.
   The fear of deception
   The fear of being hurt again or not receiving at all
   The fear of losing control. (This can often be seen when people try to step backward rather than fall.)

4. Focus on the Lord, not on falling. Give the Holy Spirit permission to do with you what he wants to do.

Notes

1. Acts 3:19. In the Greek literally translated: 'Repent ye therefore and turn so that your sins may be wiped away, so as may come times of refreshing from the presence of the Lord.' Nestle and Marshall, *RSV Interlinear Greek-English New Testament* (Bagster, 1975).
2. I was at the meeting: Church Development Council of the AIDS organisation I founded.
3. *The Sunday Telegraph* (19th June 1994).
4. *HTB in Focus* (12th June 1994).
5. *HTB in Focus* (12th June 1994).
6. *Alpha* magazine (September 1994). A fuller account is to be found in the Appendix.
7. John Wimber and team: 'Let the Fire Fall', Wembley Conference Centre (20th-23rd September 1994). Around 800 attended the day time conference on church planting, while perhaps 1,200 attended in the evenings (the place seats around twice the number).
8. David Dewey, *Baptist Times* (30th June 1994).
9. David Dewey, *Baptist Times* (30th June 1994).
10. David Dewey, *Baptist Times* (30th June 1994).
11. *The Sunday Telegraph* (19th June 1994).
12. Personal communication.
13. Prophecy Word Ministries prayer letter (July 1994).
14. *Pioneer People Life* and *Times* magazine (June 1994).
15. *Alpha* magazine (July 1994).
16. Personal communication.
17. *Jesus Army* magazine (August 1994).
18. Personal communication.
19. *HTB in Focus* (10th July 1994).
20. 'At your service – association of Vineyard churches', *The Times* (2nd July 1994).
21. I was present at the meeting.
22. Personal communication.
23. *Challenge Weekly*, New Zealand (20th July 1994).
24. *Challenge Weekly,* New Zealand (10th August 1994).
25. *The Independent* (12th August 1994).
26. 'Roman Catholic affected by charismatic blessing', *The Daily Telegraph* (22nd August 1994).
27. Personal communication from Stuart Bell.
28. Personal communication.
29. *The Observer* (4th September 1994).
30. Geoffrey Levy, 'This man has just been given the Toronto Blessing. What in God's name is going on?', *Daily Mail* (2nd September 1994).
31. John 14:6.
32. Personal communication.
33. *HTB in Focus* (10th July 1994).
34. *HTB in Focus* (10th July 1994).
35. *HTB in Focus* (10th July 1994).
36. *HTB in Focus* (10th July 1994).
37. Member of Thames Community Church.
38. I am not certain of her name – Thames Community Church.
39. Roger Ellis, leader of Revelation group of churches based in Chichester.

40. Personal communication.
41. G. Coates, *The Vision* (Kingsway Publications, 1995).
42. Andrew Brown, 'Evangelicals concerned over increase in supernatural beliefs', *The Independent* (15th September 1990).
43. Reuters News Service (25th October 1989).
44. 'Evangelical movement threatens to promote dangerous intolerance', *Independent on Sunday* (13th January 1991).
45. 'Evangelical movement threatens to promote dangerous intolerance', *Independent on Sunday* (13th January 1991).
46. 'Anglican Pentecostals – the growing popularity of evangelism', *Economist* (30th March 1991 – UK).
47. 'Church failing to attract young as congregations fall 500,000 in decade', *The Daily Telegraph* (4th March 1991).
48. Clifford Longley, 'Why the church is wary of Carey – the new Archbishop of Canterbury', *The Times* (8th April 1991).
49. 'George Carey now inherits the Church of England', *The Guardian* (19th April 1991).
50. *Sunday Times* (16th February 1992).
51. Damian Thompson, 'New churches flourish for born-again Christians', *The Daily Telegraph* (29th March 1993).
52. *The Daily Telegraph* (31 January 1992).
53. 'Opting out for Jesus – Christian teaching in school', *Independent on Sunday* (13th September 1992).
54. 'Linkman for God's own CNN – Morris Cerullo's planned Cable TV service for Britain and Europe', *The Guardian* (22nd August 1992).
55. Andrew Brown, 'UK: Priest embraces path of change', *The Independent* (18th September 1993).
56. Ruth Gledhill, 'Evangelicals ditch tambourines for community action', *The Times* (10th April 1993).
57. 'The new religious anatomy of Britain – worship moves in mysterious ways', *Economist* (13th March 1993).
58. Bridge Church, Brentford, linked to Pioneer (figures unpublished).
59. Jamie Dettmer, 'Bishop warns of "intoxicating worship" – Branch Davidian Cult – Waco, Texas', *The Times* (21st April 1993).
60. Michael De-la-Noy, 'O ye church of little faith – Church of England', *The Independent* (16th September 1993).
61. *Media Week* (1st April 1994).
62. *Idea Magazine* (October 1994).
63. John Capon, 'The gospel hits the mat with a Bonnke', *The Sunday Telegraph* (3rd October 1993).
64. *Idea Magazine* (October 1994).
65. '100 vicars do not believe in supernatural God', *Sunday Times* (31st July 1994).
66. A. A. Gill, 'Spiritual uplift', *Sunday Times* (4th September 1994).
67. BBC radio news, 6pm (4th September 1994).
68. 'The Protestant surge in Latin America', *Economist* (17th April 1993).
69. *Financial Times* (29th December 1990).
70. 'Ex-bouncer becomes spiritual midwife for new South Africa', *Reuters News Service* (28th July 1991).
71. P. Johnstone, *Operation World* (OM Publishing, 1993).

72. G. Taylor, *Sex in History* (Thames and Hudson, 1953) – quoting early Persian writings about Christians.

73. John Gillies, *Historical Collections of the Accounts of Revival* (1754).

74. Desiderius Erasmus, *On the Amiable Concord of the Church* (1540).

75. Revd William Reid, *Authentic Records of Revival Now in Progress in the United Kingdom* (republished by Richard Owen, 1980).

76. C. E. Vulliamy, *John Wesley* (London: Geoffrey Bles, 1931).

77. F. Cross, *Oxford Dictionary of the Christian Church* (Oxford University Press, 1974).

78. Jonathan Edwards, *Distinguishing Marks of a Work of the Spirit of God* (1741).

79. C. Whittaker, *Great Revivals* (Marshall Pickering, 1990).

80. Arthur Wallis, *In the Day of Thy Power* (Christian Literature Crusade, 1956).

81. C. Vulliamy, *Wesley* (Geoffrey Bles, 1931).

82. C. Whittaker, *Great Revivals* (Marshall Pickering, 1990).

83. C. Whittaker, *Great Revivals* (Marshall Pickering, 1990).

84. Charles Finney, *Revivals of Religion* (Morgan and Scott, 1913), p.133.

85. Edwin Orr's estimates quoted in C. Whittaker, *Great Revivals* (Marshall Pickering, 1990).

86. Revd William Reid, *Authentic Records of Revival Now in Progress in the United Kingdom* (Reprinted Richard Owen, 1980).

87. Revd Samuel Moore, *The Great Revival in Ireland* (Marshall Brothers, 1859). Written at the time.

88. C. Whittaker, *Great Revivals* (Marshall Pickering, 1990).

89. C. Whittaker, *Great Revivals* (Marshall Pickering, 1990).

90. William Bramwell Booth, *Echoes and Memories.*

91. Donald Gee, *Wind and Flame* (Heath Press, 1967).

92. Arthur Goodrich, *The Story of the Welsh Revival* (Fleming Revell Co., 1905).

93. Eifion Evans, *The Welsh Revival of 1904* (Evangelical Press, 1969).

94. Eifion Evans, *The Welsh Revival of 1904* (Evangelical Press, 1969).

95. Revd Vyrnwy Morgan, *The Welsh Religious Revival – 1904-5* (Chapman and Hall, 1909). A retrospect and a criticism.

96. Frank Bartleman, *Azusa Street* (reprinted Logos International, 1980).

97. George Jeffreys, *Pentecostal Rays – The Baptism and Gifts of the Holy Spirit* (Elim Publishing Company, 1933). Founder and leader of the Elim Foursquare Gospel Alliance.

98. *Independent on Sunday* (13th January 1991).

99. W. H. Harding in foreword to 1913 edition of Charles Finney, *Revivals of Religion*, a collection of addresses given in 1835, revised and added to in 1858.

100. Arthur Wallis, *In the Day of Thy Power* (Christian Literature Crusade, 1956).

101. *Ibid.*

102. Martyn Lloyd-Jones, *Joy Unspeakable* (Kingsway Publications, 1980).

103. J. Packer, *God in Our Midst* (Word, 1987).

104. Edited version of talk, reproduced in *Baptist Times* (July 1994).

105. Newsletter of Prophecy Word Ministries (July 1994).

106. All biblical quotations are from the NIV or AV. Gerald Coates mentions

that he is grateful for the research done by Dr Jack Deere found in his book *Surprised by the Power of the Spirit*, published by Kingsway.

107. CiPC Newsletter (September 1994).

108. Alan Morrison, *We all Fall Down* (Diakrisis Publications, The Manse, Market Place, Crich, Nr Matlock, Derbyshire DE4 5DD).

109. Fr Seraphim Rose, *Orthodoxy and the Religion of the Future* (St Herman Brotherhood, 1979), pp.190-191.

110. *Church of England Newspaper* (25th August 1994).

111. *Church of England Newspaper* (18th August 1994).

112. L. Berk et al, 'Neuroendocrine and stress hormone changes during mirthful laughter', *American Journal of Medical Science* 298/6 (1989), pp.390-396.

113. W. Fry, 'Humour, physiology and the aging process' in L. Nahemow et al, *Humour and Aging* (Orlando, Florida: Academic Press, 1986), pp.81-98.

114. W. Fry, 'The physiologic effects of Humour, Mirth and Laughter', *Journal of the American Medical Association*, 267 (1992), 13, pp.1857-8.

115. W. Fry: 'Learning with humour', presented at the 4th International Conference on Humour, Tel Aviv (June 1984).

116. William James, *Varieties of Religious Experience* (1903).

117. *The Times* (30th October 1992).

118. A. Ludwig, 'Altered States of Consciousness', *Archives of General Psychiatry*, 15 (1966), pp.225-234.

Index

The Truth About AIDS

by Dr Patrick Dixon

With over 15 million people already HIV-infected worldwide, AIDS is an illness no one can ignore. When this book was first launched in 1987, it made the headlines by revealing the truth about the epidemic. As a direct result a major new national and international AIDS initiative was born. Since then, major new problems relating to the disease have emerged, governments' statistics have been drastically revised and some 19,000 research papers have been published.

In 1994, aware of the need for a practical, compassionate response, Dr Dixon updated his original research with over 200 extra pages of new material. He writes of God's call to each of us to accept all kinds of people and to extend his love to them regardless of whether or not we agree with what they do. He adds, 'My hope and prayer is that this new edition will further stimulate a massive, yet sensitive, worldwide response to AIDS.'

This book addresses the practical aspects of setting up community care, deals with the use of condoms, the safety of a shared communion cup, and the issue of travel and work in developing countries.

Fully indexed and referenced.

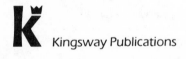

Kingsway Publications

The Genetic Revolution

by Dr Patrick Dixon

... researcher
... Christian medical doctor
... respected AIDS expert
... active church leader

A unique contribution to the debate about the ethics of genetic engineering. Within days of publication over thirty British MPs signed a motion calling for this book's Gene Charter to be adopted by Parliament. But nothing short of international regulation will do.

'As a doctor I know we urgently need gene technology to cure diseases like cystic fibrosis, cancer and AIDS, and to help feed the world, but we also need to ask what kind of future we are creating, now we have the ability to alter the very basis of life itself,' writes the author.

Already the 'genetic revolution' is being driven on by curiosity and commercial interest based on urgent human need. No one is immune from the consequences. The challenge to consider the cost faces us all as we look into this fascinating yet alarming world of experiment and discovery.

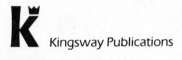 Kingsway Publications